ADVANCES IN QUANTITATIVE ANALYSIS OF FINANCE AND ACCOUNTING

ADVANCES IN QUANTITATIVE ANALYSIS OF FINANCE
AND ACCOUNTING VOLUME 10

ADVANCES IN QUANTITATIVE ANALYSIS OF FINANCE AND ACCOUNTING

EDITED BY

CHENG-FEW LEE
Department of Finance,
Rutgers University,
New Brunswick, NJ, USA

2002

JAI
An Imprint of Elsevier Science

Amsterdam – Boston – London – New York – Oxford – Paris
San Diego – San Francisco – Singapore – Sydney – Tokyo

ELSEVIER SCIENCE Ltd
The Boulevard, Langford Lane
Kidlington, Oxford OX5 1GB, UK

First edition 2002

Library of Congress Cataloging in Publication Data
A catalog record from the Library of Congress has been applied for.

British Library Cataloguing in Publication Data
A catalogue record from the British Library has been applied for.

ISBN: 0-7623-0969-5

♾ The paper used in this publication meets the requirements of ANSI/NISO Z39.48-1992 (Permanence of Paper).
Printed in The Netherlands.

CONTENTS

LIST OF CONTRIBUTORS

Ren-Raw Chen	Department of Finance, School of Business, Rutgers University, USA
Michael Impson	COBA/FIREL, University of North Texas Denton, USA
George M. Jabbour	George Washington University, USA
Marat V. Kramin	Fannie Mae Portfolio Strategy Department, Washington D.C., USA
Timur V. Kramin	Santel Tatarstan American Investment Fund, Kazan, Russia
Wikikl Kwak	College of Business Administration, University of Nebraska, USA
Alice C. Lee	Department of Finance, School of Management, Syracuse University, USA
Cheng-few Lee	Department of Finance, Rutgers University School of Business, USA
Heeseok Lee	Department of Management Information Systems, Korea Advanced Institute of Science and Technology, South Korea
Seok Weon Lee	Department of Finance and Insurance, Soonchunhyang University, South Korea
Charlotte Pryor	School of Business, University of Southern Maine, USA
Jason S. Rich	Merrill Lynch & Co. Inc., USA

Kaustav Sen	Lubin School of Business, Pace University, USA
Yong Shi	College of Info Science and Technology, University of Nebraska, USA
Bin Srinidhi	City University of Hong Kong, Accountancy Department, Hong Kong
Joseph V. Terza	Department of Economics, Pennsylvania State University, USA
Stephen D. Young	Wachovia Securities, USA
Peter Zhang	Chase Manhattan Bank, Akasaka Park Building, Japan

1. THE DETERMINANTS OF CURRENT AND LONG-TERM COMPONENTS OF CEO COMPENSATION

Kaustav Sen

ABSTRACT

This paper examines the relative contribution of accrual measures and investment opportunities in simultaneously explaining the various current and long-term components of compensation. We find that not all components of the compensation function are affected similarly by these factors. Non-discretionary accruals and investment opportunities matter for both current as well as long-term compensation. However, it is found that discretionary accruals are only relevant for current compensation. This suggests that given all available information, compensation committees are functionally fixated on reported earnings in the short-term but not otherwise.

1. INTRODUCTION

Researchers have been studying executive compensation for more than a decade. The findings indicate that accounting and market measures of financial performance (for example, see Lambert & Larker, 1987) as well as investment opportunities explain the compensation function (see Smith & Watts, 1992).

Advances in Quantitative Analysis of Finance and Accounting, Volume 10, pages 1–22.

ISBN: 0-7623-0969-5

Furthermore, Balsam (1998) finds that discretionary accruals are factored into the cash based compensation as well, indicating that the choice of accounting method matters for executive compensation. However, the simultaneous role of accruals and investment opportunities in current and long-term compensation has not been examined. It is important to study this issue in order to understand the relative importance of these factors from a short and long-term perspective.

Long-term compensation in the form of stock options is used for risk sharing and alignment of incentives in the long-term (Hemmer, 1995), whereas cash compensation in the form of salary and bonus meets the current needs of the executive and provides short-term incentives.[1] If different factors determine the current and long-term compensation, it indicates that different issues matter to shareholders in the short and long-term. Whereas value maximization is the shareholder's objective, such a situation would indicate that different factors are relevant based on the time horizon.

This study provides evidence of the relative importance of two unrelated factors, accruals and investment opportunities, for contracting purposes. Balsam (1998) notes that discretionary accruals are relevant for cash based compensation, and more strongly when reporting a loss is avoided. Smith and Watts (1992) and later Gaver and Gaver (1993) and Skinner (1993) find evidence that firm characteristics, in particular its investment opportunity set, determines the firm's corporate policies including the structure of the executive compensation. The simultaneous consideration of these distinct issues on current and long-term components of executive compensation would indicate their relative importance.

In this study, we study how accruals and the investment opportunity set can explain executive compensation. Following Balsam (1998) we first examine the relation how income before accruals and total accruals explain compensation. Next, total accruals are disaggregated into discretionary and non-discretionary accruals. We estimate the investment opportunity set using factor analysis as in Gaver and Gaver (1993) and Baber et al. (1996). We then introduce the investment opportunity set as an additional explanatory variable.

Our empirical results indicate that both non-discretionary accruals and the investment opportunity set are important for both current and long-term compensation. However, it is found that discretionary accruals are relevant for current compensation. From these results, we conclude that given all available information, compensation committees are functionally fixated on reported earnings in the short-term but not otherwise.

The rest of the paper is organized as follows. Section 2 presents three hypotheses that are subject of the data analysis. Section 3 describes the sample selection steps and the construction of variables used for the analysis. The results are discussed in Section 4. Section 5 concludes the paper.

2. DETERMINANTS OF EXECUTIVE COMPENSATION AND HYPOTHESIS DEVELOPMENT

Agency theory offers insights into issues that should determine executive compensation. The standard agency model (Jensen & Meckling, 1976; Holmstrom, 1979) suggests that compensation should be based on firm performance to mitigate monitoring problems due to moral hazard. Performance measures based on accounting numbers have been found to validate this theory (Murphy, 1985; Lambert & Larcker, 1987; Sloan, 1993). Smith and Watts (1992) use the agency framework to argue that management of investment opportunities by executives is difficult to monitor and thus executive compensation should be based on performance indicators of investment opportunities. We investigate whether short and long-term compensation depends on performance indicators using accounting numbers and investment opportunities. Furthermore, we investigate the role of accounting method choice in affecting any performance measure of executive action.

Investment opportunities typically take time to add value to a firm. However, it stands to reason that if incentives are not provided, the executive can pass up such investment opportunities. The executive is rewarded not only for the existence of investment opportunities, but also for successfully executing these opportunities. Based on this reasoning, we hypothesize that the investment opportunity set should be a determinant of the value of both the current as well as the long-term compensation.[2] Smith and Watts (1992) and Gaver and Gaver (1993) test for the existence of incentive compensation plans based on the investment opportunity set. In contrast, Baber et al. (1996) test for the sensitivity of the compensation amount to the measure of investment opportunity. We test our hypothesis in a fashion similar to the latter.

Hypothesis 1: The existing investment opportunity set impacts both the current and long-term executive compensation.

Agency based contracting theory suggest that if compensation is used to share risk and alleviate moral hazard, then the executive should be rewarded on the basis of observable outcome (Holmstrom, 1979). Earnings and cash flows are the contractible proxies for such an outcome. In the literature, return on equity (which is based on earnings) has been used as the accounting based performance measure to explain compensation (Lambert & Larcker, 1987). The market return is another performance measure used in executive compensation.

It is well known that earnings are subject to the discretionary accounting method choice of the executive and thus can be managed. Nevertheless, this should not affect the economic value and over multiple periods, the effect of the accounting method should normally reverse.[3] We thus hypothesize that discretionary accruals do not affect long-term compensation. However, in the short-term, discretionary accruals can be useful if the compensation committee believes that the investors are functionally fixated on reported earnings in the short term i.e. cannot separate out discretionary from non-discretionary accruals. We hypothesize that investors are functionally fixated and cannot see through the effect of discretionary accruals on the short-term performance.

On the other hand, non-discretionary earnings are indicators of economic performance and should be relevant for both current and long-term compensation. This is because non-discretionary earnings are not due to the accounting method choice that can eventually reverse itself but rather are realized profits, which benefit the company permanently.

Although Balsam (1998) examines a cross-sectional model with levels of compensation, in order for us to assess the impact of the investment opportunity set, we examine the multi-period impact on compensation by examining changes in compensation. However, we expect the nature of the results to be similar for compensation components examined by Balsam (1998).

> *Hypothesis 2:* Functional fixation on earnings is exhibited in the short-term only. Thus the change in non-discretionary accruals affects both current and long-term compensation, whereas the change in discretionary accruals affects the current compensation only.

To summarize, Hypothesis 1 predicts only investment opportunities matter for valuing both current and long-term compensation and hypothesis 2 predicts that:

(a) only non-discretionary accruals matter for valuing both current and long-term compensation; and
(b) discretionary accruals impact only current compensation.

3. SAMPLE SELECTION AND DATA COLLECTION

The executive compensation data is obtained from Standard and Poor's Compustat Execucomp database. It consists of more than one hundred variables from 1992–1998, with information on more than sixteen thousand executives.

Panel A of Table 1 shows the steps in selecting the sample. The Execucomp database consists of 57,795 firm-executive-years, which yields 1,915 firms. We only keep data related to the CEO, since the incentive structure for other executives including outside board members may be different. This yields 7,992 firm-executive-years (1,870 firms). We examine the compensation function at the firm level and not the executive level. Thus we do not restrict a minimum tenure for a CEO to qualify in the sample. Aggregating the compensation variables to firm level yields 7,747 firm-year records. Of these 731 observations have insufficient data for computing accruals and another 1,730 are eliminated due to first-difference computations. The final sample has 5,286 firm years or 1,569 firms. Panel B shows the distribution of firms across calendar years.

Panel A of Table 2 shows that the mean value of stock options ($1.5 million) is the largest portion (55%) of the total salary. The mean salary ($0.56 million)

Table 1. Sample Selection and Year-wise Distribution.

Panel A: Sample selection	Firm-executive-years	Firm-years	Firms
Observations in Execucomp database	57,795	10,182	1,915
Less: Non-CEO data	49,803	2,429	45
Observations with individual CEO data	7,992	7,753	1,870
Less: Multiple observations per firm	245	6	1
Summarized at the firm level		7,747	1,869
Less: Missing accrual data		731	139
		7,016	1,730
Less: Computation of first differences		1,730	161
Total number of observations		5,286	1,569

Panel B: Year-wise distribution	Year	Frequency
	1993	342
	1994	652
	1995	396
	1996	100
	1997	79

Table 2. CEO Compensation Descriptive Statistics.[8]

Panel A: Descriptive statistics

	Mean	Median	Quartile-1	Quartile-3
Salary	563.0	508.3	357.2	704.2
Bonus	553.6	300.0	91.1	625.0
Options	1517.3	403.2	0	1324.8
Grants	174.0	0	0	0
Total comp	2750.8	1509.5	793.0	2893.3
Years to vest grants	1.1	1.0	1.0	1.0

Panel B: Correlation coefficients[#1]
(Pearson Correlations above and Spearman Correlations below the diagonal)

	Salary	Bonus	Options	Grants	Total comp
Salary		0.18	0.22	0.15	0.33
Bonus	0.50		0.20	0.12	0.51
Options	0.35	0.33		0.08	0.81
Grants	0.15	0.15	0.10		0.27
Total comp	0.69	0.68	0.70	0.28	

[#1] All correlations are significant at 0.0001.

and the mean bonus ($0.55 million) are 20% each of the total compensation. However, as expected there is greater variation in bonus than salary. About 5% of the total compensation consists of other non-cash compensation including restricted stock grants. Furthermore, we find that the median time for a grant to vest is one year. This makes us conclude that stock grants do not behave as instruments of long-term compensation, but rather a non-cash form of short-term compensation.

The Pearson correlations in Panel B of Table 2 indicate that none of the basic components show a high degree of correlation. It is intuitive that these show a low degree of correlation, since otherwise the purpose of having different instruments of compensation would be moot.

4. METHODOLOGY

4.1. Estimating Discretionary Accruals

Discretionary accruals are proxies for the aggregate effect of accounting choices on income. The aggregate effect of accounting choice is the best candidate for studying the effect of executive discretion, since individual accounting choices can have a small effect on the bottom line and any specific accounting choice has to be disclosed. Thus the effect of a particular accounting choice on the income and consequently compensation has to be adjusted or reversed (see Balsam, 1998; Healy et al., 1987). On the other hand, the aggregate effect is not disclosed and thus can be used to the executive's benefit.

Dechow et al. (1995) outlines estimating discretionary accruals using five different approaches. Panel A of Table 3 outlines how to estimate the discretionary accruals for each of these approaches. Defond and Jiambalvo (1994) and Subramanyam (1996) have used yet another method, a cross-sectional version of the Jones model. However, Bernard and Skinner (1996) argue that the cross-sectional Jones model suffers from problems including the wide variation in firm characteristics within the same industry (defined using the two digit SIC code). For these reasons, we do not present the cross-sectional Jones model.

From Panel B of Table 3 we see that the DeAngelo (1986) model has the widest dispersion and the Jones (1991) model has the minimum dispersion. The mean and median values for the Healy (1985) model are the farthest from zero and for the Jones model are closest to zero. The correlation coefficients in Panel C indicate that the Healy and the Industry model are highly correlated (0.86). The Jones and the Industry model show the minimum correlation (0.56). Following Balsam (1998), we use the Jones model for all the subsequent analysis.[4]

4.2. Measuring Investment Opportunities

Smith and Watts (1992) were the first to construct a proxy for a firm's investment opportunity set. They measured it as the ratio of book value of assets to firm value. The higher this ratio, the lower are the investment opportunities for the firm. However, they also suggest alternative measures for investment opportunities including ratio of depreciation to firm value, ratio of research and development to firm value, the variance of the rate of return on the firm, the earnings price ratio and the ratio of capital expenditures to firm value.

Instead of using any one of the above measures, Gaver and Gaver (1993) suggest using factor analysis on all these measures to estimate investment opportunities. In settings where observable variables are presumed to have a common unobservable construct, the pair-wise correlations between these observable variables are condensed into measures called factors.[5] These factors

Table 3. Accrual Measures.

Panel A: Model definitions

Healy (Healy, 1985):	$NDA_\tau = \frac{\sum_t TA_t}{T}$
DeAngelo (DeAngelo, 1986):	$NDA_\tau = TA_{\tau-1}$
Jones (Jones, 1991):	$NDA_\tau = \alpha_1(1/A_{\tau-1}) + \alpha_2(\Delta REV_\tau) + \alpha_3(PPE_\tau)$
Modified Jones (Dechow et al., 1995):	$NDA_\tau = \alpha_1(1/A_{\tau-1}) + \alpha_2(\Delta REV_\tau - \Delta REC_\tau) + \alpha_3(PPE_\tau)$
Industry (Dechow and Sloan, 1991):	$NDA_\tau = \gamma_1 + \gamma_2 \text{median}(TA_\tau)$

where

$TA_t = (\Delta CA_t - \Delta CL_t - \Delta Cash_t + \Delta STD_t - Dep_t)/(A_{t-1})$,
ΔCA = change in current assets (5),
ΔCL = change in current liabilities (6),
$\Delta Cash$ = change in cash and cash equivalents (1),
ΔSTD = change in debt in current liabilities (34),
Dep = depreciation (14),
A = total assets (6),
ΔREV = change in revenues (12),
ΔREC = change in receivables (2),
PPE = property, plant and equipment (7),
median(TA_τ) = median value of total accruals for all non-sample firms in the same 2 digit SIC code

Note: (i) All of the above variables are scaled by total assets at $t-1$, (ii) Compustat data items are in parentheses.

Panel B: Descriptive statistics

	Mean	Median	Quartile-1	Quartile-3
DA_H[#1]	0.066	–0.005	–0.039	0.023
DA_D[#2]	–0.005	–0.001	–0.040	0.037
DA_J[#3]	–0.003	–0.000	–0.021	0.019
DA_MJ[#4]	–0.003	–0.000	–0.022	0.020
DA_I[#5]	–0.011	–0.003	–0.033	0.022

Table 3. Continued.

Panel C: Correlation coefficients[#6]
(Pearson Correlations above and Spearman Correlations below the diagonal)

	DA_H	DA_D	DA_J	DA_MJ	DA_I
DA_H		0.03	0.01	0.02	0.18
DA_D	0.63		0.31	0.56	0.04
DA_J	0.58	0.60		0.79	0.02
DA_MJ	0.61	0.60	0.92		0.03
DA_I	0.86	0.57	0.56	0.57	

[#1] Discretionary accruals using the Healy model (1985) as a percentage of lagged total assets.
[#2] Discretionary accruals using the DeAngelo model (1986) as a percentage of lagged total assets.
[#3] Discretionary accruals using the Jones model (1991) as a percentage of lagged total assets.
[#4] Discretionary accruals using the modified Jones model (Dechow et al., 1995) as a percentage of lagged total assets.
[#5] Discretionary accruals using the Industry model (Dechow and Sloan, 1991) as a percentage of lagged total assets.
[#6] All correlations are significant at 0.0001.

capture the variation existing in the observable variables. The investment opportunity of a firm is essentially a single underlying variable but is measured through a variety of observable variables as mentioned above. Using factor analysis becomes appealing in such a case, where the observable measures can be reduced to a single factor representing the investment opportunity set.

Baber et al. (1996) report that the set of measures used in Gaver and Gaver (1993) are often unavailable. An alternate set of measures that is more readily available is used to estimate the investment opportunity set. Further, they confirm the validity of the factor scores by testing their correlation with ex-post investment activities. Panel A of Table 4 provides the definitions for the observable measures of investment opportunity. Baber et al. (1996) provide a detailed explanation of the steps to arrive at the four measures used to estimate the investment opportunity set FACIOS. For the sake of completeness, the factor derived in Gaver and Gaver (1993), FACGAV and its related observable measures are also presented in Table 4. The main improvement in the Baber et al. (1996) specification is that a measure of investment intensity (INVINT) is used to predict FACIOS. The investment intensity is interpreted to represent the realization of prior investment opportunities (Baber et al., 1996, p. 302). It should be noted that this measure represents the investment opportunities that have been utilized and not the outcome of these investments.

Table 4. Investment Opportunity Set Measures.

Panel A: Definitions

1. Investment intensity ($INVINT_t$)

$$\frac{\sum_{i=t-2}^{i=t} [\text{Capital expenditure (30)} + \text{R\&D Expense (46)} + \text{Acquisitions (129)}]_i}{\sum_{i=t-2}^{i=t} \text{Depreciation (14)}_i}$$

2. Geometric mean annual growth rate of market value of assets ($MVAGR_t$)

$$\sqrt[n]{\frac{\text{Market value of assets } (6 - 60 + 199x25)}{\text{Market value of assets } (6 - 60 + 199x25)_{t-n}}}$$

where n = max[1, 2, 3], for which data is available

3. Market-to-book value of assets ($MKTBKASS_t$)

$$\frac{\text{Market value of assets } (6 - 60 + 199x25)_t}{\text{Book value of assets } (6)_t}$$

4. R & D expenditure to total assets ($R\&D_t$)

$$\frac{\text{R\&D Expense } (46)_t}{\text{Book value of assets } (6)_t}$$

Table 4. Continued.

Panel A: Definitions – Continued

5. Market-to-book value of equity ($MKTBKEQ_t$)

$$\frac{\text{Market value of equity } (199x25)_t}{\text{Book value of equity } (60)_t}$$

6. Earnings-to-price ratio (EP_t)

$$\frac{\text{Earnings per share } (58)_t}{\text{Price per share } (199)_t}$$

7. Variance of return on market value (VAR_t)

$$\sigma^2\left(\frac{[\Delta(\text{Market value of equity}) + \text{Common \& Preferred dividends } (26x25+19) + \text{Interest Expense } (15)]_t}{\text{Total assets } (6) - \text{Common equity } (60) + \text{Market value of equity } (199x25)_{t-1}}\right)$$

Notes:

1. Compustat data items are indicated in parentheses.
2. FACIOS is calculated using variables $INVINT_t$, $MVAGR_t$, $MKTBKASS_t$ and $R\&D_t$.
3. FACGAV is calculated using variables $MKTBKASS_t$, $R\&D_t$, $MKTBKEQ_t$, EP_t and VAR_t.

Table 4. Continued.

Panel B: Descriptive statistics

	Mean	Median	Quartile-1	Quartile-3
INVINT	2.98	2.30	1.47	3.66
MVAGR	1.15	1.11	1.03	1.23
MKTBKASS	1.91	1.51	1.18	2.12
R&D	0.03	0	0	0.03
MKTBKEQ	3.06	2.30	1.59	3.45
EP	0.02	0.05	0.03	0.07
VAR	0.78	0.07	0.03	0.17
FACIOS	0.05	–0.17	–0.46	0.27
FACGAV	0.08	–0.18	–0.33	0.10

Table 4. Continued.

Panel C: Correlation coefficients
(Pearson Correlations above and Spearman Correlations below the diagonal)

	FACIOS	FACGAV	INVINT	MVAGR	MKT-BKASS	MKT-BKEQ	EP	VAR	R&D
FACIOS		0.61	0.58	0.72	0.85	0.17	0.04	0.09	0.40
FACGAV	0.78		0.19	0.20	0.49	0.28	0.023	0.43	0.30
INVINT	0.65	0.39		0.29	0.30	0.05	–0.01	0.09	0.50
MVAGR	0.72	0.34	0.32		0.45	0.08	0.07	0.21	0.00
MKTBKASS	0.78	0.90	0.36	0.39		0.21	0.01	0.04	0.37
MKTBKEQ	0.70	0.83	0.24	0.43	0.86		0.01	0.01	0.06
EP	–0.23	–0.25	–0.23	–0.09	–0.28	–0.26		–0.01	–0.05
VAR	0.39	0.43	0.38	0.13	0.42	0.23	–0.32		0.13
R&D	0.40	0.57	0.46	0.08	0.40	0.29	–0.19	0.32	

We notice from Panel B of Table 4 that there is wider variation in FACIOS than FACGAV. However, at an aggregate level, the FACIOS measure is slightly lower. The correlation coefficients in Panel C indicate that both FACIOS and FACGAV are comparably related to the earnings-price ratio. However, FACIOS relates better to investment intensity and growth rate of market value of assets, whereas FACGAV relates better to ratios of market to book values of assets and equity, research and development ratio and variance of the rate of return.

5. EMPIRICAL RESULTS

The model for executive compensation has been specified as both a level and a change measure in the literature. We first replicate the regressions from Balsam (1998) and Baber et al. (1996) before considering the effects of accruals and investment opportunities simultaneously.

Table 5 presents the results of the empirical tests. The regressions are run with different components of compensation as the dependent variable. These are presented across the columns. The total cash compensation is given in column 3, and the total compensation in column 6. The first two models replicate regressions from Balsam (1988), the third model replicates the regression from Baber et al. (1996) and the last two models are a joint test of the role of accruals and investment opportunity set in executive compensation.

The first model we test considers only levels of operating cash flows and total accruals as the determinants of compensation levels. It is presented in Table 5, Panel A as

$$\text{Comp}_{it} = \beta_0 + \beta_1 \text{OCF}_{it} + \beta_2 \text{TA}_{it},$$

where OCF is operating cash flow and TA is total accrual. We notice from Panel A that both OCF and TA are significant at the 0.0001. These results indicate that both operating cash flows and earnings are relevant for current and long-term compensation and confirm with Balsam (1998).

The second model decomposes total accruals into discretionary and non-discretionary components. It is presented in Table 5, Panel B as

$$\text{Comp}_{it} = \beta_0 + \beta_1 \text{OCF}_{it} + \beta_2 \text{DA}_{it} + \beta_3 \text{NDA}_{it},$$

where DA is discretionary accruals using the Jones (1991) model and NDA is the non-discretionary accruals. Both types of accruals are significant for all the compensation components. These results suggest that discretionary accruals are significant for cash compensation (similar to Balsam, 1998).

Table 5. Regression Results.[9]

Panel A: $Comp_{it} = \beta_0 + \beta_1 OCF_{it} + \beta_2 TA_{it}$

	Salary	Bonus	Salary + Bonus	Options	Grants	Total
β_0	515.4*	437.8*	953.2*	1148.4*	135.9*	2213.8*
	(126.3)	(16.3)	(34.4)	(15.7)	(12.3)	(28.0)
β_1	0.22*	0.54*	0.76*	1.71*	0.18*	2.57*
	(33.9)	(12.7)	(17.4)	(14.8)	(10.3)	(20.6)
β_2	0.22*	0.59*	0.80*	1.78*	0.21*	3.10*
	(32.7)	(13.6)	(18.0)	(15.2)	(11.7)	(24.4)
Adj-R^2	0.179	0.034	0.058	0.042	0.029	0.134

Panel B: $Compit = \beta_0 + \beta_1 OCF_{it} + \beta_2 DA_{it} + \beta_3 NDA_{it}$

	Salary	Bonus	Salary + Bonus	Options	Grants	Total
β_0	513.5*	441.9*	955.3*	1147.7*	128.2*	2206.0*
	(120.4)	(15.4)	(32.5)	(14.8)	(12.4)	(26.9)
β_1	0.22*	0.51*	0.73*	1.74*	0.17*	2.4*
	(31.3)	(11.0)	(15.2)	(13.9)	(10.5)	(18.1)
β_2	0.20*	0.59*	0.79*	1.63*	0.25*	2.34*
	(24.1)	(10.5)	(13.8)	(10.9)	(12.2)	(14.7)
β_3	0.21*	0.60*	0.81*	1.55*	0.234*	2.38*
	(27.8)	(12.1)	(15.8)	(11.6)	(13.1)	(16.9)
Adj-R^2	0.182	0.031	0.052	0.042	0.038	0.067

Table 5. Continued

Panel C: $\Delta Comp_{it} = \beta_0 + \beta_1 RET_{it} + \beta_2 dROE_{it} + \beta_3 RET{*}FACIOS_{it} + \beta_4 dROE{*}FACIOS_{it} + \beta_5 FACIOS_{it}$

	Salary	Bonus	Salary + Bonus	Options	Grants	Total
β_0	–0.01*	–0.01*	–0.02*	–0.02	–0.00**	–0.04*
	(–12.2)	(–5.3)	(–9.3)	(–2.1)	(–2.2)	(–3.6)
β_1	0.01*	0.032	0.04	0.06**	0.02*	0.01*
	(7.7)	(12.6)	(13.2)	(3.0)	(5.4)	(6.0)
β_2	–0.00	0.00	0.00	–0.00	–0.00	–0.01
	(–0.4)	(1.2)	(0.8)	(–0.4)	(–0.2)	(–0.9)
β_3	0.01*	0.02*	0.03*	0.04**	0.01*	0.07*
	(7.4)	(12.0)	(12.6)	(2.8)	(5.5)	(5.7)
β_4	–0.00**	–0.00	–0.00	–0.00	–0.00	–0.02**
	(–3.2)	(–0.2)	(–1.5)	(–0.2)	(–0.5)	(–2.3)
β_5	–0.02*	–0.02*	–0.03*	–0.04**	–0.00	–0.08*
	(–16.0)	(–7.5)	(–12.6)	(–2.9)	(–1.2)	(–5.8)
Adj-R^2	0.053	0.035	0.051	0.002	0.006	0.012

Table 5. Continued

Panel D: $\Delta Comp_{it} = \beta_0 + \beta_1 \Delta OCF_{it} + \beta_2 \Delta DA_{it} + \beta_3 \Delta NDA_{it} + \beta_4 FACIOS_{it} + \beta_5 RET + \beta_6 RET*FACIOS_{it} + \beta_7 dROE + \beta_8 dROE*FACIOS_{it}$

	Salary	Bonus	Salary + Bonus	Options	Grants	Total
β_0	–0.01	–0.01*	–0.02*	–0.02	–0.00	–0.03
	(–10.6)	(–3.6)	(–7.3)	(–1.5)	(–2.1)	(–2.4)
β_1	–0.00	0.14*	0.14*	–0.94*	0.02	–0.44*
	(–0.4)	(7.8)	(6.1)	(–7.0)	(0.7)	(–3.8)
β_2	0.09*	0.26*	0.36*	–0.04	0.01	0.35
	(7.4)	(10.5)	(11.5)	(–0.2)	(0.2)	(2.2)
β_3	0.08*	0.24*	0.33*	0.66*	0.02	0.74*
	(7.8)	(11.7)	(12.6)	(4.4)	(0.9)	(5.6)
β_4	–0.02*	–0.02*	–0.03*	–0.04**	–0.00	–0.07*
	(–16.1)	(–7.4)	(–12.6)	(–2.6)	(–1.5)	(–5.2)
β_5	0.01*	0.03*	0.04*	0.05**	0.02*	0.08*
	(7.4)	(11.3)	(12.1)	(2.7)	(5.4)	(5.1)
β_6	0.01*	0.02*	0.03*	0.03***	0.01*	0.06*
	(7.2)	(11.0)	(11.8)	(2.2)	(5.5)	(4.6)
β_7	–0.00	0.00	–0.00	–0.00	–0.00	–0.00
	(–0.9)	(0.3)	(–0.1)	(–0.2)	(–0.2)	(–0.7)
β_8	–0.00**	–0.00	–0.00**	0.00	–0.00	–0.02**
	(–3.0)	(–1.0)	(–2.0)	(0.3)	(–0.6)	(–2.1)
Adj-R^2	0.112	0.073	0.109	0.084	0.006	0.072

Table 5. Continued

Panel E: $\Delta Comp_{it} = \beta_0 + \beta_1 \Delta OCF_{it} + \beta_2 \Delta DA_{it} + \beta_3 \Delta NDA_{it} + \beta_4 FACGAV_{it} + \beta_5 RET + \beta_6 RET*FACGAV_{it} + \beta_7 dROE + \beta_8 dROE*FACGAV_{it}$

	Salary	Bonus	Salary + Bonus	Options	Grants	Total
β_0	–0.01*	–0.01	–0.01*	–0.02	–0.00	–0.02
	(–10.6)	(–3.0)	(–6.7)	(–1.5)	(–1.7)	(–2.3)
β_1	–0.00	0.15*	0.15*	–0.91*	–0.02	–0.44*
	(–0.2)	(8.3)	(6.5)	(–6.9)	(1.0)	(–3.8)
β_2	0.09*	0.27*	0.36*	–0.03	0.01	0.34
	(7.2)	(10.8)	(11.6)	(–0.1)	(0.4)	(2.2)
β_3	0.08*	0.25*	0.34*	0.67*	0.03	0.74*
	(7.7)	(12.1)	(12.8)	(4.5)	(1.1)	(5.6)
β_4	–0.00**	–0.00	–0.01	–0.03	–0.00	–0.00
	(–2.6)	(–1.8)	(–2.5)	(–0.3)	(–0.3)	(–0.7)
β_5	0.00**	0.01*	0.02*	0.03**	0.01*	0.04**
	(3.2)	(7.2)	(7.0)	(1.9)	(3.7)	(3.0)
β_6	0.00***	0.02*	0.03*	0.03	0.02*	0.04**
	(2.5)	(6.4)	(6.1)	(1.3)	(3.7)	(2.1)
β_7	–0.00	0.00	0.00	–0.00	0.00	–0.00
	(–0.3)	(0.6)	(0.4)	(–0.5)	(0.0)	(–0.6)
β_8	–0.00	–0.00	–0.00	0.00	–0.00	–0.00
	(–0.4)	(–0.8)	(–0.8)	(0.2)	(–0.3)	(–0.5)
Adj-R^2	0.060	0.053	0.072	0.082	0.002	0.064

The third model considers the role of the investment opportunity set as an explanatory variable. This model, exactly as in Baber et al. (1996) is presented in Table 5, Panel C as

$$\Delta Comp_{it} = \beta_0 + \beta_1 RET_{it} + \beta_2 dROE_{it} + \beta_3 RET{*}FACIOS_{it} + \beta_4 dROE{*}FACIOS_{it} + \beta_5 FACIOS_{it}$$

where RET_{it} is the stock return, $dROE_{it}$ is the change in the return on equity and $FACIOS_{it}$ is the investment opportunity set as defined in Baber et al. (1996).

First we examine β_3 and β_4 to confirm the results of Baber et al. (1996). Essentially, they hypothesize and find that $\beta_3 > 0$ and $\beta_4 = 0$[6] leads to conclude that the investment opportunity set is relevant for executive compensation. As pointed out by Baber et al. (1996), the relation between compensation and investment opportunity set (IOS) is not straightforward. Thus no expectations to the sign or significance of β_4 are offered. Results from Panel C of Table 5 confirm with the expected results. We find that β_3 is significantly positive for all compensation components, whereas $\beta_4 = 0$ for all of them (except total compensation).

The last two models consider the joint effect of earnings accruals and the investment opportunities on CEO compensation. Following Baber et al. (1996), we use changes in compensation as our dependent variable in these regressions for the joint examination of accruals and investment opportunity measures in determining compensation.[7] Accordingly, the independent variables are change measures. The fourth model is presented in Table 5, Panel D as

$$\Delta Comp_{it} = \beta_0 + \beta_1\, \Delta OCF_{it} + \beta_2\, \Delta DA_{it} + \beta_3\, \Delta NDA_{it} + \beta_4 FACIOS_{it} + \beta_5 RET + \beta_6 RET{*}FACIOS_{it} + \beta_7\, dROE + \beta_8\, dROE{*}FACIOS_{it}$$

We find that with the exception of grants, changes in non-discretionary accruals are significantly positive for all other compensation components. Furthermore, we find β_6 significantly positive for all the components and $\beta_8 = 0$ for all the components except total compensation. This essentially confirms that the investment opportunity set is relevant for all compensation components. Furthermore, market and not accounting based performance measures are relevant for investment opportunities. Finally, we note that changes in discretionary accruals are significantly positive only for cash, bonus and their total. This result indicates that there is functional fixation in the short-term but not in the long-term.

The fifth and final model is similar to the fourth model, except the measure of the investment opportunity set is as defined in Gaver and Gaver (1993). The results from this model are presented in Table 5, Panel E and are similar to those in Panel D with one exception. We find that the value of β_6 is not significantly positive for options. We interpret it as a low association between the factors influencing the FACGAV measure and the value of options used for compensation.

The results above confirm both hypotheses. The adjusted R^2 for the total cash compensation varied from 5% to 11%. Salary was explained better by our choice of independent variables, ranging from 5% to 22%. Bonus was not explained that well, ranging from 3% to 7%. The R^2 of the total compensation varied between 6% and 13%. This is expected as there are many other variables influencing equity compensation (see Core & Guay, 1999). Our motive was not to get high R^2, but to examine the relative role of the selected independent variables in influencing the various compensation components. The significance of the parameter estimates discussed earlier satisfies this goal. Compared to Balsam (1998), the R^2 are low which may be due to the sample sizes. However, the R^2 values are comparable with Baber et al. (1996).

6. CONCLUSION

This paper attempts to determine the factors relevant for the determining the current and long-term components of executive compensation. We focus on two distinct factors – accruals as well as the investment opportunity set after controlling for operating cash flows. We find that when accruals and investment opportunities are considered simultaneously, the following are true:

(i) non-discretionary accruals changes and investment opportunities are relevant for determining both current and long-term compensation changes; and
(ii) discretionary accruals changes are relevant for determining both only current compensation changes.

This suggests that compensation committees are functionally fixated for the short-term but not for the long-term. These findings further our understanding of how incentive compatible compensation policies are designed to motivate the executive in the short and long-term. It remains an interesting research question to examine the motives for such a behavior by the compensation committee.

NOTES

1. Hemmer (1993) finds that options that are hedged using other components of the compensation package can be an effective compensation instrument to eliminate moral

hazard and maintain optimal risk sharing. The hedged option is risk-free to the agent as long as he takes the desired action.

2. Stock options and restricted stock grants can be instruments of long-term compensation. Core and Guay (1999) predict equity grants are used in compensation to manage optimal equity incentive levels and find that deviation from the optimum level is a determinant of the grant. However, the vesting period of a restricted stock grant ultimately decides whether it is indeed a form of long-term compensation.

3. There are exceptions to this situation e.g. a company is growing forever.

4. Gaver (1998) alert us that a particular model or discretionary accrual may suffer from a measurement error problem. She suggests considering all models using factor analysis. Alternatively, she rationalizes use of a particular model if it is assumed that the errors in measurement are correlated across models. We use this insight to justify using the Jones model.

5. Two conditions mentioned in Baber et al. (1996) are used to retain the relevant number of factors: (i) the minimum eigenvalue of the principal components is greater than one; and (ii) the starting communalities of the composite variables (computed as the squared multiple correlation of each variable with the remaining composite variables) are explained by the factors retained (see Harman, 1976; Gaver & Gaver, 1993).

6. See note 15, page 307 in Baber et al. (1996).

7. Balsam (1998) use level form of the variables. However, to test the role of the investment opportunity set, we need to follow a structure similar to Baber et al. (1996). Thus the change form is used in our final set of regressions.

8. All compensation values are in thousand of dollars.

9. Values in parenthesis are *t*-statistics. Also: * denotes 0.0001, ** denotes 0.05 and *** denotes 0.10 level of significance.

REFERENCES

Baber, W., Janakiraman, S., & Kang, S. (1996). Investment opportunities and the structure of executive compensation. *Journal of Accounting and Economics*, *21*, 297–318.

Balsam, S. (1998). Discretionary Accounting Choices and CEO Compensation. *Contemporary Accounting Research*, *15*, 229–252.

Bernard, V., & Skinner, D. (1996). What motivates managers' choice of discretionary accruals?, *Journal of Accounting and Economics*, *22*, 313–326.

Core, J., & Guay, W. (1999). The use of equity grants to manage optimal equity incentive levels. *Journal of Accounting and Economics*, *28*, 151–184.

DeAngelo, L. (1986). Accounting numbers as market valuation substitutes: A study of management buyouts of public stockholders. *The Accounting Review*, *61*, 400–420.

Dechow, P., & Sloan, R. (1991). Executives incentives and the horizon problem: An empirical investigation. *Journal of Accounting and Economics*, *14*, 51–89.

Dechow, P., Sloan, R., & Sweeney, A. (1995). Detecting earnings management. *The Accounting Review*, *70*, 193–226.

Defond, M., & Jiambalvo, J. (1994). Debt covenant violation and manipulation of accruals: Accounting choices in troubled companies. *Journal of Accounting and Economics*, *17*, 145–176.

Gaver, J. (1998). Discussion of "Discretionary Accounting Choices and CEO Compensation". *Contemporary Accounting Research*, *15*, 253–260.

Gaver, J., & Gaver, K. (1993). Additional evidence on the association between the investment opportunity set and corporate financing, dividend, and compensation policies. *Journal of Accounting and Economics*, *16*, 125–160.

Harman, H. (1976). *Modern factor analysis* (3rd ed.). Chicago, IL: University of Chicago Press.

Healy, P. (1985). The effect of bonus schemes on accounting decisions. *Journal of Accounting and Economics*, *7*, 85–107.

Healy, P., Kang, S., & Palepu, K. (1987). The effect of accounting procedure changes on CEO's cash salary and bonus compensation. *Journal of Accounting and Economics*, *9*, 7–34.

Hemmer, T. (1993). Risk-free incentive contracts: Eliminating agency cost using option-based compensation schemes. *Journal of Accounting and Economics*, *16*, 447–473.

Holmstrom, B. (1979). Moral hazard and observability. *Bell Journal of Economics*, *10*, 74–91.

Jensen, M., & Meckling, W. (1976). Theory of the firm: Managerial behavior, agency costs and ownership structure. *Journal of Financial Economics*, *3*, 305–360.

Jones, J. (1991). Earnings management during import relief investigations. *Journal of Accounting Research*, *29*, 225–264.

Lambert, R., & Larker, D. (1987). An analysis of the use of accounting and market measures of performance in executive compensation contracts. *Journal of Accounting Research*, *25*, 85–123.

Murphy, K. (1985). Corporate performance and managerial remuneration. *Journal of Accounting and Economics*, *7*, 11–42.

Skinner, D. (1993). The investment opportunity set and accounting procedure choice: Preliminary evidence. *Journal of Accounting and Economics*, *16*, 407–445.

Sloan, R. (1993). Accounting earnings and top executive compensation. *Journal of Accounting and Economics*, *16*, 55–100.

Smith, C., & Watts, R. (1992). The investment opportunity set and corporate financing, dividend, and compensation policies. *Journal of Financial Economics*, *32*, 263–292.

Subramanyam, K. R. (1996). The pricing of discretionary accruals. *Journal of Accounting and Economics*, *22*, 249–282.

2. OPTION PRICING AND HIGHER ORDER MOMENTS*

Stephen D. Young, George M. Jabbour, Marat V. Kramin and Timur V. Kramin

ABSTRACT

This article revisits the valuation of options while incorporating higher-order moments. It is well known that real world option prices are not readily reconciled with the assumptions in the Black-Scholes paradigm. One explanation is that returns sometimes depart from normal. This article contains a review of this topic, followed by an elaboration of a simplified model, which can be used to value plain vanilla options while incorporating higher-order moments via Edgeworth expansion applied directly to the probability density function. Option values and comparative statics (the "Greeks") are explored for skewness and kurtosis values consistent with the S&P 500 Index market.

1. INTRODUCTION

It is well known that the value of a derivative security is simply the present value of the expected payoff discounted at the risk-free rate of interest, where the expectation is calculated using risk-neutral probabilities. Despite

* The views expressed in this article are those of the authors and do not necessarily reflect the position of Wachovia Securities, Fannie Mae, or Santel.

Advances in Quantitative Analysis of Finance and Accounting, Volume 10, pages 23–39.

ISBN: 0-7623-0969-5

well-known deficiencies, the Black-Scholes (BS) (1973) framework has been the most widely used method for analytically deriving option prices. The foundation of these deficiencies lies directly in the assumptions surrounding the evolution of the stock price over the life of the option contract. The BS model assumes that prices are lognormally distributed and subsequently returns are normally distributed with constant variance over all times and market levels. This assumption cannot be satisfied by the empirical world and is not scientifically corroborated. Thus the model tends to be biased because it does not allow for asymmetries.

In many financial theories, an underlying return distribution is assumed. More often than not, it is the normal distribution which may be fully described by its mean (first moment) and variance (second moment). Another characteristic of the normal distribution is its symmetry and standard degree of peakedness. Under a null hypothesis of normality, measures of skewness and kurtosis are distributed with a mean of zero and three respectively. The skewness and kurtosis characterize the third and fourth moments respectively and allow one to model asymmetric and peaked data.[1]

While most derivative pricing models rely on the normality assumption, strict observance of this is flawed. Returns often exhibit non-zero skewness and greater-than-three kurtosis. In fact, empirical findings reveal that log share returns typically have fat-tails. This implies that extreme asset returns occur more frequently than described by the normal distribution. Some of the earliest work, which supported this thesis, is Mandelbrot (1963) and Fama (1965). More recently, Singleton and Wingender (1986) document significantly positive skewness in a time series of monthly return data from the CRSP file over the period 1961–1980. Their work focuses on single equities and not indices. Similarly, Aggarwal and Rao Ramesh (1990) examine weekly return distributions for 1,200 common stocks. In all of the time periods examined – 1974, 1977, 1980, and 1983 – a large portion of the 300 randomly selected stocks exhibited positive skewness. They also document positive excess kurtosis. More importantly, for this paper, Turner and Weigel (1992) document negative skewness and positive excess kurtosis in the S&P 500 and Dow Jones indices over the 1928–1989 period. According to their research, returns in the 1980s had far more negative skewness and positive excess kurtosis than any other decade considered in the study. In addition, all decades in their study are consistent with "fat-tailed" distributions. Campbell and Hentschel (1992) report skewness and kurtosis for log excess stock returns on the Center for Research in Securities Prices (CRSP) value-weighted index of stocks from the New York Stock Exchange and American Stock Exchange for the period from 1926 to 1988. Consistent with previous research on stock indices, they find strong empirical support for the negative skewness and positive excess kurtosis for the CRSP Index.

Not surprisingly, numerous authors document pricing biases in the BS framework. Most notably, Macbeth and Merville (1979) report that the BS model undervalues in-the-money options and overvalues out-of-the money options using implied volatilities. Other research confirms biases related to strike price and time to maturity.

Deviations from normality and the implications for option pricing have not been lost on academics. One of the earliest attempts to correct for biases is in the jump- diffusion model of Merton (1976). This model augments the BS return distribution with a Poisson-driven jump process, which allows for discontinuous stock prices. However, the model is difficult to parameterize as it calls for the estimation of two additional values: the number of jumps per annum and the percentage of the total volatility explained by the jumps.

Jarrow and Rudd (1982) incorporate deviations from normality by taking the correct value of an option to be the sum of the BS value plus adjustment terms, which depend on the second and higher order moments of the underlying diffusion process. Their approach is similar to the one expressed in this paper yet it is more complicated in its implementation and understanding. The pricing specification expressed in the Jarrow and Rudd paper, uses a series of adjustment terms which represent the differences between the approximate and true distributions for the second, third, and fourth moments respectively. Thus the Jarrow and Rudd approach provides a methodology for approximating option values for arbitrary stochastic processes.

Rithchey (1990) delineates a mixture call option-pricing model to examine the impact of a non-normal density function. The model is taken as the weighted sums of BS solutions. Their research finds discrepancies between market prices and values derived via BS. In short, values of in the money options and options with longer maturities are closely approximated by the BS model. Low-priced, and out-of-the-money options are found to have significant mispricing using the BS framework.

Corrado and Su (1996) apply a Gram-Charlier series expansion to the normal density function and provide skewness and kurtosis adjustment terms for the BS model. Their approach allows for an analytical solution. However, the Gram-Charlier and Edgeworth expansion, are infinite series. Thus, while their work admits an analytical solution via Hermite polynomials, if one chooses to include more terms in the series expansion beyond Gram-Charlier and Edgeworth this method becomes quite complicated. Lastly, by minimizing the sum of squared errors, Corrado and Su solve for implied volatility, skewness, and kurtosis measures. Their findings are consistent with non-normal skewness and kurtosis implied in S&P 500 Index option prices.

Johnson, Pawlukiewicz, and Mehta (1997) present a binomial model for options pricing which incorporates asymmetric end-of-period return distributions. More specifically, this model presents a binomial specification that allows for non-normal skewness. Again, the results indicate that a failure to account for this deviation from normality results in mispricing.

Tian (1998) develops a trinomial option-pricing model that allows for the first four moments of the underlying asset distribution. This represents an improvement over the Johnson, Pawlukiewicz, and Mehta specification as it accounts for non-normal skewness and kurtosis, which allows one to address both "fatter tails" and "peakedness" in observed stock returns distributions. However, this parameterization admits a limited range of skewness and kurtosis values. In fact, because of this the numerical results omit many combinations of skewness and kurtosis values that are characteristic of real world market data.

Rubinstein (1998) significantly decreased the complexity of incorporating non-normal skewness and kurtosis by applying Edgeworth expansion in a binomial framework in order to incorporate these higher-order moments. There is one major drawback to this approach. The resulting skewness and kurtosis will only approximate the pre-specified levels. Further, consistent with Tian's (1998) specification, this method only admits a limited locus of skewness and kurtosis parameters – under an Edgeworth expansion the locus is more constricted than if one reverts to a Gram-Charlier expansion. Outside this locus, one cannot ensure that the adjusted risk-neutral probabilities are everywhere non-negative, and on the interval between zero and one inclusive.

Corrado (2000) utilizes a generalized lambda distribution for generating option values where the underlying return distribution exhibits non-normal skewness and kurtosis. In contrast to the other methods, which augment the assumptions of BS by transforming the density function to account for higher-order moments, this approach relies on a completely different density. The generalized lambda distribution is well known among statisticians, but has not yet been embraced by the financial community. As a consequence, it adds an additional layer of complexity to an already involved procedure.

In an attempt to reconcile real world option prices with theory, Das and Sundaram (1999) use two extensions of the BS model – introducing jumps into the return process and stochastic volatility – to examine the extent to which either of these methods is capable of resolving observed anomalies. In short, their research finds that neither approach is sufficient but the stochastic volatility model fares marginally better.

As the above literature suggests, over time, it has become clear that the market does not price all options according to the BS paradigm. In the options market implied volatility frequently increases with decreasing strike. This is the familiar "negative" skew commonly observed in the market for S&P 500 Index options. Typically, traders adjust for this by quoting volatilities that correspond to the consensus of the market for a given maturity and strike. Yet only one index underlies all the options on a particular underlying asset and it can only have a unique volatility. The pattern of implied volatilities with variation in time is known as the "term structure of volatility" and the pattern associated with strike prices the "skew". Together, they combine to create what is called the "implied volatility surface".[2] This variation with maturity and strike does imply that volatility (σ) may be some complicated function of both spot and time $\sigma(S, T)$ and has been explored by numerous researchers. In fact, there has been a proliferation of alternative volatility specifications since the original constant volatility posited by BS.

Most notably, Cox and Ross (1976) delineate the option pricing formula for the deterministic case where there is a constant elasticity relationship between volatility and the underlying security price $\sigma(S)$. In this model, volatility is proportional to the level of the stock price raised to a power. Other methods of deterministic volatility structures include autoregressive conditional heteroscedasticity (ARCH), generalized autoregressive conditional heteroscedasticity (GARCH), the exponential GARCH (EGARCH), and exponentially weighted moments models.

Stochastic volatility posits that the future level of volatility cannot be perfectly predicted from currently available information and is typically some complicated function of spot and time $\sigma(S, T)$. From a stochastic perspective, among others, Hull and White (1987), Scott (1987), and Wiggins (1987) were among the first to develop models and explore this issue. Stein and Stein (1991) and Heston (1993), also worked on the stochastic volatility issue but with models that are simpler and computationally more efficient than their predecessors.[3]

Recently, academics and practitioners have elaborated "implied" lattice methods – see Derman and Kani (1994), Dupire (1994), and Rubinstein (1994). If one knows the standard index option prices for all strikes and maturities, then, the local volatility surface $\sigma(S, T)$ can be determined. The essence of this approach is that the market is correct and that one can both recover the implied risk-neutral probabilities and implied volatilities from the liquid options market. Recovering the risk-neutral probabilities proves very powerful as these probabilities are immutable with respect to option type and so this method allows one to price not only plain vanilla but also exotic options in a manner consistent with the liquid market. Derman, Kani, and Zou (1996, p. 25) discuss the notion of local volatility, which according to their research can be used to "measure market sentiment, to compute the evolution of implied volatilities through time, to calculate the index exposure of standard index options, and to value and hedge exotic options."

The real phenomenon underlying term structures, smiles, and surfaces may be that either market forces prevent prices from taking their true BS values or that share returns are not normally distributed. The thrust of this paper is to present a simple methodology for pricing options while incorporating higher-order moments, which allows for non-normal share returns. These moments may be derived from a priori econometric analysis.[4] Daily returns for the S&P 500 Index from 1999 through 2001 are considered. Values and comparative statics computed from the higher-order moment parameterization are compared to those of the BS model.

The outline of the remainder of this paper is as follows: Section 2 delineates a simplified model, which can easily be implemented in practice. Section 3 presents numerical results related to this simplification including empirical observations, option values and comparative statics, the final section, Section 4, presents conclusions.

2. THE PRICING MODEL

In the case of a European call option, the final payoff is $(S_T - X)^+$, with the option value given by the expected present value payoff, in a risk-neutral world:

$$V_c = e^{-rT}\hat{E}[(S_T - X)^+] \tag{1}$$

where r is the continuously compounded risk-free rate of interest, T the time to expiration, $\hat{E}$ is the expectation operator in a risk-neutral economy, S_T is the underlying asset value at maturity, and X is the strike price. Under a Geometric Brownian Motion diffusion process, our related expression for S_T is given by:

$$S_T = S_0 e^{[((r-d)-\frac{\sigma^2}{2})T + \sigma\sqrt{T}X]} \tag{2}$$

where S_0 is the current underlying asset value, d is the continuous dividend yield, σ is the instantaneous volatility rate of the underlying return distribution, T is the time to expiration, and Z is a standard normal variable with a mean of zero and variance of T. Thus by substituting for S_T and simplifying V_c may be written as:

$$V_{BS,c} = \frac{e^{-rT}}{\sqrt{2\pi}} \int_a^{\infty} (e^{t \cdot s + m} - X) \cdot e^{-\frac{1}{2}t^2} \cdot dt \tag{3}$$

with

$$a = \frac{\ln(X) - m}{s},\ s = \sigma\sqrt{T},\ \text{and}\ m = \ln(S_0) + (r - d) \cdot T - \frac{\sigma^2}{2} T.$$[5]

Similarly, with a change in the limits of integration, and the boundary condition to $(X - S_T)^+$, the value of a European put is given by:

$$V_{BS,p} = \frac{e^{-rT}}{\sqrt{2\pi}} \int_{-\infty}^{a} (X - e^{t \cdot s + m}) \cdot e^{-\frac{1}{2}t^2} \cdot dt \tag{4}$$

with a, s, and m previously defined. Equations (3) and (4) represent the BS formula for European calls and puts in integral form.

To adjust the above for higher-order terms, one applies a series expansion. More specifically, a generalized Edgeworth expansion will transform the standardized density given a prespecified skewness and kurtosis. This expansion $f(t)$ is defined accordingly:

$$f(t) = 1 + \frac{1}{6}\xi(t^3 - 3t) + \frac{1}{24}(\kappa - 3)(t^4 - 6t^2 + 3) + \frac{1}{72}\xi^2(t^5 - 10t^3 + 15t) \tag{5}$$

where ξ is skewness and κ represents kurtosis. Thus for a European call (put) option, under an Edgeworth expansion, the value is given by the following:

$$V_{Edge,c} = \frac{e^{-rT}}{\sqrt{2\pi}} \int_a^{\infty} (e^{t \cdot s + m} - X) \cdot e^{-\frac{1}{2}t^2} \cdot f(t) \cdot dt \tag{6}$$

$$V_{Edge,p} = \frac{e^{-rT}}{\sqrt{2\pi}} \int_{-\infty}^{a} (X - e^{t \cdot s + m}) \cdot e^{-\frac{1}{2}t^2} \cdot f(t) \cdot dt \tag{7}$$

If $\xi = 0$ and $\kappa = 3$ then $f(t) = 1$, the density function is standard normal $N(0, 1)$ and option values are consistent with the BS paradigm. The above integrals are easily evaluated via numerical integration – a trapezoidal or parabolic (Simpson's rule) method works well.[6]

Analogously, for European calls and puts, the following partial derivatives (delta, gamma, vega, theta, and rho)

$$\Delta = \frac{\partial V}{\partial S}, \ \Gamma = \frac{\partial^2 V}{\partial S^2}, \ \upsilon = \frac{\partial V}{\partial \sigma}, \ \Theta = \frac{\partial V}{\partial t}, \ \rho = \frac{\partial V}{\partial r}$$

may be calculated numerically (the partial derivatives with respect to skewness

$$\frac{\partial V}{\partial \xi}$$

and kurtosis

$$\frac{\partial V}{\partial \kappa}$$

may also be numerically obtained). In addition, one may also determine the total change in value due to skewness by setting the kurtosis value equal to three and comparing this value to the BS output.

$$V_{Edge}(S, X, \sigma, T, r, d, \xi, \kappa = 3) - V_{BS}(S, X, \sigma, T, r, d)$$

The total change in value due to kurtosis may similarly be determined by setting the skewness parameter equal to zero and comparing the resulting value to the BS output.

$$V_{Edge}(S, X, \sigma, T, r, d, \xi = 0, \kappa) - V_{BS}(S, X, \sigma, T, r, d)$$

The values, as well as the comparative statics provide insight into the pricing and hedging biases introduced in an environment characterized by non-normal underlying returns.

3. NUMERICAL RESULTS

From an empirical perspective, one can choose to calculate a measure for skewness and kurtosis and use these values in the Edgeworth model. In examining the phenomenon of S&P 500 Index return data and negative skewness and positive excess kurtosis, the period from 12/29/89–11/02/01 is considered. Daily returns are calculated as the natural logarithm of the price relatives:

$$r_i = \ln(P_t / P_{t-1}) \tag{8}$$

The sample mean, standard deviation, skewness, and excess kurtosis are as follows:

$$\bar{r} = \frac{1}{n}\sum_{i=1}^{n} r_i \tag{9}$$

$$s = \sqrt{\frac{n\sum_{i=1}^{n} r_i^2 - \left(\sum_{i=1}^{n} (r_i)\right)^2}{n(n-1)}} \tag{10}$$

$$\xi = \frac{n}{(n-1)(n-2)}\sum_{i=1}^{n}\left(\frac{r_i - \bar{r}}{s}\right)^3 \tag{11}$$

$$\kappa_{Excess} = \left\{\frac{n(n+1)}{(n-1)(n-2)(n-3)}\sum_{i=1}^{n}\left(\frac{r_i - \bar{r}}{s}\right)^4\right\} - \frac{3(n-1)^2}{(n-2)(n-3)} \tag{12}$$

where r_i, the daily return, is given by Eq. (8), $\bar{r}$ is the mean of the return series defined by Eq. (9), n is the number of observations, and s is the sample standard deviation of returns. Daily return data for the S&P 500 Index collected over the period 12/29/89–11/02/01 is consistent with negative skewness and positive excess kurtosis – (–0.2562, and 4.3463 respectively). Table 1 contains S&P 500 Index rolling values for means, maximum, and minimum values of skewness (11) and excess kurtosis (12) for 1-month, 3-month, and 6-month periods. Consistent with the research on indices by Turner and Weigel (1992) and Campbell and Hentschel (1992), which cover the periods from 1928 through 1989 and from 1926 through 1988 respectively, the data over the 1989 to 2001 period points to negative skewness and positive excess kurtosis in S&P 500 Index returns.

The S&P 500 Index options market (these options trade European style exercise) is characterized by academics and practitioners as having a negative skew. Perhaps, the most noticeable implication from a trading perspective is that out of the money puts typically trade at high-implied volatilities relative to other options. However, if one uses a constant volatility as assumed by the BS model, a graphic of strike vs. implied volatility would show a flat line. Typically, traders adjust the valuation of options for this negative skew by applying different volatilities across strikes and time. Some solve for the volatility surface by observing prices and inverting the BS equation to derive volatility measures while others have a particular view of the market.

Table 1. S&P 500 Index Returns Skewness and Excess Kurtosis Values 12/29/89–11/02/01.

1 – Month Rolling Skewness and Excess Kurtosis (24 observations per period)

	Mean	Max	Min
Skewness	–0.0151	1.8921	–2.8161
Excess Kurtosis	0.5608	11.0215	–1.3175

Total Observations in Rolling Period: 2,966

3 – Month Rolling Skewness and Excess Kurtosis (64 observations per period)

	Mean	Max	Min
Skewness	–0.1217	0.9686	–1.9138
Excess Kurtosis	1.1549	10.2886	–0.7653

Total Observations in Rolling Period: 2,926

6 – Month Rolling Skewness and Excess Kurtosis (127 observations per period)

	Mean	Max	Min
Skewness	–0.1847	0.6683	–2.0355
Excess Kurtosis	1.6842	10.6264	–0.6273

Total Observations in Rolling Period: 2,863

The above table depicts the mean, maximum, and minimum values for skewness and excess kurtosis over 1, 3, and 6 month rolling periods.

According to Rubinstein (1998, p. 23), the S&P 500 Index options market has been left-skewed since the crash of 1987. This is an empirical observation. Thus rather than relaxing the constant volatility assumption in the BS model one may estimate the skewness and kurtosis from market data. Consistent with Rubinstein's (1998, p. 22) empirical observations, the values and partial derivatives, which are compared to the BS model in this section, assume a leptokurtic distribution – ($\xi = -0.8, \kappa = 4.8$).[7] Figure 1 depicts a normal distribution and a left skewed – leptokurtic – density.

The distinguishing characteristics of the left skewed – leptokurtic density include fatter tails and a higher peak. In short, given a leptokurtic distribution, there is a greater likelihood for more extreme events than what is suggested by the normal density.

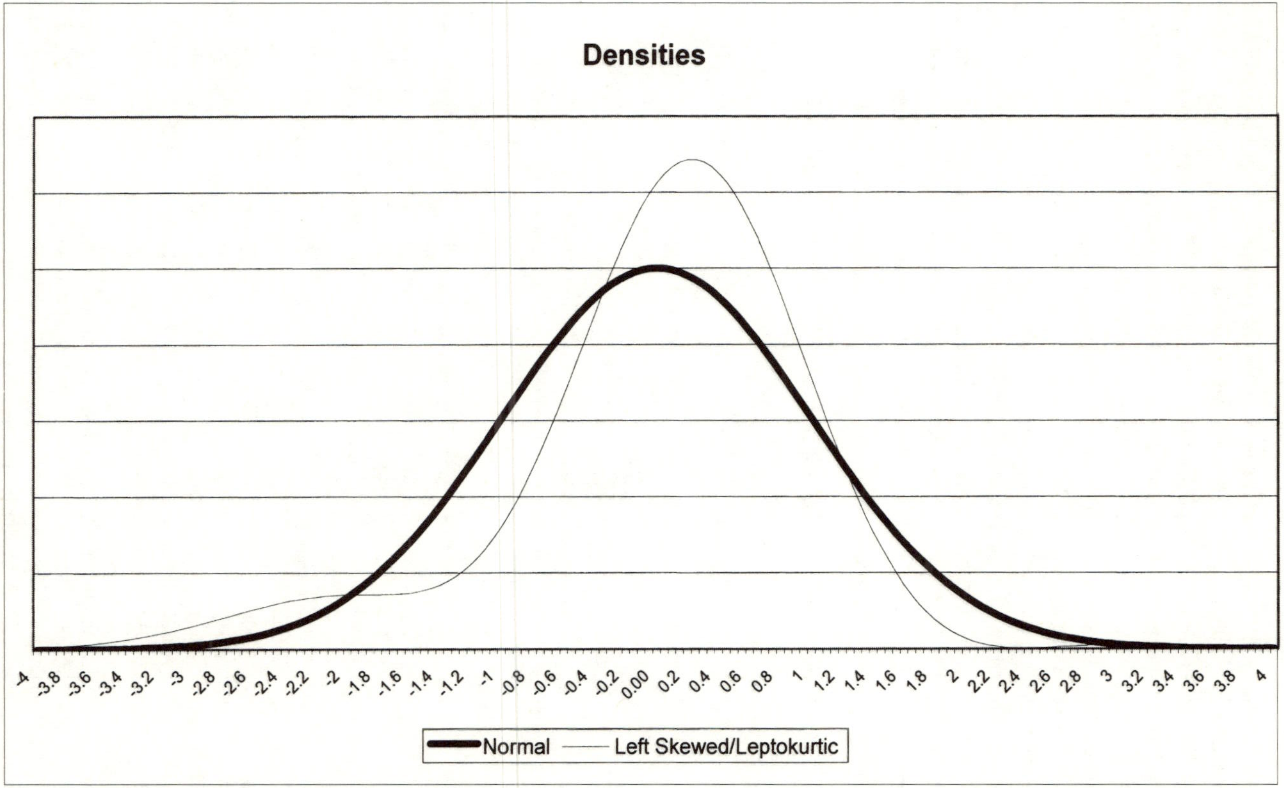

The normal distribution is a standard density with a mean of zero, variance of one, skewness of zero and kurtosis of three.
The left-skewed distribution has a mean of zero, variance of one, skewness of –0.8, and kurtosis of 4.8.

Fig. 1.

Tables 2 and 3 depict the values as well as partial derivatives for both European call and put options.[8] The assumptions include an underlying index value of 100, strikes of 80, 90, 100, 110, and 120, a 4% per-annum risk-free rate of interest, six-month time to maturity, 25% per annum volatility, and a continuous dividend yield of 1.25% per annum. For the Edgeworth call and put the skewness and kurtosis are –0.8 and 4.8 respectively.

Consistent with the market for S&P 500 Index options, the results in Tables 2 and 3 suggest that given the values chosen for skewness and kurtosis, using a constant volatility the BS model undervalues low-strike options and overprices high-strike options. This is the case for both call and put options. Practitioners usually adjust for this by disregarding the constant volatility assumption and applying a higher volatility for lower strike options. This

Table 2. Comparison of Call Option and Comparative Static Values.

Strike	BS	Edge	BS	Edge
	Call Value		Vega	
80	21.611	22.026	10.106	10.119
90	13.625	13.639	20.967	16.589
100	7.651	6.927	27.649	23.255
110	3.835	2.807	26.150	21.194
120	1.734	0.964	19.281	12.514
	Delta		Theta	
80	0.918	0.925	–4.186	–4.193
90	0.772	0.836	–6.820	–5.900
100	0.562	0.617	–8.153	–7.233
110	0.352	0.340	–7.353	–6.120
120	0.192	0.135	–5.280	–3.461
	Gamma		Rho	
80	0.008	0.004	35.078	35.249
90	0.017	0.014	31.796	34.965
100	0.022	0.027	24.298	27.379
110	0.021	0.028	15.701	15.575
120	0.015	0.018	8.746	6.268

The above table depicts the values of a European Call option with the following parameters: ($s = 100$, $r = 4\%$, $T = 0.5$, $\sigma = 25\%$, $d = 1.25\%$) for strikes of 80, 90, 100, 110, and 120. The Edgeworth Call is valued with the same parameters except a skewness and kurtosis of –0.8, and 4.8 respectively. Comparative statics for the Edgeworth Call are computed numerically.

Table 3. Comparison of Put Option and Comparative Static Values Strike.

Strike	BS	Edge	BS	Edge
	Put Value		Vega	
80	0.650	1.131	10.106	10.878
90	2.466	2.546	20.967	17.348
100	6.294	5.636	27.649	24.014
110	12.280	11.318	26.150	21.953
120	19.981	19.276	19.281	13.273
	Delta		Theta	
80	–0.076	–0.068	–2.291	–2.488
90	–0.222	–0.157	–4.534	–3.802
100	–0.431	–0.376	–5.474	–4.743
110	–0.641	–0.654	–4.282	–3.238
120	–0.802	–0.858	–1.817	–0.187
	Gamma		Rho	
80	0.008	0.004	–4.130	–3.959
90	0.017	0.014	–12.313	–9.144
100	0.022	0.027	–24.712	–21.631
110	0.021	0.028	–38.210	–38.336
120	0.015	0.018	–50.066	–52.544

The above table depicts the values of a European Put option with the following parameters: ($s=100$, $r=4\%$, $T=0.5$, $\sigma=25\%$, $d=1.25\%$) for strikes of 80, 90, 100, 110, and 120. The Edgeworth Put is valued with the same parameters except a skewness and kurtosis of –0.8, and 4.8 respectively. Comparative statics for the Edgeworth Put are computed numerically.

practice has come to characterize the S&P 500 Index options market. Additionally, the comparative statics are noticeably different given a non-normal distribution.

Table 4 separates out the value that is contributed by each of skewness and kurtosis consistent with a non-normal density function. It is interesting to note that given a negative skewness, the results attributed to this are monotonically decreasing with strike. This is consistent with the BS model underpricing low-strike options and overpricing high-strike options. Similarly, there is a pattern related to the results for kurtosis. Given a value for kurtosis, which is greater than three, option prices are less than suggested by BS for at or near the money but greater for strikes far out or in the money. This is consistent with the thesis

Table 4. Value Attributed to Non-normal Skewness and Kurtosis.

Strike	Call Value	
	Skewness	Kurtosis
80	0.336	0.078
90	0.295	–0.281
100	–0.227	–0.497
110	–0.751	–0.277
120	–0.881	0.110
	Put Value	
	Skewness	Kurtosis
80	0.409	0.071
90	0.368	–0.288
100	–0.153	–0.504
110	–0.678	–0.284
120	–0.808	0.103

Values attributed to skewness and kurtosis are computed by setting one variable to its normal density specification and observing the effect vis-à-vis the BS model value. For example, setting kurtosis equal to three and skewness to –0.8. Analogously, setting skewness equal to zero and kurtosis to 4.8. The BS value is subtracted from the corresponding Edgeworth model value.

that the leptokurtic distribution implies that extreme events are more likely than what is suggested by the normal density.

Figure 2 depicts the volatility smiles consistent with option values obtained via the Edgeworth model. These values are obtained by inverting the BS model and solving via bisection for the volatility that is consistent with the price given by the proposed Edgeworth model. The downward sloping smile is consistent with the market for S&P 500 Index options.

4. CONCLUSIONS

In general, models are simplifications of reality typically based on assumptions with varying degrees of truth. One such model is the BS option-pricing model. This paper revisits the assumption of normally distributed returns consistent with the BS option-pricing paradigm. While numerous researchers have refuted this claim, and have proposed alternatives, practitioners still rely heavily on BS because of its simplicity. The proposed model addresses higher order moments in the context of options pricing. The model is simple to implement and affords

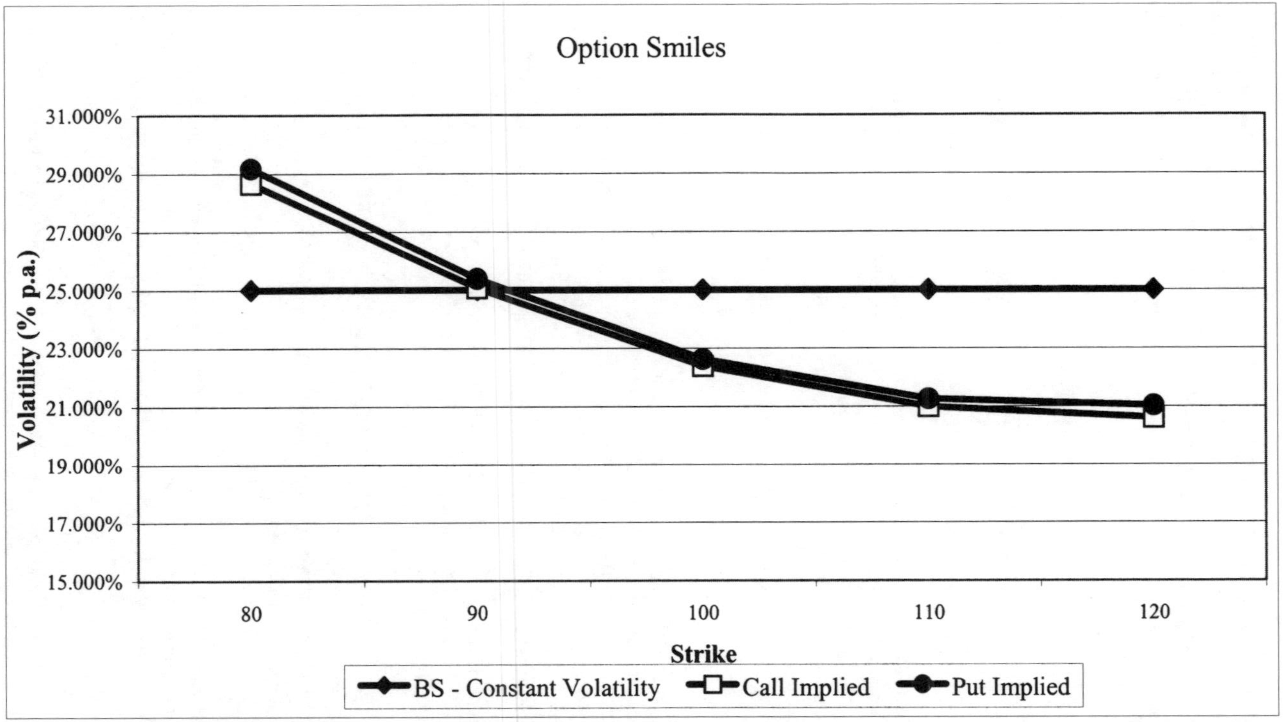

The above smiles are computed by assuming a constant 25% per annum volatility for the BS model and solving via bisection for the implied volatility associated with the Call and Put values in Tables 1 and 2 obtained from the Edgeworth model.

Fig. 2.

one the ability to transform the standard normal distribution into a distribution consistent with the first four moments. This allows one to value and hedge options while having an opinion about skewness and kurtosis. In particular, the market for S&P 500 Index options may be more realistically modeled by taking these moments into account.

NOTES

1. Kritzman (1994) is a good reference for higher order moments and their relevancy in finance.
2. Mayhew (1995) provides an excellent literature review related to implied volatility and smiles.
3. For an extensive discussion on options and volatility, and models, which address the deterministic and stochastic nature of volatility, see Abken and Nandi (1996).
4. In contrast to the two additional parameters necessary for the jump-diffusion process, skewness, and kurtosis values are more readily available and understood by academics and practitioners.
5. For currency options, one may substitute the foreign risk-free rate r_f for d in

$$m = \ln(S_0) + (r - d)T - \frac{\sigma^2}{2}T.$$

6. MATLAB provides an excellent environment for evaluating integrals numerically. It contains built in functions, which facilitate this process.
7. Corrado and Su (1996) also observe a market for S&P 500 Index options in which there exists a negative skew and a kurtosis greater than three. More specifically, for November 1990, they find an average value for skewness and kurtosis of –1.72 and 3.47 respectively. Similarly, for December 1993 Corrado and Su report skewness and kurtosis values of –1.66 and 5.75.
8. Analytical formulae for the Black-Scholes option pricing model and partial derivatives may be found in almost any comprehensive text on investments or book related to derivatives pricing.

REFERENCES

Abken, P., & Nandi, S. (1996). Options and Volatility. *Federal Reserve Bank of Atlanta – Economic Review*, (December), 21–35.

Aggarwal, R., & Rao Ramesh, P. (1990). Institutional Ownership and Distribution of Equity Returns. *The Financial Review*, *25*. 211–229.

Black, F., & Scholes, M. (1973). The Pricing of Options and Corporate Liabilities. *Journal of Political Economy*, *81*(3), 637–654.

Campbell, J. Y., & Hentschel, L. (1992). No News is Good News: An Asymmetric Model of Changing Volatility in Stock Returns. *Journal of Financial Economics*, *31*, 281–318.

Corrado, C. J. (2001). Option Pricing Based on the Generalized Lambda Distribution. *Journal of Futures Markets*, (February).

Corrado, C. J., & Su, T. (1996). Skewness and Kurtosis in S&P 500 Index Returns Implied by Option Prices. *Journal of Financial Research*, *19*, 175–192.

Cox, J., & Ross, S. (1976). The Valuation of Options for Alternative Stochastic Processes. *Journal of Financial Economics*, *3*, 145–166.

Das, S. R., & Sundaram, R. K. (1999). Of Smiles and Smirks: A Term Structure Perspective. *Journal of Financial and Quantitative Analysis*, *34*(2), 211–239.

Derman, E., & Kani, I. (1994). Riding on the Smile. *Risk*, *7* (February), 32–39.

Derman, E., Kani, I., & Zou, J. (1996). The Local Volatility Surface: Unlocking the Information in Index Option Prices. *Financial Analysts Journal*, (July/August), 25–36.

Dupire, B. (1994). Pricing with a Smile. *Risk*, *7* (January), 18–20.

Fama, E. F. (1965). The Behavior of Stock Market Prices. *Journal of Business*, *38*, 34–105.

Heston, S. (1993). A Closed-Form Solution for Options with Stochastic Volatility with Applications to Bond and Currency Options. *Review of Financial Studies*, *6*, 327–343.

Hull, J., & White, A. (1987). The Pricing of Options on Assets with Stochastic Volatilities. *The Journal of Finance*, *42*(2), 281–300.

Jarrow, R., & Rudd, A. (1982). Approximate Option Valuation for Arbitrary Stochastic Processes. *Journal of Financial Economics*, *10*(3), 347–369.

Johnson, R. S., Pawlukiewicz, J. E., & Mehta, J. M. (1997). Binomial Option Pricing with Skewed Asset Returns. *Review of Quantitative Finance and Accounting*, *9*, 89–101.

Kritzman, M. (1994). What Practitioners Need to Know About Higher Moments. *Financial Analysts Journal*, (September/October), 10–17.

Macbeth, J., & Merville, L. (1979). An Empirical Examination of the Black-Scholes Call Option Pricing Model. *The Journal of Finance*, *34*(5), 1173–1186.

Mandelbrot, B. (1963). The Variation of Certain Specultaive Prices. *Journal of Business*, *36*, 394–419.

Merton. R. C. (1976). Option Pricing with Discontinuous Returns. *Journal of Financial Economics*, *3*, 125–144.

Mayhew, S. (1995). Implied Volatility. *Financial Analysts Journal*, (July/August), 8–19.

Ritchey, R. (1990). Call Option Valuation for Discrete Normal Mixtures. *Journal of Financial Research*, *13*(4), 285–296.

Rubinstein, M. (1994). Implied Binomial Trees. *Journal of Finance*, *49*(3), 771–818.

Rubinstein, M. (1998). Edgeworth Binomial Trees. *Journal of Derivatives*, *5*, 20–27.

Scott, L. O. (1987). Option Pricing When the Variance Changes Randomly: Theory, Estimation, and Application. *Journal of Financial and Quantitative Analysis*, *22*, 419–438.

Singleton, J. C., & Wingender, J. (1986). Skewness Persistence in Common Stock Returns. *Journal of Financial and Quantitative Analysis*, *21*, 335–341.

Stein, E. M., & Stein, J. C. (1991). Stock Price Distributions with Stochastic Volatility: An Analytic Approach. *Review of Financial Studies*, *4*, 727–752.

Tian, Y. S. (1998). A Trinomial Option Pricing Model Dependent on Skewness and Kurtosis. *International Review of Economics and Finance*, *7*(3), 315–330.

Turner, A. L., & Weigel, E. J. (1992). Daily Stock Return Volatility: 1928–1989. *Management Science*, *38*, 1586–1609.

Wiggins, J. B. (1987). Option Values under Stochastic Volatilities. *Journal of Financial Economics*, *19*, 351–372.

3. ADDITIONAL EVIDENCE ON ABNORMAL RETURNS AND RETURN VOLATILITY AROUND STOCK SPLITS

Michael Impson

ABSTRACT

Previous research on stock splits has shown that conventional splits that increase the number of shares outstanding are typically associated with positive abnormal returns around the split effective date and reverse splits are associated with negative abnormal returns around the reverse split effective date. Other studies have documented volatility changes around the stock split effective date. After adjusting for event-induced variance changes, I find that although significance levels are reduced, significant abnormal returns still persist around the split effective date. Using a technique that is robust to departures from normality, I also find that long term variance increases following split effective dates and that long term variance decreases following reverse split effective dates, consistent with results of previous studies.

1. INTRODUCTION

Stock splits, both conventional and reverse, should in theory be non-events in the life of the firm, since changing the size of a fractional share of the firm's

Advances in Quantitative Analysis of Finance and Accounting, Volume 10, pages 41–56.

ISBN: 0-7623-0969-5

equity should have no effect on the earning power of its assets. However, as has been well documented previously, apparently significant market reactions do occur in response to stock splits, both at the announcement date and the ex date. Fama, Fisher, Jensen and Roll (1969) in their classic study, concluded that splits per se had no effect on shareholder wealth. The reactions that are observed have been accounted for by institutional factors and information content of the announcements. However, information content does not appear to be a viable explanation for the abnormal returns observed on the ex date, since the impending split is well publicized and seldom canceled, as documented by Grinblatt, Masulis and Titman (1984). Maloney and Mulherin (1992) advanced the idea that ex date abnormal returns are driven at least in part by changes in bid ask spreads.

An increase in the volatility of stock returns after the ex date of stock splits has been documented in previous studies (Ohlson & Penman, 1985; French & Dubofsky, 1986; Conroy, Harris & Benet, 1990). The volatility changes appear to persist long after the split effective date. Sheikh (1989) finds that implied volatilities extracted from call option prices increase on the ex day of the split. None of these studies find variance increases at the announcement date, however.

Dravid (1987) found that return variance decreased following reverse splits. Woolridge and Chambers (1983), document negative abnormal returns on the proposal date and effective date of reverse splits.

This study examines both mean and volatility changes on the days around stock splits and considers them jointly. Since previous studies found return variance increased following splits, I investigate the possibility that when these variance changes are accounted for, the previously documented abnormal returns on and around the split effective date will disappear and the split effective date becomes a non-event as it is expected to be. I also examine longer term variance changes as a result of the split using an alternative methodology to that used in prior studies.

2. DATA AND SAMPLE

Splits and reverse splits were identified from the Center for Research in Security Prices (CRSP) database. CRSP distribution codes 5523, 5533, and 5543 were included. Over the period 1971–1999, 5,898 splits by NYSE/AMEX and 4,843 splits by NASDAQ firms were identified. Over the same period, 48 reverse splits by NYSE/AMEX firms and 69 reverse splits by NASDAQ firms were identified. In keeping with the convention of distinguishing stock splits from stock dividends, only distributions that increased the number of shares outstanding by 25% or more are included in the split sample. Because of the small number of observations available, any distributions that reduced the number of shares outstanding were considered reverse splits. The sample was also screened to include only observations with less than 50 days elapsed between the split announcement date and split effective date. The screened sample still includes the vast majority of observations available. The 50 day limit was imposed to assure that no split announcements fell within the market model regression interval discussed below.

3. METHODOLOGY

The objective of the tests performed is to detect shifts in mean returns and variance of returns around the ex date of stock splits and reverse splits. Previous research has documented shifts in both parameters. Based on the work of Sanders and Robbins (1991), these tests are also designed to detect the effect that event-induced variance changes have on tests of shifts in the mean. In addition, tests to detect long term variance changes are performed.

3.1. Market Model

The Sanders and Robbins technique utilizes market model prediction errors around the split effective date. In estimating the parameters, it is assumed that the underlying security return generating process is completely described by the single index market model (SIMM):

$$R_{jt} = \hat{\alpha}_j + \hat{\beta}_j R_{mt} + e_{jt};\ t = 1, \ldots, t;\ j = 1, \ldots, j \qquad (1)$$

where:

R_{jt} = return to security j on day t

$\hat{\alpha}_j$ = the intercept

$\hat{\beta}_j$ = the slope coefficient

R_{mt} = the return to the CRSP value weighted index on day t

e_{jt} = the disturbance on day t consistent with OLS assumptions

Defining the event date (split effective date) as day 0, for each security j, Eq. (1) is estimated with ordinary least squares over a 250 day interval, days –300 to –51 relative to the event date. Results reported in Tables 1–4 are based on the use of the CRSP value weighted index for the market index, but tests not reported using the CRSP equally weighted index produce essentially the same results. For each day in the desired forecast interval, the prediction error or abnormal return is defined as the actual minus predicted security return:

$$PE_{jt} = R_{jt} - \hat{\alpha}_j - \hat{\beta}_j R_{mt} \tag{2}$$

where $\hat{\alpha}_j$ and $\hat{\beta}_j$ are estimated using data from the estimation interval and R_{jt} and R_{mt} are from the interval of interest. For each security j, the cumulative prediction error is defined as the sum of the prediction errors over the interval t_1 to t_2.

$$CPE_j = \sum_{t=t_1}^{t_2} PE_{jt} \tag{3}$$

3.2. *Variance of CPE*

The variance of the cumulative prediction error is given by the following expression. Note that this expression collapses to the usual variance of the forecast error format for single day intervals.

$$\left[\sigma^2_{CPE} = \hat{\sigma}^2_j \quad N_2 + \frac{N_2^2}{N_1} + N_2^2 \frac{(\bar{R}_{m2} - \bar{R}_{m1})^2}{\sum_{t=1}^{N_1} (R_{mt} - \bar{R}_{m1})^2} \right] \tag{4}$$

where

$\hat{\sigma}^2_j$ = the variance of OLS residuals from Eq. (2)

N_1 = the number of observations in the estimation interval

N_2 = the number of observations in the forecase interval

$\bar{R}_{m1}$ = the mean value of the market return in the estimation interval

$\bar{R}_{m2}$ = the mean value of the market return in the forecast interval

3.3. *Weighted CPE*

Following the Collins and Dent (1984) methodology, weighted prediction errors are calculated. In all the equations and discussion that follow, the expression is stated using CPE, but applies equally well for single day intervals and prediction errors. For the vector of cumulative prediction errors, the weighted cumulative prediction error is the sum of the weighted CPE's for each firm. The weight is the reciprocal of the variance of the cumulative prediction error. The equation is:

$$WCPE = \sum_{j=1}^{J} \frac{CPE_j}{\sigma^2_{CPE}} \tag{5}$$

3.4. Test Statistics

In order to test for mean and variance changes as a result of the event, the method described by Sanders and Robbins (1991) is used. Based on the work of Ross (1989), the variance change is of interest in its own right, since Ross demonstrated that the rate of information flow and variance of returns are related. In addition, variance changes are of interest because variance changes can affect the results of the more common tests of shifts in the mean. Thus, variance changes should be investigated both to determine any changes in the rate of information flow and also to check the validity of wealth (mean) effects tests.

To implement the technique, a vector of cumulative prediction errors for each of the sample firms for the period of interest is created. Predicted returns are based on the market model regression described above. Statistics developed by Collins and Dent (1984) are used to test for mean shifts assuming cross sectional independence. Since market model prediction errors are both serially and crosssectionally hetereoscedastic, the Collins and Dent (1984) mean estimator should be the best linear unbiased estimator.

The mean cumulative prediction error using the Collins and Dent (1984) technique is:

$$M_3 = \frac{WCPE}{\sum_{j=1}^{J} \frac{1}{\sigma^2_{CPE_j}}} \tag{6}$$

where J is the number of firms in the sample. The associated test statistic is:

$$Z_3 = \frac{M_3 - \mu}{(\sigma^2_{M3})^{0.5}} \tag{7}$$

where μ is the mean of a normal distribution of cumulative prediction errors and:

$$\sigma^2_{M3} = \frac{1}{\sum_{j=1}^{J} \frac{1}{\sigma^2_{CPE_j}}} \tag{8}$$

However, the Z-statistics related to those mean estimators require that variance is unchanged by the event. Prior studies have found that variance of prediction errors is changed by the event, rendering the Z-statistic incorrect (e.g. Dann, 1981; Kalay & Lowenstein, 1985; Patel & Wolfson, 1979). Sanders and Robbins observe that the variance estimate used for the t-statistic is useful in this instance since it impounds variance changes resulting from the event, while the one for the Z-statistic does not. For the t-statistic, the variance estimator is given by:

$$s_{M3}^2 = \frac{\sum_{j=1}^{J} (CPE_j - M_3)^2 / \sigma_{CPE_j}^2}{(J-1) \sum_{j=1}^{J} \frac{1}{\sigma_{CPE_j}^2}} \tag{9}$$

The associated t-statistic is:

$$t_3 = \frac{M_3 - \mu}{(s_{M3}^2)^{0.5}} \tag{10}$$

If there is no variance change, the ratio of s_{M3}^2/σ_{M3}^2 should be equal to one. However, if there is an event-induced variance increase, s_{M3}^2 will increase and the ratio will exceed one. Collins and Dent (1984) propose a chi-square statistic utilizing this variance ratio as a basis for detecting variance changes. However, departures of the sample from normality significantly impact the power of this test. Since previous research has demonstrated that market model prediction errors typically demonstrate significant departures from normality (Brown & Warner (1985), Jain (1986)), the usefulness of the Collins and Dent test is questionable for this application.

The departure from normality is identified as excess kurtosis by Sanders and Robbins (1991). As they point out, this excess kurtosis is firm specific thus creating a problem in the use of a parametric procedure or a Monte Carlo procedure utilizing a random sampling of firms. The alternative proposed is to generate an empirical distribution of the variance ratio using the sample firms over a period outside the event period of interest. The actual variance ratio calculated for the day or period of interest can then be compared to the empirical distribution. Variance ratios for the day or period of interest that lie above the 95th percentile or below the 5th percentile of the empirical distribution indicate a significant change in variance. In this study, the empirical distribution is generated using two 100-day periods immediately preceding and following the event period.

3.5. Variance Differences between Periods

In order to examine longer term variance changes, a 100 day pre-event period is compared with a 100 day post-event period. The pre-event period ends five days prior to the split effective date and the post-event period begins five days after the effective date in order to exclude any localized reaction to the event.

The conventional F-test may not yield reliable results as a basis for examining variance changes if the data exhibits significant non-normality. An alternative test that is robust to departures from normality is described by Van Valen (1978) and utilized by Lockwood and McInish (1990) in testing for equality of variances across bull and bear markets. Variations about the sample median are employed in the test as follows:

$$D_k = \frac{\sum_{i=1}^{N_k} \left[\sum_{j=1}^{J_k} (|R_{ijk} - Md_K| - \bar{D}_{ij})^2 \right]}{J_k} \tag{11}$$

where:

R_{ijk} = return to firm i on day j in period k

Md_k = median return for all firms in period k

$\bar{D}_{ik}$ = mean return for firm i in period k

J_k = number of days in period k

N_k = number of firms in period k

A t- test performed on D values for the pre-event and post-event periods is used to detect any difference in variance between periods.

4. RESULTS

4.1. Daily Returns

4.1.1. Splits

For splits, daily variances for a period beginning 100 days before the split ex date and ending 100 days after the split ex date are shown pictorially in Fig. 1. The variance measure shown here is the variance of raw returns; however, almost identical results are obtained used the variance of the prediction error or the Sanders and Robbins t-statistic variance estimator. There is a large variance

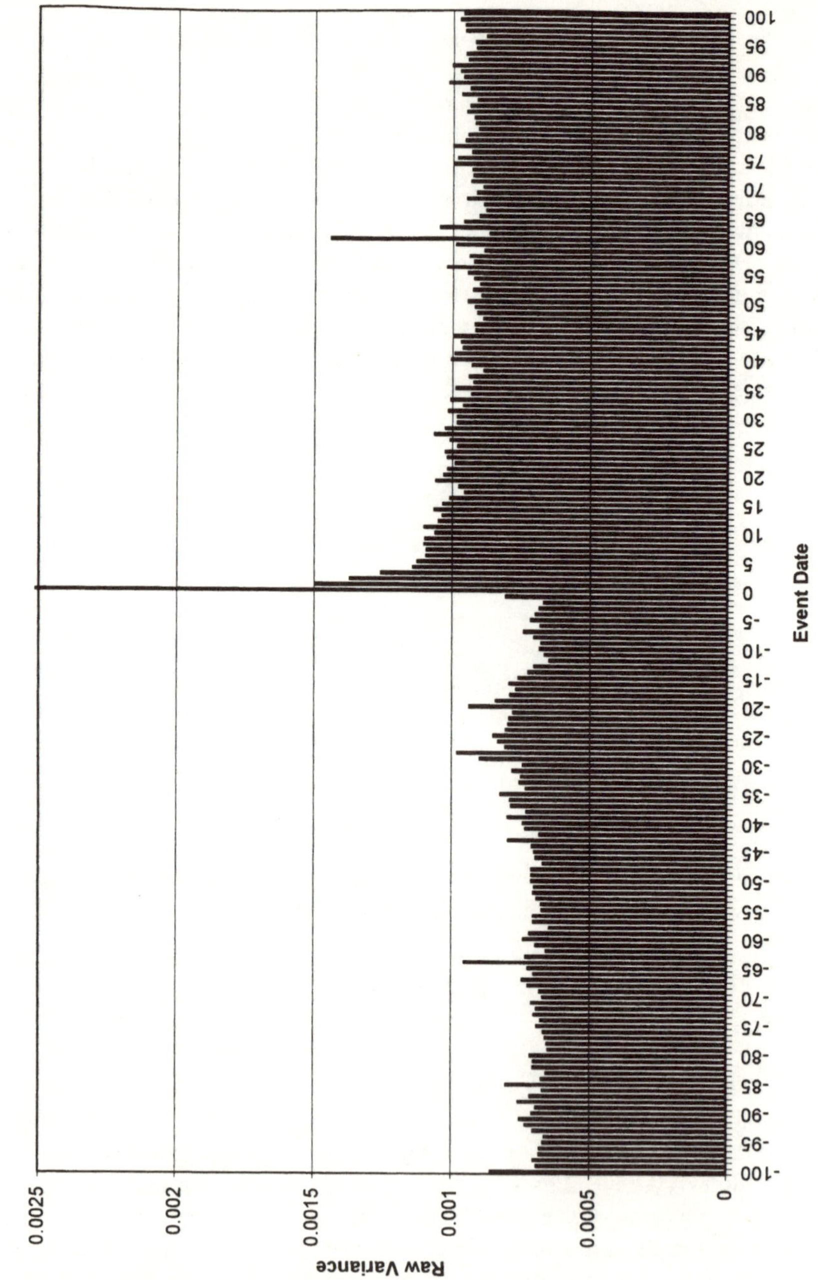

Fig. 1. Variance Changes Around Split Ex Date.

increase on the split effective date and variances are clearly larger after the split effective date.

Table 1 shows the prediction errors, test statistics, variance estimators, and variance ratios for a period beginning 15 days before the spit ex date and ending 15 days after the split ex date. The table confirms the highly significant variance increase on the split effective date and a significant variance increase on the three days following, based on the 95th percentile of the empirical distribution. In fact, variance ratios for 16 days in the period exceed the 95th percentile of the empirical distribution.

Table 1 also shows that there are significant positive abnormal returns on the day preceding through three days following the split effective date, conditionally based on the *Z*-statistic assumption of constant variance. Although the significance level is reduced unconditionally, based on the *t*-statistic, there are still significant abnormal returns over this period.

4.1.2. Reverse Splits

Figure 2 depicts the pattern of variance changes for reverse splits for a similar period again using variance of raw returns. The large spike around the event date is again apparent. It also appears that there is some reduction in variance following the split effective date.

Table 2 documents abnormal returns and variance changes for the reverse split sample. Around the event date, a pattern similar to that of the conventional splits is also observed here. Based on the variance ratio measure compared to the empirical distribution, significant variance increases occur on days –2 through the split effective date, but following the effective date variances and variance ratios decline.

Table 2 also shows significant negative abnormal returns on the reverse split effective date and two days following, both conditionally based on the *Z*-statistic and unconditionally based on the *t*-statistic, although at reduced significance levels. There are also significant negative abnormal returns on days +5 and +6.

4.2. Intervals

Table 3 shows abnormal returns and variance changes for intervals around the split effective date. The empirical distribution of variance ratios for each interval was generated using two periods, a 100-day pre-event period immediately preceding the 101-day forecast interval (days –50 to +50) and a 100-day post-event period immediately following the 101-day forecast interval. Pre- and post-event intervals were used to impound any pre- or post-event

Table 1. Daily Abnormal Returns and Variance Changes Around Forward Split Effective Date.

Day	Prediction Error	Z	t	Collins-Dent Z Variance Estimator	Collins-Dent t Variance Estimator	Variance Ratio
–15	–0.000267	–1.586	–1.442	0.00000002841	0.00000003439	1.210
–14	0.000504	–2.995**	–2.793**	0.00000002837	0.00000003263	1.150
–13	–0.000329	–1.954*	–1.827	0.00000002836	0.00000003244	1.144
–12	–0.000902	–5.355**	–5.190**	0.00000002837	0.00000003022	1.065
–11	–0.000437	–2.593**	–2.469**	0.00000002838	0.00000003130	1.103
–10	–0.000674	–3.999**	–3.831**	0.00000002837	0.00000003091	1.090
–09	0.000681	–4.045**	–3.946**	0.00000002837	0.00000002981	1.051
–08	–0.000196	–1.162	–1.090	0.00000002838	0.00000003225	1.136
–07	–0.000423	–2.513*	–2.320*	0.00000002838	0.00000003332	1.174
–06	–0.000481	–2.852**	–2.650*	0.00000002839	0.00000003289	1.159
–05	–0.000270	–1.605	–1.475	0.00000002841	0.00000003362	1.183
–04	–0.000026	0.153	0.139	0.00000002841	0.00000003407	1.199
–03	–0.000171	–1.013	–0.970	0.00000002838	0.00000003097	1.091
–02	0.000327	1.939	1.805	0.00000002840	0.00000003277	1.154
–01	0.001643	9.752**	8.642**	0.00000002839	0.00000003616	1.273
00	0.008528	50.516**	24.296**	0.00000002850	0.00000012321	4.323##
01	0.002823	16.754**	10.412**	0.00000002839	0.00000007351	2.589##
02	0.001625	9.644**	6.233**	0.00000002839	0.00000006798	2.394##
03	0.000887	5.268**	3.483**	0.00000002838	0.00000006493	2.288##
04	–0.000379	–2.249*	–1.544	0.00000002839	0.00000006026	2.123##
05	–0.000628	–3.724**	–2.529*	0.00000002841	0.00000006160	2.168##
06	–0.000615	–3.648**	–2.570**	0.00000002839	0.00000005720	2.015##
07	–0.000760	–4.509**	–3.251**	0.00000002837	0.00000005459	1.924#
08	–0.001006	–5.969**	–4.317**	0.00000002839	0.00000005426	1.911#
09	–0.001212	–7.196**	–5.156**	0.00000002839	0.00000005530	1.948#
10	–0.001022	–6.067**	–4.342**	0.00000002839	0.00000005543	1.952##
11	–0.000643	–3.814**	–2.768**	0.00000002838	0.00000005389	1.899#
12	–0.000664	–3.939**	–2.688**	0.00000002840	0.00000006096	2.147##
13	–0.000912	–5.410**	–3.924**	0.00000002839	0.00000005396	1.901#
14	–0.000748	–4.441**	–3.229**	0.00000002840	0.00000005372	1.892#
15	–0.001154	–6.835**	–4.961**	0.00000002853	0.00000005416	1.899#

* Significant at the 5% level.
** Significant at the 1% level.
# 95th percentile of the empirical distribution is 1.83.
99th percentile of the empirical distribution is 1.95.

effects. Interval statistics were generated by stacking non-overlapping intervals of the desired length through both of the 100 day periods. Five days was the

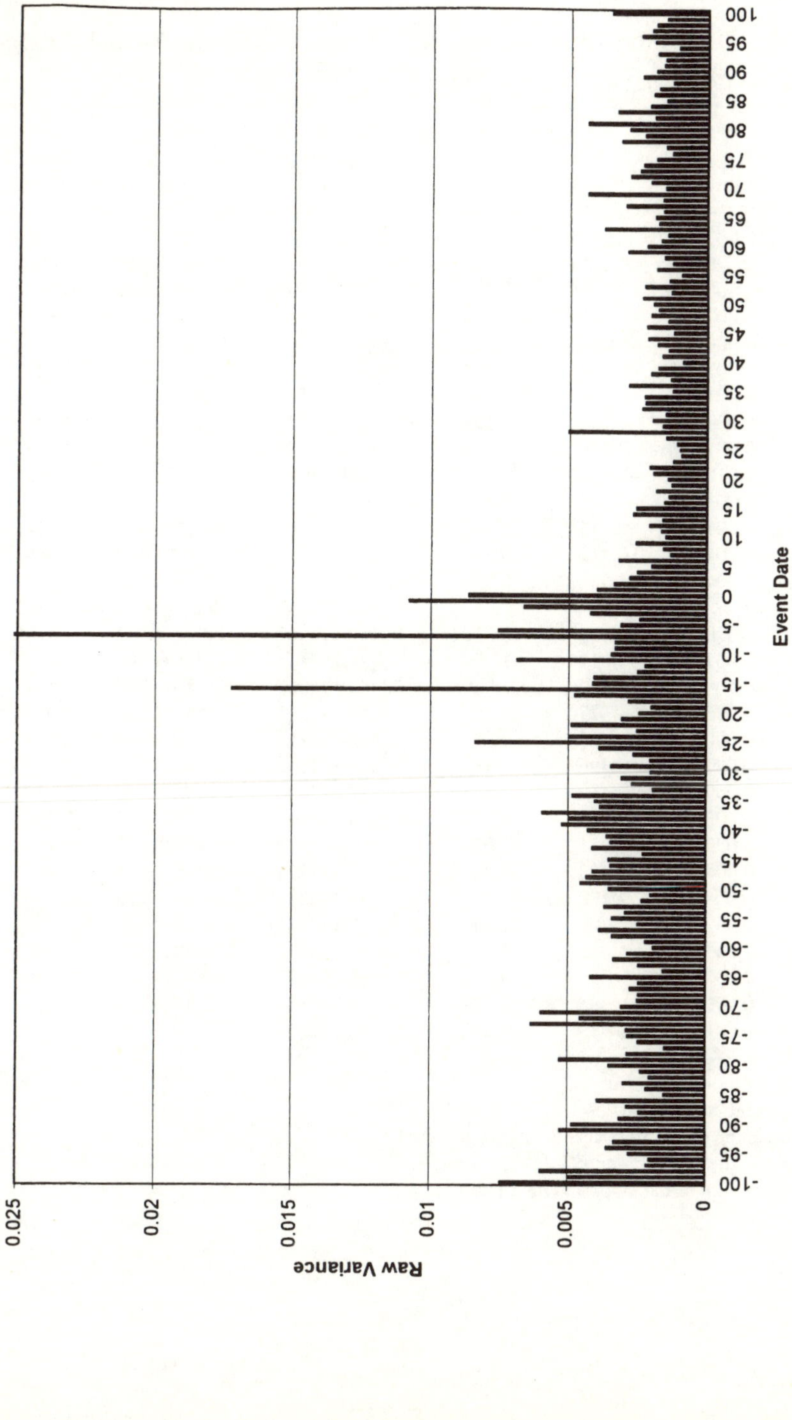

Fig. 2. Variance Changes Around Reverse Split Ex Date.

Table 2. Daily Abnormal Returns and Variance Changes Around Reverse Split Effective Date.

Day	Prediction Error	Z	t	Collins-Dent Z Variance Estimator	Collins-Dent t Variance Estimator	Variance Ratio
–15	0.003613	0.995	0.913	0.0000131942	0.0000156735	1.188
–14	0.000458	0.126	0.120	0.0000131727	0.0000144658	1.098
–13	–0.008419	–2.302*	–2.418*	0.0000133753	0.0000121249	0.907
–12	0.002990	0.823	0.909	0.0000132029	0.0000108274	0.820
–11	–0.000527	–0.145	–0.124	0.0000132822	0.0000179877	1.354
–10	–0.007137	–1.964*	–1.854	0.0000132081	0.0000148214	1.122
–09	–0.001443	–0.397	–0.434	0.0000131921	0.0000110326	0.836
–08	0.004428	1.220	1.198	0.0000131824	0.0000136581	1.036
–07	0.001829	0.504	0.231	0.0000131770	0.0000629409	4.777##
–06	–0.010304	–2.836**	–2.429*	0.0000131999	0.0000179911	1.363
–05	–0.002792	–0.769	–0.815	0.0000131954	0.0000117423	0.890
–04	0.001499	0.413	0.497	0.0000131959	0.0000091134	0.691
–03	0.001152	0.317	0.271	0.0000132069	0.0000180143	1.364
–02	0.004947	1.362	0.833	0.0000131906	0.0000352690	2.674##
–01	–0.002339	–0.637	–0.357	0.0000134969	0.0000429782	3.184##
00	–0.020789	–5.405**	–3.519**	0.0000147962	0.0000348911	2.358#
01	–0.007757	–2.019*	–1.903	0.0000147547	0.0000166102	1.126
02	–0.008088	–2.112*	–1.969*	0.0000146607	0.0000168779	1.151
03	–0.006627	–1.727	–1.785	0.0000147247	0.0000137856	0.936
04	–0.002629	–0.698	–0.746	0.0000141759	0.0000124354	0.877
05	–0.009379	–2.496*	–2.416*	0.0000141143	0.0000150653	1.067
06	–0.009355	–2.482*	–2.435*	0.0000142050	0.0000147587	1.039
07	–0.003128	–0.833	–1.160	0.0000141064	0.0000072721	0.516
08	–0.003495	–0.931	–1.073	0.0000140971	0.0000106102	0.753
09	0.004447	1.183	1.081	0.0000141274	0.0000169155	1.197
10	0.004499	1.190	1.394	0.0000142863	0.0000104222	0.730
11	0.002988	0.790	0.994	0.0000143245	0.0000090360	0.631
12	0.003864	1.021	1.167	0.0000143172	0.0000109567	0.765
13	0.001381	0.365	0.461	0.0000143153	0.0000089865	0.628
14	0.001441	0.381	0.387	0.0000142836	0.0000138814	0.972
15	–0.001550	–0.410	–0.447	0.0000142877	0.0000120118	0.841

* Significant at the 5% level.
** Significant at the 1% level.
◆ 5th percentile of the empirical distribution is 0.512.
\# 95th percentile of the empirical distribution is 1.63.
\## 99th percentile of the empirical distribution is 2.17.

longest interval used, since this produces 40 interval observations across the two 100 day periods. Longer intervals would not produce an adequate number of observations for analysis.

4.2.1. Splits

As shown in Table 3, results of the interval tests for splits indicate highly significant positive market reactions for all of the intervals considered, based on the *Z*-statistic. Significance levels are reduced for the *t*-statistic, but the interval reaction is still highly significant. Variance ratios for each of the intervals show that there is a significant variance change over each of the intervals.

Table 3. Cumulative Abnormal Returns and Variance Changes For Intervals Around Split Effective Date.

Interval	Cumulative Prediction Error	*Z*	*t*	Collins-Dent *Z* Variance Estimator	Collins-Dent *t* Variance Estimator	Variance Ratio
Panel A: Splits						
–5 to 5	0.014196	25.432**	18.291**	0.0000003116	0.0000006024	1.933[a]
–1 to 0	0.010070	42.279**	25.410**	0.0000000567	0.0000001570	2.769[b]
–1 to 1	0.012907	44.222**	27.591**	0.0000000852	0.0000002189	2.569[c]
Panel B: Reverse Splits						
–5 to 5	–0.043691	–3.790**	–3.529**	0.0001328913	0.0001533093	1.154[d]
–1 to 0	–0.020098	–4.155**	–2.777**	0.0000233941	0.0000523915	2.240[e]
–1 to 1	–0.025246	–4.417**	–3.416**	0.0000326665	0.0000546086	1.672[f]

* Significant at the 5% level.

** Significant at the 1% level.

[a] 95th percentile of the variance ratio empirical distribution for conventional splits, interval –5 to 5, is 1.59.

[b] 95th percentile of the variance ratio empirical distribution for conventional splits, interval –1 to 0, is 1.73.

[c] 95th percentile of the variance ratio empirical distribution for conventional splits, interval –1 to 1, is 1.71.

[d] 95th percentile of the variance ratio empirical distribution for reverse splits, interval –5 to 5, is 1.60.

[e] 95th percentile of the variance ratio empirical distribution for reverse splits, interval –1 to 0, is 1.44.

[f] 95th percentile of the variance ratio empirical distribution for reverse splits, interval –1 to 1, is 1.44.

Table 4. Van Valen Tests for Variance Changes For 100 Day Intervals Before and After Split Effective Date.

Split Type	Van Valen *t*-statistic
Conventional	3.269**
Reverse	–4.271**

* Significant at the 5% level.
** Significant at the 1% level.

4.2.2. Reverse Splits
Results of the interval tests for reverse splits also indicate highly significant but negative market reactions based on the *Z*-statistic and less negative but still significant reactions based on the *t*-statistic. The variance ratio tests show significant variance changes for the day –1 to day 0 and day –1 to day 1 intervals, but not for the day –5 to day 5 interval. This is consistent with the results of the long interval tests below and inspection of Fig. 2. There is a variance spike around the reverse split effective date, but after the reverse split, variances appear to decline below the levels prior to the split.

4.3. Long Intervals

Van Valen *t*-tests to detect variance changes are performed comparing a 100-day interval preceding the split effective date (days –105 to –6) with a 100-day interval following the split effective date (days 6 to 105). The period from 5 days preceding the split until 5 days after the split was excluded to avoid the period where the large variance spike occurs. As seen in Table 4, the Van Valen statistic indicates a significant variance increase comparing the 100-day period preceding the conventional split effective date with the 100-day period following the split effective date. For reverse splits, there is a significant decrease in variance when comparing these two periods.

5. SUMMARY

This study documents significant variance changes around the effective date of both splits and reverse splits. However, even when these variance changes are incorporated using the *t*-statistic to examine significance levels of test of shifts of the mean return, there are still significant abnormal returns on and around the split effective date. Thus, the significant abnormal returns found by previous studies still persist when the more rigorous unconditional tests are performed.

A test of variance changes comparing 100-day intervals prior to and after the effective date, but excluding the 11-day interval around the split effective date shows that there is a significant long term variance increase following the conventional split effective date. Using the same technique and intervals indicates that long term variance decreases following reverse splits. Both these results are consistent with results from prior studies like those of Ohlson and Penman (1985) and Dravid (1987).

ACKNOWLEDGMENT

An anonymous referee provided helpful comments and suggestions.

REFERENCES

Brown, S. J., & Warner, J. B. (1980). Using Daily Stock Returns: The Case of Event Studies. *Journal of Financial Economics*, *14*(1985), 3–31.

Collins, D. W., & Dent, W. T. (1984). A Comparison of Alternative Methodologies Used in Capital Market Research. *Journal of Accounting Research*, *24*, 48–84.

Conroy, R. M., Harris, R. S., & Benet, B. A. (1990). The Effects of Stock Splits on Bid-Ask Spreads. *Journal of Finance*, *45*, 1285–1295.

Dann, L. (1981). Common Stock Repurchases: An Analysis of Returns to Bondholders and Stockholders. *Journal of Financial Economics*, *9*, 113–138.

Dravid, A. R. (1987). A Note on the Behavior of Stock Returns around Ex-Dates of Stock Distributions. *Journal of Finance*, *42*, 163–168.

Fama, E. F., Fisher, L., Jensen, M., & Roll, R. (1969). The Adjustment of Stock Prices to New Information. *International Economic Review*, *10*, 1–21.

French, D., & Dubofsky, D. (1986). Stock Splits and Implied Stock Price Volatility. *Journal of Portfolio Management*, *12*, 55–59.

Grinblatt, M., Masulis, R., & Titman, S. (1984). The Valuation Effects of Stock Splits and Stock Dividends. *Journal of Financial Economics*, *13*, 461–490.

Jain, P. C. (1986). Analysis of the Distribution of Security Market Model Prediction Errors for Daily Returns Data. *Journal of Accounting Research*, *24*, 76–96.

Kalay, A., & Lowenstein, U. (1985). Predictable Events and Excess Returns: The Case of Dividend Announcements. *Journal of Financial Economics*, *14*, 423–449.

Lockwood, L., & McInish, T. (1990). Tests of Stability for Variances and Means of Overnight/Intraday Returns During Bull and Bear Markets. *Journal of Banking and Finance*, *14*, 1243–1253.

Maloney, M. T., & Mulherin, J. H. (1992). The Effects of Splitting on the Ex: A icrostructure Reconciliation. *Financial Management*, *21*, 44–59.

Ohlson, J. A., & Penman, S. (1985). Volatility Increases Subsequent to Stock Splits: In Empirical Aberration. *Journal of Financial Economics*, *14*, 251–266.

Patel, J., & Wolfson, M. (1979). Anticipated Information Releases Reflected in Call Option Prices. *Journal of Accounting and Economics*, *1*, 117–140.

Ross, S. A. (1989). Information and Volatility: The No-Arbitrage Martingale Approach to Timing and Resolution Irrelevancy. *Journal of Finance*, *44*, 1–17.

Sanders, R. W., & Robbins, R. P. (1991). Discriminating Between Wealth and Information Effects in Event Studies in Accounting and Finance Research. *Review of Quantitative Finance and Accounting*, *1*, 307–329.

Sheikh, A. M. (1989). Stock Splits, Volatility Increases, and Implied Volatilities. *Journal of Finance*, *44*, 1361–1372.

Woolridge, J., & Chambers, D. (1983). Reverse Splits and Shareholder Wealth. *Financial Management*, *12*, 5–15.

Van Valen, L. (1978). The Statistics of Variation. *Evolutionary Theory*, *4*, 33–43.

4. A FUZZY SET APPROACH IN INTERNATIONAL TRANSFER PRICING PROBLEMS

Wikil Kwak, Yong Shi, Heeseok Lee and Cheng-few Lee

ABSTRACT

Managers and regulators have great interest in transfer pricing problems since today's multinational corporations cannot be successful without dealing with environmental factors such as cultural and political differences, tax regulations, customs duties, restrictions on the transfer of funds, and foreign currency gains and losses, to compete in the global market strategically.

The review of existing transfer pricing models shows that three major shortcomings, from a management point of view, need to be overcome in the previous mathematical models of transfer pricing problems. First, most previous mathematical models cannot provide a comprehensive scenario of all possible optimal trade-offs between multiple criteria (objectives) under consideration for a given transfer pricing problem. Second, none of the past mathematical models can deal with the organizational differentiation problems. Third, most previous approaches implicitly assume that only one decision maker (DM) sets up the transfer price.

The MC^2 linear programming framework can resolve the above shortcomings inherent in the previous transfer pricing models. To reduce the complexity in computing the trade-offs among multiple criteria and

Advances in Quantitative Analysis of Finance and Accounting, Volume 10, pages 57–74.

ISBN: 0-7623-0969-5

multiple DMs' preferences, this paper adopts a fuzzy set approach to solve Multiple Criteria Multiple Decision Maker (MCMDM) international transfer pricing problems. A solution procedure is proposed to systematically identify a satisfying selection of possible prices that cannot only reach the best compromise value for the multiple criteria, but also use the best price range according to the multiple decision makers' preferences. The selection can help the firm make a realistic decision regarding its overall firm's strategic management.

1. INTRODUCTION

Recently, transfer pricing issues have become more important because most corporations increased the transfer of goods or services dramatically among their divisions as a result of increased outsourcing of products or services due to restructuring or downsizing of their organizations. In addition, transfer pricing guidelines are an important element of the international tax system because 60% of world trade is done by multinational corporations (Organization for Economic Cooperation and Development, 1995). Lin et al. (1993) also suggest that the harmonization of international accounting and taxation is necessary to deter the manipulation of international transfer pricing in Asian Pacific countries. Therefore, designing a good systematic transfer pricing strategy should be a major concern for both top management and divisional managers of multinational corporations as well as government regulators.

Transfer pricing problems have been extensively studied by a number of scholars. Many of them have recognized that a successful transfer pricing strategy should consider multiple criteria or objectives, such as overall profit after tax, total market share, divisional autonomy, performance evaluation, and utilized production capacity (Abdel-khalik et al., 1974; Bailey & Boe, 1976; Merville & Petty, 1978; Yunker, 1983; Lecraw, 1985; Lin et al., 1993). Emmanual (1999) and Rushinek and Rushinek (1988) empirically support that maximization of global after-tax income through the choice of transfer prices is the most important goal of international transfer pricing. Other important variables include the competitive position of foreign subsidiaries, divisional performance evaluation, foreign restrictions on repatriation of profits, and the maintenance of adequate cash flows in foreign subsidiaries (Tang, 1992). However, multiple criteria approaches implicitly assume that only one decision maker sets up the transfer price. This assumption is not realistic in most real-world transfer pricing problems. For example, Toyota assembles and sells automobiles in the U.S. using most parts made in Japan, multiple DMs, such as all parties of managers including central management for the transferred goods or services, must be involved in the determination of the transfer price. In order to remove this unrealistic assumption of one decision maker, Kwak et al. (1996) proposed a model with multiple criteria and multiple decision makers (MCMDM). This model originally adopted the framework of multiple criteria and multiple constraint level (MC^2) linear programming to consider both multiple criteria and multiple DMs' preferences in formulating capital budgeting problems. The well-known analytic hierarchy process (AHP) approach (Saaty, 1980) was employed in the solution procedure to reduce the complexity in computing the trade-offs among multiple criteria and multiple DMs' preferences, respectively.

As an alternative methodology, this paper proposes a fuzzy set approach to solve MCMDM transfer pricing problems. This approach is based upon two fundamental human cognitive processes:

(i) all DMs involved in the transfer pricing decision making have goal setting and compromising behavior for seeking multiple criteria; and
(ii) each DM has a preference for the transfer price level.

The solution procedure systematically identifies a fuzzy optimal selection of possible transfer prices that cannot only reach the best-compromised value for the multiple criteria, but also use the best price range according to the multiple decision makers' preferences. In comparison with the AHP approach of Kwak et al. (1996), the fuzzy set approach does not have to elicit weights of importance for both multiple criteria and multiple DMs' preferences. Furthermore, the fuzzy set approach is easier for a firm to apply, because it can be implemented by using any available commercial computer software that solves linear programming problems.

The remainder of the paper proceeds as follows. The next section reviews the existing transfer pricing methods. Section 3 presents how the MC^2 framework is used in formulating transfer pricing problems and shows how to apply the fuzzy set approach to solve MCMDM transfer pricing problems. Section 4 uses a numerical example to illustrate the fuzzy optimal solution for transfer pricing problems and its managerial implications. The last section concludes the paper with some future research considerations.

2. EXISTING TRANSFER PRICING METHODS

Generally, transfer pricing problems can be determined based on three factors:

(i) is there a similar product available in the market? If so, the best transfer price is market-based pricing. If not, cost or negotiated pricing should be used;

(ii) is the variable cost of the seller less than the market price? If not, the seller does not operate efficiently, and the buyer should buy from outside; and
(iii) is the selling unit operating at full capacity? If not, the selling division should provide for the internal buyer and the transfer price should fall somewhere between variable cost and market price from top management's point of view (Bolcher et al., 1999, p. 777).

These guidelines generally provide motivations for divisional managers as well as overall company strategic perspectives. However, other decision makers' interests also should be considered. If this is the case, marginal cost (or opportunity cost) or negotiated transfer prices can be used. Empirical research has found that some corporations prefer cost-based prices to market-based prices, because market-based pricing method is recommended when the emphasis is on the motivation of divisional managers (Borkowski, 1990, 1997). Pricing intermediate goods based on the market price will motivate the supplying division to reduce its costs to achieve efficiency and to allow divisional autonomy for both the supplying division and the purchasing division if there is no extra capacity for the supplying division. Statistics show that almost a third of corporations actually use market-based transfer pricing (Tang, 1992).

However, if there is no outside market for intermediate goods or services and there is extra capacity for the supplying division, then accounting-based pricing, marginal cost pricing (economic models and mathematical programming techniques), or negotiated transfer pricing (behavioral approach) is commonly recommended for finding a good transfer pricing system. Accounting-based transfer prices may not be globally optimal for the corporation as a whole because the supplying division's inefficiency can be built into the determination of transfer prices (Abdel-khalik et al., 1974; Eccles, 1983).

Hirschleifer (1956) recommended using an economic model to set a transfer price at a supplying division's marginal cost to achieve the global optimal output. A problem with this economic model is that it can destroy the divisional manager's autonomy, and the supplying division may not get the benefit of efficiencies. Moreover, the supplying division manager in this case should be evaluated based on cost, not on profit. To alleviate this problem of destroying the divisional manager's autonomy, Ronen and McKinney (1970) suggested dual prices in which a subsidy is given to the supplying division by the central office in addition to marginal costs. This subsidy would not be added to the price charged to the purchasing division. They believed that autonomy is enhanced because the corporate office is only a transmitter of information, not a price setter, and that the supplying division has the same autonomy as an independent supplier. However, there might be a gaming chance where all divisions are winners but the central office is a loser. There is also a "marginal cost plus" approach that charges variable manufacturing costs (usually standard variable costs) and is supplemented by periodic lump-sum charges to the transferees to cover the transferor's fixed costs, or their fixed costs plus profit, or some kind of subsidy. It is difficult, however, to set a fixed fee which will satisfy both the supplying division and the purchasing division. This method enables the purchasing division to absorb all the uncertainties caused by fluctuations in the market place. Moreover, the system begins to break down if the supplying division is operating at or above the normal capacity since variable costs no longer represent the opportunity costs of additional transfers of goods and services (Onsi, 1970).

As an alternative method to identify marginal costs as the transfer prices, a mathematical programming approach becomes more attractive for the transfer pricing problem because it handles complex situations in trade setting (Dopuch & Drake, 1964). The application of linear programming to the transfer pricing problem is based on the relationship between the primal and dual solutions in the linear programming problem. Shadow prices, which reflect the input values of scarce resources (or opportunity cost) implied in the primal problem, can be used as the basis for a transfer price system. However, these transfer prices have the following limitations for decision making:

(i) those transfer prices based on dual values of a solution tend to reward divisions with scarce resources;
(ii) the linear formulation requires a great deal of local information; and
(iii) transfer prices based on shadow prices do not provide a guide for performance evaluation of divisional managers.

Ruefli (1971) proposed a generalized goal decomposition model for incorporating multiple criteria (objectives) and some behavioral aspects within a three-level hierarchical organization into the mathematical formulation of transfer pricing problems. Bailey and Boe (1976) suggested another goal programming model as a supplement of Ruefli's model. Both models overcome the shortcoming of linear programming in dealing with multiple criteria and the organizational hierarchy. Merville and Petty (1978) used a dual formulation of goal programming to directly find the shadow price as the optimal transfer price for multinational corporations. However, the optimal solution of these models that results in the transfer prices is determined by a particular distance (norm) function because of the mathematical structure of goal programming. Thus, the optimal solution represents only a single optimal trade-off of the multiple criteria, not all possible optimal trade-offs.

Watson and Baumler (1975) and Thomas (1980) criticized the lack of behavioral considerations in the mathematical programming approaches. They suggested a negotiated transfer pricing to further the integration of differentiation within the organization. The differentiation of the organization exists because, for example, different managers can interpret the same organizational problem differently. Generally, the negotiated transfer pricing will be successful under conditions such as the existence of some form of outside markets for the intermediate product, freedom to buy or sell outside, and sharing all market information among the negotiators. Negotiated prices may require iterative exchanges of information with the central office as a part of a mathematical programming algorithm.

In an international setting, tax or regulation is major issues for setting transfer prices. The OECD or the U.S. government recommends to use "arm's length" method as a standard for transfer pricing (Radaelli, 1998; Armstrong, 1998). However, it is not easy to apply this method if there is no similar products or services available in the market.

3. METHODOLOGY

MC^2 Linear Programming

Practically speaking, since linear programming has only a single criterion (objective) and a single resource availability level (right hand side), it has limitations in handling real-world transfer pricing problems. For instance, linear programming cannot be used to solve the problem in which a corporation tries to maximize overall profit after tax and the total market share simultaneously. This dilemma is overcome by a technique called multiple criteria (MC) linear programming (Zeleny, 1974; Goicoechea et al., 1982; Steuer, 1986; Yu, 1985). To extend the framework of MC linear programming, Seiford and Yu (1979) and Yu (1985) formulated a model of multiple criteria and multiple constraint levels (MC^2) linear programming. This model is rooted by two facts. First, from the linear system structure's point of view, the criteria and constraints may be "interchangeable." Thus, like multiple criteria, multiple constraint (resource availability) levels can be considered. Second, from the application's point of view, it is more realistic to consider multiple resource availability levels (discrete right hand sides) than a single resource availability level in isolation. The philosophy behind this perspective is that the availability of resources can fluctuate depending on the decision situation changes, such as the desirability levels believed by the different managers. For example, if the differentiation of budget among managers in transfer pricing problems

(Watson & Baumler, 1975) is represented by different levels of budget, then this differentiation can be resolved by identifying some best compromises of budget levels as the consensus budget.

The theoretical connections between MC linear programming and MC^2 linear programming can be found in Gyetvan and Shi (1992). Decision problems related to MC^2 linear programming has been extensively studied (Lee et al., 1990; Shi, 1991; Shi & Yu, 1992). Key ideas of MC^2 linear programming, a primary theoretical foundation of this paper, are outlined as follows.

An MC^2 linear programming problem can be formulated as

$$\begin{aligned} &\text{Max } \lambda^t Cx \\ &\text{s.t. } Ax \leq D\gamma \\ &\quad x \geq 0, \end{aligned}$$

where $C \in \mathbf{R}^{q \times n}$, $A \in \mathbf{R}^{m \times n}$, and $D \in \mathbf{R}^{m \times p}$ are matrices of $q \times n$, $m \times n$, and $m \times p$ dimensions, respectively; $x \in \mathbf{R}^n$ are decision variables; $\lambda \in \mathbf{R}^q$ is called the *criteria parameter* and $\gamma \in \mathbf{R}^p$ is called the *constraint level parameter*. Both (λ, γ) are assumed unknown.

Denote the index set of the basic variables $\{x_{j_1}, \ldots, x_{j_m}\}$ for the MC^2 problem by $J = \{j_1, \ldots, j_m\}$. Note that the basic variables may contain some slack variables. Without confusion, J is also called a basis for the MC^2 problem. Since a basic solution J depends on parameters (λ, γ), define that:

(i) a basic solution J is *feasible* for the MC^2 problem if and only if there exists a $\gamma^0 > 0$ such that J is a feasible solution for the MC^2 problem with respect to γ^0; and

(ii) J is *potentially optimal* for the MC^2 problem if and only if there exist a $\lambda^0 > 0$ and a $\gamma^0 > 0$ such that J is an optimal solution for the MC^2 problem with respect to (λ^0, γ^0).

For an MC^2 problem, there may exist a number of potentially optimal solutions {J} as parameters (λ, γ) vary depending on decision situations.

Seiford and Yu (1979) derived a simplex method to systematically locate the set of all potentially optimal solutions {J}. The computer software of the simplex method (called MC^2 software) was developed by Hao and Shi (1996). This software consists of five subroutines in each iteration:

(i) pivoting;
(ii) determining primal potential bases;
(iii) determining dual potential bases;
(iv) determining the effective constraints for the primal weight set; and
(v) determining the effective constraints for the dual weight set (Chapter 8 of Yu, 1985).

It is written in PASCAL and operates in a man-machine interactive fashion. The user cannot only view the tableau of each iteration but also trace the past iterations. In the next section, the framework of the MC^2 problem, as well as its software, will be used to formulate and solve using the fuzzy set approach for international transfer pricing problems.

Multiple Factor Transfer Pricing Model

The review of existing transfer pricing models shows that two major shortcomings, from a management point of view, need to be overcome in the previous mathematical models of transfer pricing problems. First, neither the linear programming approach nor the goal programming approach can provide a comprehensive scenario of all possible optimal trade-offs between multiple objectives under consideration for a given transfer pricing problem, such as maximizing the overall profits for a corporation and minimizing the underutilization of production capacity (Tang, 1992). A transfer pricing scheme by linear programming only reflects a single objective of a corporation. As a result, the linear programming approach cannot help the corporation seek to simultaneously achieve several objectives, some in conflict, in business competition. The transfer price determined by the goal programming approach is an optimal compromise (i.e. trade-off) among several objectives of the corporation. However, it misses other possible optimal compromises of the objectives which are results from some linear combinations of objective weights. These compromises lead to different optimal transfer prices for different decision situations that the corporation may face. Second, none of the past mathematical models can deal with the organizational differentiation problems, as Watson and Baumler (1975) pointed out. In real-world cases, when a corporation designs its transfer prices for the divisions, the involved decision makers (executives or divisional managers) can give different opinions on the same issue, such as production capacity and customer's demand. In mathematical models, these different interpretations can be represented by different "constraint levels." Because both linear programming and goal programming presume a fixed single constraint level, they fail to mathematically describe such an organizational differentiation problem.

The MC^2 linear programming framework can resolve the above shortcomings inherent in the previous transfer pricing models. Based on Al-Eryani et al. (1990), Yunker (1983), Tang (1992), and Rushinek and Rushinek (1998) the four important objectives of transfer pricing problems in most corporations are considered:

(i) maximizing the overall profit after tax;
(ii) maximizing the total market share;
(iii) maximizing the subsidiary profit (note that the subsidiary profit maximization is used to reflect the degree of the subsidiary autonomy in decision making. It may differ from the overall profit); and
(iv) maximizing the utilized production capacity.

Even though the following model contains only these four specific objectives, the generality of the modeling process fits in all transfer pricing problems with multiple criteria and multiple constraint levels.

To mathematically formulate the MCMDM transfer pricing model, let k be the number of divisions in a corporation under consideration, and t be the index number of the products that each division of the corporation produces.

Define x_{ij} as the units of the jth product made by the ith division, $i = 1, \ldots, k; j = 1, \ldots, t$. For the coefficients of the objectives, let p_{ij} be the unit overall profit generated from the jth product made by the ith division; m_{ij} be the market share value for the jth product made by the ith division in the market; s_{ij} be the unit subsidiary profit generated from the jth product made by the ith division; and c_{ij} be the unit utilized production capacity of the ith division to produce the jth product. For the coefficients of the constraints, let b_{ij} be the budget allocation rate for producing the jth product by the ith division. For the coefficients of the constraint levels, let b_{ij}^s be the budget availability level believed by the sth manager (or executive) for producing the jth product by the ith division, $s = 1, \ldots, h$; let d_i^s be the production capacity level believed by the sth manager for the ith division; d_{ij}^s be the production capacity level believed by the sth manager for the ith division to produce the jth product; e_{ij}^s be the initial inventory level believed by the sth manager for the ith division to hold the jth product. Then, the multiple factor transfer pricing model is:

$$\text{Max} \sum_{i=1}^{k} \sum_{j=1}^{t} p_{ij} x_{ij}$$

$$\text{Max} \sum_{i=1}^{k} \sum_{j=1}^{t} m_{ij} x_{ij}$$

$$\text{Max} \sum_{i=1}^{k} \sum_{j=1}^{t} s_{ij} x_{ij}$$

$$\text{Max} \sum_{i=1}^{k} \sum_{j=1}^{t} c_{ij} x_{ij} \tag{1}$$

Subject to:

$$\sum_{i=1}^{k} \sum_{j=1}^{t} b_{ij}x_{ij} \leq (b_{ij}^{l}, \ldots, b_{ij}^{h})$$

$$\sum_{j=1}^{t} x_{ij} \leq (d_{i}^{l}, \ldots, d_{i}^{h})$$

$$x_{ij} \leq (d_{ij}^{l}, \ldots, d_{ij}^{h})$$

$$-x_{ij} + x_{i+1,j} \leq (e_{ij}^{l}, \ldots, e_{ij}^{h})$$

$$x_{ij} \geq 0, i = 1, \ldots, k, j = 1, \ldots, t. \quad (2)$$

Note that even though this MCMDM transfer pricing model includes only four specific groups of objectives for presentation purpose, the modeling process easily adapts to all international transfer pricing problems with multiple criteria and multiple constraint levels such as maximization of after tax profit for the parent company as another criteria or minimization of foreign taxes and tariffs as additional constraints.

The above model (1–2) is an MC^2 problem with four objectives and four constraint levels. Solving this type of real-world problem is quite complicated. Therefore, this paper proposes a fuzzy set approach to make computational task as practical as possible.

A Fuzzy Solution Method

Based on a compromised solution approach for multiple objective decision making problems, Shi and Liu (1993) propose fuzzy MC linear programming. Their fuzzy approach adopts the compromised solution or the "satisficing solution" between upper and lower bounds of acceptability for objective payoffs. The following section presents the fuzzy set approach for an international transfer pricing problem:

Step 1

Given the model (1–2), we may use any available computer software to solve the following series of LP programs. For illustration purposes, let's assume $t = 5$, $i = 5$, and $u = 5$:

(i) Max(and Min) $\sum_{j=1}^{5} P_j X_j$ (3)

subject to:

$$\sum_{j=1}^{5} b_{ij}x_j \le (c_{1_i}, \ldots, c_{5_i})(\gamma_1, \ldots, \gamma_5)t \quad (4)$$

$$\sum \gamma_p = 1, \gamma_p > 0, p = 1, \ldots, 5,$$

and $x_j \ge 0$, for $j = 1, \ldots, 5$.

(ii) Max(and Min) $\sum_{j=1}^{5} m_{ij}x_j$, $i = 1, \ldots, 5$ (5)

subject to: (4)

(iii) Max(and Min) $\sum_{j=1}^{5} s_{ij}x_j$, $i = 1, \ldots, 5$ (6)

subject to: (4)

(iv) Max(and Min) $\sum_{j=1}^{5} c_{ij}x_j$, $i = 1, \ldots, 5$ (7)

subject to: (4)

Group (i) of the above LP problems has two types of optimization: one is maximization and the other is minimization. Groups (ii), (iii) and (iv) have 6 problems, respectively. All of them use the same constraints (4). The total number of problems is 8. We define the objective value of the maximization problems by $\mathbf{U}_i$ as the upper bound of DMs' acceptability for the objective payoff; and the objective value of the minimization problems by $\mathbf{L}_i$ as the lower bound of DMs' acceptability for the objective payoff, $\mathbf{i} = 1, \ldots, 12$.

Step 2

Let $f(x)_i$, $i = 1, \ldots, 12$, be the objective functions in Step 1. Then, we solve the following linear program:

$$\text{Max } \beta \tag{8}$$

subject to:

$$\beta \leq (f(x)_i - L_i)/(U_i - L_i), i = 1, \ldots, 12, \tag{9}$$

$$\beta \geq 0,$$

$$\sum_{j=1}^{5} b_{ij}x_j \leq (c_{1i}, \ldots, c_{5i})(\gamma_1, \ldots, \gamma_5)^t$$

$$\sum \gamma_p = 1, \gamma_p > 0, p = 1, \ldots, 5,$$

and $x_j \geq 0$, for $j = 1, \ldots, 5$.

The resulting values of x_j are the fuzzy optimal solution and the value of β is the satisficing level of the solution for the DMs.

The above fuzzy solution method has systematically reduced the complexity of the MCMDM capital budgeting model (1–2) because it transforms the MC^2 LP problem into a LP problem. The above two solution steps can be easily implemented by employing available commercial computer software. In the next section, a prototype of the transfer pricing model in a multinational corporation will be illustrated to demonstrate the implications for decision makers.

4. MODEL IMPLICATIONS

Numerical Example

As an illustration of the multiple factor transfer pricing model, the Union Plastic Corporation has two divisions that process raw materials into intermediate or final products. Division 1, which is located in Taipai, Taiwan, manufactures two kinds of plastics, called Products 1 and 2. Product 1 in Division 1 is an intermediate product and cannot be sold externally. It can, however, be processed further by Division 2 into a final product. Division 2, which is located in Omaha, Nebraska, USA, processes Product 2 and finalizes Product 1 in Division 1. Central management and two divisional managers agree on the following multiple objectives:

(i) Maximize the overall company's after tax profit.

(ii) Maximize the market share goal of Product 2 in Division 1, and Products 1 and 2 in Division 2.
(iii) Maximize the utilized production capacity of the company so that each division manager can avoid any underutilization of normal production capacity.

The data related to these objectives is given in Table 1.

In Table 1, Product 1 of Division 1 is a by-product which has no sale value in Division 1 at all. The unit profit – $4 of this product means its production cost. All other products generate profits. We use a market price of each product to maximize the market share goal. Note that the market prices of three products in Table 1 are different.

In this example, besides central management, the selling divisional manager and the purchasing divisional manager may have different interpretations of the same resource availability across the divisions. The selling divisional manager views the constraint level based on the material, manpower, and equipment under control, while the purchasing divisional manager views the constraint level based on the available cash flow. Central management will make the final decision for the company's transfer price setting on the basis of the compromises of both managers. All divisional managers will carry out central management's decision, although they have their autonomy to provide the information about the divisional profits and costs for central management. The interpretations of both managers for the resource constraint levels are summarized in Table 2.

All executives and divisional managers agree on the units of resources consumed to produce the products. The data is given in Table 3.

Table 1. Data of the Objectives in the United Chemical Corporation.

	Division 1		Division 2	
	Product 1	Product 2	Product 1	Product 2
Unit Profit ($):	–4	8	13	5
Market Price:	0	40	46.2	38
Unit Utilizing Production Capacity (hours):	4	4	3	2

Table 2. The Constraint Levels of the Vice Presidents.

	The Selling Divisional Manager	The Purchasing Divisional Manager
Transfer Product Constraint:	0	100
Budget Constraint ($):	45,000	40,000
Production Capacity of Product 2 in Division 1:	38,000	12,000
Production Capacity of Product 1 in Division 2:	45,000	50,000
Production Capacity of Product 2 in Division 2:	36,000	10,000

Let x_{ij} be the units of the jth product produced by the ith division, $i = 1, 2$; $j = 1, 2$.

Then:

Step 1

We use the LINDO (Schrage, 1991) computer software to solve 3 maximization problems and 3 minimization problems for 3 objectives, respectively. The

Table 3. The Unit Consumptions of Resources.

	Division 1		Division 2	
	Product 1	Product 2	Product 1	Product 2
Transfer Product Constraint:	–1.0	0	1.0	0
Budget Constraint ($):	0	0.4	0.4	0.4
Production Capacity of Product 2 in Division 1:		1.0		
Production Capacity of Product 1 in Division 2:			1.0	
Production Capacity of Product 2 in Division 2:				1.0

results are: $\mathbf{U}_1 = 856{,}900$, $\mathbf{U}_2 = 4720{,}000$, $\mathbf{U}_3 = 546{,}000$; and $\mathbf{L}_1 = -20{,}000$, $\mathbf{L}_2 = 0$, $\mathbf{L}_3 = 0$. To see more concentrated value on γ_1 and γ_2, we add $\gamma_1 \geq 0.3$ and $\gamma_2 \geq 0.3$ on each problem. Then, the results are: $\mathbf{U}_1^* = 801{,}380$, $\mathbf{U}_2^* = 442{,}7900$, $\mathbf{U}_3^* = 516{,}700$; $\mathbf{L}_1^* = -20{,}000$, $\mathbf{L}_2^* = 0$, $\mathbf{L}_3^* = 0$. The LINDO software yields slack and dual prices which is an opportunity cost or marginal cost of transfer prices. When $\gamma_1 + \gamma_2 = 1$, objective function value of this example is \$856,900 for the first objective maximization. Slacks for $\gamma_1 = 6{,}500$ and transfer prices of $\{x_{11}, x_{12}, x_{21}, x_{22}\}$ are \$4.00, \$12.50, \$3.00, and \$4.00, respectively. When $\gamma_1 > 0.3$ and $\gamma_2 > 0.3$, the objective function value is \$801,380. Slacks for $x_{12} = 1{,}540$ and transfer prices of $x_{11} = \$4.00$, $x_{21} = \$8.00$.and $x_{22} = \$9.00$ will be produced to achieve the objective payoff $V(J_1)$ and the resource of x_{22} has the amount of s_5 unused. Generally, if we let $p_q(J_i)$, $q = 1, \ldots, 5$; $i = 1, 2$, be the shadow price of J_i for the qth constraint. According to the marginal cost pricing approach, the optimal transfer prices of $\{J_1, J_2\}$ are designated as the shadow prices of $\{J_1, J_2\}$.

Step 2

Let β be the satisficing level of the fuzzy optimal solution for the DMs. Then, we have the fuzzy solution problem as shown in the Appendix. Solving this problem, we obtain: $\beta = 0.987$, $x_{11} = 48{,}262.7$, $x_{12} = 38{,}000$, $x_{21} = 45{,}000$, and $x_{22} = 29{,}500$ units and $\gamma_1 = 1$ and $\gamma_2 = 0$. If we impose the preference parameter of the decision makers $\gamma_i \geq 0.3$, then the solution will be $\beta = 0.991$, $x_{11} = 48{,}784$, $x_{12} = 30{,}200$, $x_{21} = 46{,}500$, and $x_{22} = 28{,}200$ units and $\gamma_1 = 0.7$ and $\gamma_2 = 0.3$. Here γ_1 = the preference of the selling divisional manager and γ_2 = the preference of the purchasing divisional manager. However, the current fuzzy solution does not provide shadow prices. For the current solution with both managers' preferences, we only find fuzzy optimum units for each product. For example, if we transfer x_{11} at \$4.00, x_{12} at \$12.50, x_{21} at \$3.00 and x_{22} at \$4.00, the objective functions will be \$791,964 which is less than the optimum value for the achievement of the goal of maximization of profits, but we can satisfying both managers according to their other preferences. With the above shadow prices (or transfer prices), the constraint in the Step 2 is satisfied. However, other shadow prices in Step 1 do not satisfy the constraints in the Step 2.

Managerial Implications

The fuzzy set approach for the transfer pricing problems as we discussed in this paper has some managerial implications. First, the model integrates the multiple objective transfer pricing problem with multiple DMs. In our model, multiple constraint levels are allowed to incorporate each DM's preference of budget availability. This improvement in modeling can minimize the uncertainty of determining the level of budget availability.

Second, the fuzzy set approach facilitates DMs' participation to avoid suboptimization of overall company's goals. This model supports divisional autonomy more than any other mathematical programming model by allowing differences in each decision maker's preference.

Third, solving MC^2 problems in a real-world setting is not practical because of computational complexity. The fuzzy set approach is more straightforward and easy to solve using currently available computer software.

Finally, the structure of the MCMDM international transfer pricing is flexible. We can add or delete more objectives or constraints as easily possible as economic or political environment changes which is common in international business environments.

5. CONCLUSIONS

A multiple factor international transfer pricing model has been developed to solve the transfer pricing problems in a multi-divisional corporation. This model can provide a comprehensive scenario about possible optimal transfer prices depending on multiple criteria and multiple constraint levels. This method allows to foster goals of transfer pricing such as global optimization, division autonomy, and performance evaluation. In addition, this fuzzy set approach can handle better real-world problems with uncertainty. The fuzzy set model and its solution method provide better solutions in transfer pricing problems than the previous linear programming or goal programming models by receiving input from all decision maker's preference.

We can extend the fuzzy set approach to other real-world problems in business. The framework of this model can be applied to other areas, such as financial planning, portfolio determination, inventory management, resource allocation, audit sampling objectives, and personnel planning for a CPA firm if the decision variables and formulation are expressed appropriately.

REFERENCES

Abdel-khalik, A. R., & Lusk, E. J. (1974). Transfer pricing – a synthesis. *The Accounting Review*, 8–24.

Al-Eryani, M. F., Alam, P., & Akhter, S. H. (1990). Transfer pricing determinants of U.S. multinationals. *Journal of International Business Studies*, 409–425.

Armstrong, M. A. (1998). Political economy of international transfer pricing, 1945–1994: state, capital and the decomposition of class. *Critical Perspective on Accounting*, *8*, 391–432.

Bailey, A. D., & Boe, W. J. (1976). Goal and resource transfers in the multigoal organization. *The Accounting Review*, 559–573.

Blocher E. J., Chen, K. H., & Lin, T. W. (1999). *Cost Management: A strategic Emphasis,*. New York: Irwin/McGraw-Hill.

Borkowski, S. C. (1990). Environmental and organizational factors affecting transfer pricing: a survey. *Journal of Management Accounting Research*, 78–99.

Borkowski, S. C. (1997). Factors motivating transfer pricing choices of Japanese and United States transnational corporations. *Journal of International Accounting, Auditing & Taxation*, *6*(1), 25–47.

Dopuch, N., & Drake, D. F. (1964). Accounting implications of a mathematical programming approach to the transfer price problem. *Journal of Accounting Research*, 10–24.

Eccles, R. G. (1983). Control with fairness in transfer pricing. *Harvard Business Review*, 149–161.

Emmanuel, C. R. (1999). Income shifting and international transfer pricing: a three-country example. *Abacus*, *35*(3), 252–267.

Goicoechea, A., Hansen, D. R., & Duckstein, L. (1982). *Multiobjective Decision Analysis with Engineering and Business Applications*. New York: John Wiley & Sons.

Gyetvan, F., & Shi, Y. (1992). Weak duality theorem and complementary slackness theorem for linear matrix programming problems. *Operations Research Letters*, *11*, 249–252.

Hao, X. R., & Shi, Y. (1996). Large-scale MC^2 program: version 1.0. A C++ program run on PC or Unix, College of Information Science and Technology, University of Nebraska-Omaha, Omaha, NE 68182, USA.

Hirshleifer, J. (1956). On the economies of transfer pricing. *The Journal of Business*, 172–184.

Kwak, W., Shi, Y., Lee, H., & Lee, C. F. (1996). Capital budgeting with multiple criteria and multiple decision makers. *Review of Quantitative Finance and Accounting*, *7*, 17–112.

Lecraw, D. J. (1985). Some evidence on transfer pricing by multinational corporations. In: A. M. Rugman & L. Eden (Eds), *Multinationals and Transfer Pricing*. New York: St. Martin's Press.

Lee, Y. R., Shi, Y., & Yu, P. L. (1990). Linear optimal designs and optimal contingency plans. *Management Science*, *36*, 1106–1119.

Lin, L., Lefebvre, C., & Kantor, J. (1993). Economic determinants of international transfer pricing and the related accounting issues, with particular reference to Asian pacific countries. *The International Journal of Accounting*, 49–70.

Merville, L. J., & Petty, W. J. (1978). Transfer pricing for the multinational corporation. *The Accounting Review*, 935–951.

Organization for Economic Cooperation and Development (1995). *Transfer pricing guidelines for multinational enterprises and tax administrations*. Paris: OECD Publications.

Onsi, M. (1970). A transfer pricing system based on opportunity cost. *The Accounting Review*, 535–543.

Radaelli, C. M. (1998). Game theory and institutional entrepreneurship: transfer pricing and the search for coordination in international tax policy. *Policy Studies Journal*, *26*(4), 603–619.

Ronen, J., & McKinney, G. (1970). Transfer pricing for divisional autonomy. *Journal of Accounting Research*, 99–112.

Ruefli, T. W. (1971). A generalized goal decomposition model. *Management Science*, B-505–B-518.

Rushinek, A., & Rushinek S. F. (1988). Multinational transfer-pricing factors: tax, custom duties, antitrust/dumping legislation, inflation, interest, competition, profit/dividend, and financial reporting. *The International Journal of Accounting*, *23*(2), 95–113.

Saaty, T. L. (1980). *The Analytic Hierarchy Process*. New York: McGraw-Hill.

Schrage, L. (1991). *User's Manual: Linear, Integer, and Quadratic Programming with Lindo*. San Franscio, California: The Scientific Press.

Seiford, L., & Yu, P. L. (1979). Potential solutions of linear systems: the multi-criteria multiple constraint level program. *Journal of Mathematical Analysis and Applications*, 283–303.

Shi, Y. (1991). Optimal linear production systems: models, algorithms, and computer support systems'. Ph.D. dissertation, School of Business, University of Kansas.

Shi, Y., & Liu, Y. H. (1993). Fuzzy potential solutions in multicriteria and multiconstraints levels linear programming problems. *Fuzzy Sets and Systems*, *60*, 163–179.

Shi, Y., & Yu, P. L. (1992). Selecting optimal linear production systems in multiple criteria environments. *Computer and Operations Research*, *19*, 585–608.

Steuer, R. (1986). *Multiple Criteria Optimization: Theory. Computation and Application*. New York: John Wiley & Sons.

Tang, R. Y. W. (1992). Transfer pricing in the 1990s. *Management Accounting*, *72*(8), 22–26.

Thomas, A. L. (1980). *A Behavioral Analysis of Joint-Cost Allocation and Transfer Pricing*. Stipes Publishing.

Watson, D. J. H., & Baumler, J. V. (1975). Transfer pricing: a behavioral context. *The Accounting Review*, 466–474.

Yu, P. L. (1985). *Multiple Criteria Decision Making: Concepts, Techniques and Extensions*. New York: Plenum.

Yunker, P. J. (1983). Survey study of subsidiary, autonomy, performance evaluation and transfer pricing in multinational corporations. *Columbia Journal of World Business*, 51–63.

Zeleny, M. (1974). *Linear Multiobjective Programming*. Berlin: Springer-Verlag.

APPENDIX

Maximize β

Subject to

$$-4x_{11} + 8x_{12} + 13x_{21} + 5x_{22} - 1056{,}900\beta \geq -200{,}000$$

$$40x_{12} + 46.2x_{21} + 38x_{22} - 4720{,}000\beta \geq 0$$

$$4x_{11} + 4x_{12} + 3x_{21} + 2x_{22} - 546{,}000\beta \geq 0$$

$$-x_{11} + x_{21} - 100\gamma_1 \leq 0$$

$$0.4x_{12} + 0.4x_{21} + 0.4x_{22} - 45{,}000\gamma_1 - 40{,}000\gamma_2 \leq 0$$

$$x_{12} - 38{,}000\gamma_1 - 12{,}000\gamma_2 \leq 0$$

$$x_{21} - 45{,}000\gamma_1 - 50{,}000\gamma_2 \leq 0$$

$$x_{22} - 36{,}000\gamma_1 - 10{,}000\gamma_2 \leq 0$$

$$\gamma_1 + \gamma_2 = 1$$

$\gamma_i \geq 0.3$, for $i = 1$ and 2.

and $x_j = \{0, 1\}$, for $j = 1$ and 2.

5. WHO BEARS THE RBIP (RISK-BASED INSURANCE PREMIUMS) TAX?

Seok Weon Lee

ABSTRACT

This study examines whether bank shareholders, especially those of riskier banks, bear part of the 1993 RBIP (Risk-Based Insurance Premiums) tax. Since riskier banks are charged higher insurance premiums under RBIP, RBIP may be expected to have different effects on expected profit or return for the banks with different risk positions, presumably a more negative effect on the shareholders of riskier banks. Consistent with these premises, we found over the period 1990–1996 that the positive associations between the banks' risk measures estimated from the well-known two factor return generating model (market risk and short/long-term-interest-rate risk) and stock return appeared to become weaker after RBIP. This result suggests that bank shareholders, especially those of riskier banks, may not be compensated for taking risk as much as they were under fixed-rate deposit insurance system, and therefore, bear at least part of the RBIP tax.

1. INTRODUCTION

Researchers agree that the bank and S & L failures of the 1970s and 1980s are attributed to the moral hazard risk-taking behavior associated with fixed-rate

Advances in Quantitative Analysis of Finance and Accounting, Volume 10, pages 75–87.

ISBN: 0-7623-0969-5

deposit insurance system.[1] In general, market forces prevent corporations from taking excessive risks. Debtholders demand interest rates high enough to compensate for higher default risk when a corporation holds a risky portfolio. Thus, it is difficult to exploit debtholders because the cost of debt increases with the riskiness of a corporation. However, the effectiveness of this market mechanism is limited in the banking sector because of government-backed deposit insurance. Depositors, who are the major debtholders of banks, are indifferent about the riskiness of individual banks, and hence, do not demand higher interest rates from riskier banks. Furthermore, the Federal Deposit Insurance Corporation (FDIC) charged fixed insurance premiums until the end of 1992. Under fixed-rate deposit insurance, the insurer does not assess riskiness and does not charge a risk-premium (higher insurance premium) for high risk-taking. Therefore, banks could pursue riskier strategies without paying higher insurance premiums. The growing problems of the banking sector associated with the fixed-rate deposit insurance system motivated a major regulatory change, the introduction in 1993 of Risk-Based Insurance Premium (RBIP), to discourage banks from being excessively risky. Under RBIP, of course, the insurer (FDIC) assesses the riskiness of individual banks and charges higher premiums to riskier banks.

For any social regulation, there must be some parties that bear the tax associated with it. The purpose of this study is to examine who bears the RBIP tax. Given that RBIP is levied on banks, the first candidate who might bear the RBIP tax will be the bank shareholders, especially those of the riskier banks: Under RBIP, the FDIC assesses the riskiness of individual banks and charge the riskier banks higher insurance premiums. Thus, RBIP may be expected to have some effects on banks' expected profit or return, especially a negative effect on the shareholders of riskier banks. Consistent with these premises, we found some evidence over the period 1990–1996 that the positive association between the banks' risk measures estimated from the well-known two factor return generating model (market risk and short/long-term-interest-rate risk) and stock return appeared to become weaker after RBIP. This result implies that, compared to fixed-rate deposit insurance system, stock returns of the riskier banks more decreased (or less increased) than those of the safer banks after RBIP, suggesting that the shareholders of the riskier banks may not be compensated for taking risk as much as they were under fixed-rate deposit insurance system, compared to those of the safer banks. In this way, the shareholders of the riskier banks bear at least part of the RBIP tax.[2] Note the hypotheses we are testing: that the (positive) *associations* between stock return on the one hand and risk factors on the other hand became weaker after RBIP. It was the strength and direction of these associations – not return or profit itself of the banking industry – in the pre-RBIP period. Thus we are not testing the hypothesis that U.S. banking became less (or more) profitable after RBIP or that it became less (or more) profitable because of RBIP. Testing that hypothesis would require different methods than we employ, partly because of the confounding effect of the other regulatory changes during the sample period. But there is no apparent reason why the other regulatory changes should alter the *associations*.

In the next section, we describe the sample of banks, giving the correlations for the variables used in estimating equations. Section 3 describes the hypotheses to be tested and the basic regression model used to test them. We present the empirical results for the hypothesis in section 4. In section 5, we perform panel analysis for the full sample first, and then partitioned sample to examine how the shareholders of the banks with different exposure to the probability of failure differently bear the RBIP tax. Section 6 offers concluding comments.

2. SAMPLE, DATA AND CORRELATION TESTS

Data are collected for 82 bank holding companies for which data are available on both the Standard & Poor's Stock Report and the Center for Research in Security Prices (CRSP) data tapes over the period 1990–1996. The data on capital-to-asset ratios are obtained from the Standard & Poor's Stock Report, and daily stock return data come from the CRSP data base. Daily returns are adjusted to account for dividend payouts and stock splits. Our analysis is based on those bank holding companies that traded every business day for the whole sample period.

Table 1 presents Pearson correlation coefficients among the risk characteristics for the pre- and post-RBIP periods. This table shows that the coefficients among market risk, long/short-term-interest-rate risk and the capital-to-asset ratio, though on the whole statistically significant, are not so high as to present multicollinearity problems in a regression analysis using these variables as independent variables. Market risk is the beta of daily stock returns with respect to the return on the CRSP equally-weighted market portfolio. Interest-rate risk is the beta of daily stock returns with respect to the interest rates. Two alternative daily interest rates are used to estimate the banks' exposure to interest rates: 3-month Treasury bill yield and 10-year note yield.[3] Table 1 shows that, before RBIP, stock return had a significantly positive correlation with the market risk and long-term-interest-rate-risk as implied by finance theory. After RBIP, the correlations become weaker and lose some of their statistical significance. Stock return also had a negative correlation with the capital-to-asset ratio before RBIP as expected,[4] however, it is not statistically significant. After RBIP, the relation becomes insignificantly positive.

Table 1 also shows that the capital ratio had a significantly negative correlation with both market risk and long-term-interest-rate risk before RBIP. Thus, banks seem to maintain very risky operating structures under fixed-rate deposit insurance system. After RBIP, however, these relations become weaker, suggesting that the banks seem to have changed their operating structures toward safer ones. As expected, market risk and long-term-interest-rate risk had a significantly positive coefficient for both pre- and post-RBIP period.

Table 1, also, presents somewhat less weaker and less significant correlation between stock return and the short-term-interest-rate risk before RBIP, compared to the long-term-interest-rate risk. This result might suggest that investors believe that the degree of bank mismatching the duration of its assets and liabilities would not be so serious for the banks' short-term contracts, and therefore, that they do not require as much risk premium as they did for long-term contracts. This relation has not changed after RBIP.

Table 1. Correlations.

These tables show the Pearson correlations among the risk-characteristics variables. The first number is the correlation for the pre-RBIP period; the second is the correlation for the post-RBIP period. One, two, or three asterisks indicate statistical significance at the 10, 5, or 1% level, respectively.

	Stock return	Market risk	Long-term-interest-rate risk	Capital-to-asset ratio
Stock return	1	0.1227*** 0.1097*	0.2884*** 0.1829**	–1.3155 0.6730
Market risk		1	0.3011** 0.2551**	–0.1911** –0.1881*
Long-term-interest-rate risk			1	–0.2116** –0.1276*
Capital-to-asset ratio				1

	Stock return	Market risk	Capital-to-asset Ratio
Short-term-interest-rate risk	0.1627** 0.1593*	0.1316** 0.1140**	–0.2748* –0.1926*

Overall, the results in Table 1 indicate that the shareholders of the banks seemed to be compensated for taking market-related systematic risk under the fixed-rate deposit insurance system. However, under RBIP, they do not appear to be compensated for taking risk as much as they were under fixed-rate deposit insurance system. In this way, the shareholders of the banks (especially, those of the riskier banks) bear at least part of the RBIP tax. Of course, these comparisons are only suggestive, because they do not control for other factors affecting bank stock return.

3. TESTING MODEL AND HYPOTHESES

As a stronger test to examine whether bank shareholders bear the RBIP tax, we estimate the following cross-sectional regression equations for 82 sample banks, for each year over the period of 1990–1996. We omit 1993 because 1993 is a transitional year for the introduction of the RBIP.

$$(\text{Stock return})_i = \gamma_0 + \gamma_1(\text{Market risk})_i + \gamma_2(\text{Long-term-interest-rate risk})_i + \gamma_3(\text{Capital-to-asset})_i + \varepsilon_i \quad (1)$$

$$(\text{Stock return})_i = \gamma_0 + \gamma_1(\text{Market risk})_i + \gamma_2(\text{Short-term-interest-rate risk})_i + \gamma_3(\text{Capital-to-asset})_i + \varepsilon_i \quad (2)$$

(Stock return)$_t$ is the average of the daily returns of year t. Risk is either market risk or interest rate risk. Following Flannery and James (1984), Sweeney and Warga (1986), and Saunders, Strock and Travlos (1990), etc., it was assumed that a two-factor market model was the appropriate return-generating process for bank stock returns, with the daily return on the CRSP equally-weighted market portfolio being the first factor and the daily change in interest rates being the second factor. A higher interest-rate risk indicates a greater exposure to interest-rate movement being resulted from a bank mismatching the duration of its assets and liabilities. (Capital-to-asset ratio)$_{i,t}$ is bank i's year-t end value.

As discussed above, if everything else is the same, the riskier banks (the banks with higher market and interest-rate risk) would be charged higher insurance premiums under RBIP, and hence their profits and stock returns are expected to more decline (or less increase) than those of the safer banks, compared to the pre-RBIP period. Thus, we may hypothesize that the coefficients γ_1 and γ_2 in the above equations would become less positive (or more negative) after RBIP. If everything else is the same, lower capital-ratio banks would be charged higher insurance premiums under RBIP, and hence their profits and stock returns are expected to more decline (or less increase) than those of the higher capital-ratio banks. Thus, the coefficient γ_3 is expected to become less negative after RBIP.

4. EMPIRICAL RESULTS

Table 2 shows the result for estimating the Eq. (1) in which the bank's exposure to long-term-interest rate is used as one of the risk factors affecting the bank's stock return. The results for the pre-RBIP period (1990–1992) present that the coefficient on the market risk is significantly positive for all the three years as implied by finance theory. It also presents that the coefficient on the long-term-interest-rate risk is positive for all the three years before RBIP. Of the three, two cases are statistically significant. Considering that the performance of the banks' asset portfolios are largely related to the fluctuations of the interest rates, this result can be expected. Table 1 also shows that the coefficient on the capital-to-asset ratio is negative for all the three years before RBIP, consistent

Table 2. Cross-sectional Regression Results.

This table shows the coefficients and t-statistics from OLS cross-sectional estimates of Eq. (1) over the period of 1990–1992, and 1994–1996. One, two, or three asterisks indicate statistical significance at the 10, 5, or 1% level, respectively.

$$(\text{Stock return})_i = \gamma_0 + \gamma_1(\text{Market risk})_i + \gamma_2(\text{Long-term-interest-rate risk})_i + \gamma_3(\text{Capital-to-asset})_i + \varepsilon_i$$

Independent variables	Intercept	Market risk	Long-term-interest-rate risk	Capital-to-asset ratio	Adjusted R^2	F-statistic
Year						
1990	–0.0217	0.1927***	0.3728**	–1.4184	0.19	25.38***
	(–0.26)	(2.48)	(2.41)	(–1.29)		
1991	–0.0118	0.1831***	0.2819	–1.2910	0.18	24.19***
	(–0.41)	(2.51)	(1.57)	(–1.34)		
1992	0.1204	0.1616**	0.3410**	–0.8629	0.23	26.57***
	(0.83)	(2.11)	(1.99)	(–1.07)		
1994	0.9231	0.0904	–0.0127	–0.1210	0.25	25.38***
	(1.53)	(1.18)	(0.26)	(–0.82)		
1995	0.8328	0.1210	0.1186	0.0617	0.22	24.91***
	(0.99)	(1.49)	(1.56)	(0.25)		
1996	0.7329	0.1172*	0.1527*	0.1829	0.23	26.11***
	(1.02)	(1.64)	(1.66)	(0.71)		

with the implication of finance theory. However, none of the three are statistically significant.

The last three panels of Table 2 present the results for the post-RBIP period 1994–1996. Firstly, it shows that the significantly positive relation between the stock return and the market risk over the pre-RBIP period appear to become weaker after RBIP, being reflected in only one significantly positive coefficient. Furthermore, compared to pre-RBIP period, the absolute level of the coefficient becomes less for all the three years over 1994–1996. Thus, under RBIP, the shareholders of the riskier banks may not be compensated for taking risk as much as they were under fixed-rate deposit insurance system. In this way, the shareholders of the riskier banks bear at least part of the RBIP tax. Similar to the results for the market risk, Table 1 presents some evidence that the positive relation between the stock return and the long-term-interest-rate risk over the pre-RBIP period appears to become weaker after RBIP. The coefficient on the interest-rate risk is positive for two years of which only one case is statistically significant. However, it does not appear that the shareholders of the lower-capital-ratio banks necessarily bear part of the RBIP tax.[5]

Table 3 shows the result for estimating the Eq. (2) in which the bank's exposure to short-term-interest rate is used as one of the risk factors affecting the bank's stock return. With respect to the market risk and the capital-to-asset ratio, it shows very similar results to those in Table 2. However, with respect to the interest-rate-risk, it presents weaker and less significant results compared to the case of long-term-interest-rate risk, as in the results for the correlation test. The coefficient on the short-term-interest-rate risk is significantly positive for only one case before RBIP. This result might suggest that investors do not require as much risk premium as they did for the long-term contracts. This result may deductively indicate that investors believe that the degree of bank mismatching the duration of its assets and liabilities would not be so serious for the banks' short-term contracts. This relation does not appear to have changed after RBIP.

5. PANEL ANALYSIS

Full Sample Test

To examine the extent to which the RBIP tax falls on the shareholders of the banks, we have estimated the following panel regression equations by including the dummy variable D that takes the value of 0 before the introduction of RBIP and the value of 1 afterwards. We have pooled the cross-sectional and time-series data of the sample banks and have estimated fixed

Table 3. Cross-sectional Regression Results.

This table shows the coefficients and t-statistics from OLS cross-sectional estimates of Eq. (1) over the period of 1990–1992, and 1994–1996. One, two, or three asterisks indicate statistical significance at the 10, 5, or 1% level, respectively.

$$(\text{Stock return})_i = \gamma_0 + \gamma_1(\text{Market risk})_i + \gamma_2(\text{Long-term-interest-rate risk})_i + \gamma_3(\text{Capital-to-asset})_i + \varepsilon_i$$

Independent variables	Intercept	Market risk	Long-term-interest-rate risk	Capital-to-asset ratio	Adjusted R^2	F-statistic
Year						
1990	–0.0208	0.1769***	0.2107	–1.4087	0.17	24.13***
	(–0.24)	(2.42)	(1.08)	(–1.20)		
1991	–0.0099	0.1768***	0.1927	–1.2823	0.18	23.18***
	(–0.38)	(2.54)	(1.07)	(–1.30)		
1992	0.1101	0.1559**	0.1218*	–0.6521	0.22	25.29***
	(1.01)	(2.09)	(1.65)	(–1.14)		
1994	0.8629	0.0788	0.1922	–0.0993	0.24	25.10***
	(1.49)	(1.21)	(1.27)	(–0.61)		
1995	0.8123	0.1109	0.1629*	0.0591	0.22	24.18***
	(0.79)	(1.53)	(1.67)	(0.25)		
1996	0.7129	0.1129*	0.2001	0.1717	0.24	26.07***
	(1.03)	(1.64)	(1.56)	(0.70)		

effects regression equations.[6] This specification avoids a potential omitted variable problem that could occur when the individual-specific component of the error is correlated with the regressors in the model.

$$\begin{aligned}(\text{Stock return})_{it} = {} & \gamma_0 + \gamma_{11}(\text{Market risk})_{it} + \gamma_{12}D \times (\text{Market risk})_{it} \\ & + \gamma_{21}(\text{Long-term-interest-rate risk})_{it} \\ & + \gamma_{22}D \times (\text{Long-term-interest-rate risk})_{it} \\ & + \gamma_{31}(\text{Capital-to-asset})_{it} + \gamma_{32}D \times (\text{Capital-to-asset})_{it} + \varepsilon_{it} \qquad (3)\end{aligned}$$

$$\begin{aligned}(\text{Stock return})_{it} = {} & \gamma_0 + \gamma_{11}(\text{Market risk})_{it} + \gamma_{12}D \times (\text{Market risk})_{it} \\ & + \gamma_{21}(\text{Short-term-interest-rate risk})_{it} \\ & + \gamma_{22}D \times (\text{Short-term-interest-rate risk})_{it} \\ & + \gamma_{31}(\text{Capital-to-asset})_{it} + \gamma_{32}D \times (\text{Capital-to-asset})_{it} + \varepsilon_{it} \qquad (4)\end{aligned}$$

In the above equations, the coefficients on the interaction term of the dummy variable and the explanatory variables (γ_{12}, γ_{22} and γ_{32}) measure the change in the slope of the relationship between each explanatory variable and the stock return. Thus, if part of the RBIP tax falls on the shareholders of the banks, significantly negative signs on γ_{12}, γ_{22}, and a significantly positive sign on γ_{32} are expected.

The results are presented in Table 4. We focus on interpreting the change in the coefficients with the introduction of RBIP. It shows a significantly negative coefficient on the market risk, γ_{12}, for both equations, suggesting that the shareholders of the banks bear part of the RBIP tax associated with the market risk, as hypothesized and similar to the results for the cross-sectional tests. For the capital-to-asset ratio, the table presents a positive coefficient (γ_{32}) for both equations as hypothesized. However, none of them are statistically significant. Thus, we may not be able to argue that the shareholders of the lower-capital-ratio banks necessarily bear part of the RBIP tax. Regarding the interest-rate risk, the table shows a significantly negative coefficient for the long-term-interest-rate risk, suggesting that the shareholders bear part of the RBIP tax associated with long-term interest rate risk. However, it shows an insignificant change for the short-term-interest-rate risk.

Partitioned Sample Test

To examine how the shareholders of the banks with different exposure to the probability of failure differently bear the RBIP tax, we partition the full sample into two groups, the banks with higher percentage of non-performing loans (riskier banks) vs. lower ones (safer banks). We assume that the bank's probability of failure is reasonably measured by its ratio of non-performing loans to asset. After partitioning, each year, the full sample at the median for the ratio of non-performing loans to asset, we estimate the above Eqs (3) and (4) for each group, and compare the extent to which the RBIP tax falls on the shareholders of the banks for each group.

The results in Table 5 present *negatively* more significant and greater coefficients on both variables, D × (Market risk) and D × (Long-term interest rate risk), for the banks with higher ratio of non-performing loans. This result may suggests that the shareholders of the riskier banks (the banks with higher ratio of non-performing loans) bear more of the RBIP tax associated with the market risk and long-term-interest-rate risk than those of the safer banks. This result is consistent with our hypothesis, because, under RBIP, if every thing else is the same, given the same level of increase in risk, the banks with higher ratio of non-performing loans will be charged higher insurance premiums,

Table 4. Fixed-Effects Panel Regression Results (Full sample).

This table shows the coefficients and t-statistics from fixed-effects panel regression estimates of Eqs (3) and (4) for the full sample over the period of 1990–1992, and 1994–1996. One, two, or three asterisks indicate statistical significance at the 10, 5, or 1% level, respectively.

$$(\text{Stock return})_{it} = \gamma_0 + \gamma_{11}(\text{Market risk})_{it} + \gamma_{12}D \times (\text{Market risk})_{it} + \gamma_{21}(\text{Long-term-interest-rate risk})_{it} + \gamma_{22}D \times (\text{Long-term-interest-rate risk})_{it} + \gamma_{31}(\text{Capital-to-asset})_{it} + \gamma_{32}D \times (\text{Capital-to-asset})_{it} + \varepsilon_{it}$$

$$(\text{Stock return})_{it} = \gamma_0 + \gamma_{11}(\text{Market risk})_{it} + \gamma_{12}D \times (\text{Market risk})_{it} + \gamma_{21}(\text{Short-term-interest-rate risk})_{it} + \gamma_{22}D \times (\text{Short-term-interest-rate risk})_{it} + \gamma_{31}(\text{Capital-to-asset})_{it} + \gamma_{32}D \times (\text{Capital-to-asset})_{it} + \varepsilon_{it}$$

	With long-term-interest-rate risk	With short-term-interest-rate risk
Intercept	–0.0283 (–0.42)	–0.0319 (–0.51)
$(\text{Market risk})_{it}$	0.1628*** (2.52)	0.1552*** (2.41)
$D \times (\text{Market risk})_{it}$	–0.1022** (–2.15)	–0.1018** (–2.32)
$(\text{Long-term-interest-rate risk})_{it}$	0.2561** (1.98)	
$D \times (\text{Long-term- interest-rate risk})_{it}$	–0.6763* (–1.71)	
$(\text{Short-term-interest-rate risk})_{it}$		0.1927* (1.65)
$D \times (\text{Short-term-interest-rate risk})_{it}$		–0.2893 (–1.37)
$(\text{Capital-to-asset})_{it}$	–1.3402 (–1.11)	–1.4210 (–1.26)
$D \times (\text{Capital-to-asset})_{it}$	0.8239 (0.84)	0.9028 (0.75)
Adjusted R^2	0.25	0.24
F-statistic	27.25***	27.11***

Table 5. Fixed-Effects Panel Regression Results (Partitioned Sample).

This table shows the coefficients and t-statistics from fixed-effects panel regression estimates of Eqs (3) and (4) for the partitioned sample over the period of 1990–1992, and 1994–1996. One, two, or three asterisks indicate statistical significance at the 10, 5, or 1% level, respectively.

$$(\text{Stock return})_{it} = \gamma_0 + \gamma_{11}(\text{Market risk})_{it} + \gamma_{12}D \times (\text{Market risk})_{it} + \gamma_{21}(\text{Long-term-interest-rate risk})_{it} + \gamma_{22}D \times (\text{Long-term-interest-rate risk})_{it} + \gamma_{31}(\text{Capital-to-asset})_{it} + \gamma_{32}D \times (\text{Capital-to-asset})_{it} + \varepsilon_{it}$$

$$(\text{Stock return})_{it} = \gamma_0 + \gamma_{11}(\text{Market risk})_{it} + \gamma_{12}D \times (\text{Market risk})_{it} + \gamma_{21}(\text{Short-term-interest-rate risk})_{it} + \gamma_{22}D \times (\text{Short-term-interest-rate risk})_{it} + \gamma_{31}(\text{Capital-to-asset})_{it} + \gamma_{32}D \times (\text{Capital-to-asset})_{it} + \varepsilon_{it}$$

	Higher non-performing-loans ratio banks	Lower non-performing-loans ratio banks	Higher non-performing-loans ratio banks	Lower non-performing-loans ratio banks
	With long-term-Interest-rate risk	With long-term-Interest-rate risk	With short-term-Interest-rate risk	With short-term-Interest-rate risk
Intercept	–0.0218 (–0.29)	–0.0619 (–0.33)	–0.0129 (–0.16)	–0.0422 (–0.22)
$(\text{Market risk})_{it}$	0.0992*** (2.51)	0.1827*** (2.93)	0.0829*** (2.28)	0.1628*** (2.62)
$D \times (\text{Market risk})_{it}$	–0.1527** (–2.18)	–0.0816* (–1.74)	–0.1621** (–2.31)	–0.0754* (–1.82)
$(\text{Long-term-interest-rate risk})_{it}$	0.2243* (1.72)	0.2910** (1.82)		
$D \times (\text{Long-term-interest-rate risk})_{it}$	–0.8117** (–1.96)	–0.4219* (–1.64)		
$(\text{Short-term-interest-rate risk})_{it}$			0.1827* (1.70)	0.1901* (1.65)
$D \times (\text{Short-term-interest-rate risk})_{it}$			–0.2618 (–1.41)	–0.2902 (–1.39)
$(\text{Capital-to-asset})_{it}$	–1.1028 (–1.04)	–1.2183 (–0.79)	–1.1310 (–0.89)	–1.1411 (–0.80)
$D \times (\text{Capital-to-asset})_{it}$	0.7811 (0.57)	1.0113 (0.81)	0.8729 (0.66)	0.9110 (0.73)
Adjusted R^2	0.27	0.25	0.22	0.26
F-statistic	26.54***	26.99***	25.47***	26.11***

which will be resulted in lower expected profits and lower stock returns for these banks. Regarding the capital ratio and short-term-interest-rate risk, the results do not appear to show any significant differences in the degree of bearing the RBIP tax between the shareholders of the riskier and safer banks.

6. CONCLUSION

This study examines whether bank shareholders, especially those of riskier banks, bear part of the 1993 RBIP (Risk-Based Insurance Premiums) tax. Since riskier banks are charged higher insurance premiums under RBIP, RBIP may be expected to have different effects on expected profit or return for the banks with different risk positions, presumably a more negative effect on the shareholders of riskier banks. Consistent with these premises, we found over the period 1990 that the positive associations between the banks' risk measures estimated from the well-known two factor return generating model (market risk and short/long-term-interest-rate risk) and stock return appeared to become weaker after RBIP. This result suggests that bank shareholders, especially those of riskier banks, may not be compensated for taking risk as much as they were under fixed-rate deposit insurance system, and therefore, bear at least part of the RBIP tax.

NOTES

1. See Benston, Eisenbeis, horvitz, Kane, and Kaufman (1986) for a thorough discussion and references to many studies.

2. This does not mean that the RBIP tax dose fall *wholly* on bank shareholders. The other possible candidate on whom the RBIP tax falls may be bank customers (depositors and borrowers). The intuition for this reasoning is that as long as the RBIP affects the bank profits, the banks would have some incentives to shift this cost to the bank customers through adjustments of deposit and loan interest rates. Of course, whether the banks can succeed in shifting the cost of RBIP tax to the bank customers should be related to whether the risk-taking incentives of banks decreased after RBIP. This is an interesting topic for further research.

3. These data were obtained from the Data Resources Incorporated (DRI) interest rate dada base.

4. It is generally agreed that the lower the capital-to-asset ratio of a bank is, the riskier it is, because of both leverage effect and the moral-hazard-incentives of stockholders associated with limited liability.

5. As in the case for the cross-sectional test, this result may raise an interesting question, because capital ratio is one of the important factors when assessing insurance premiums by the Federal Deposit Insurance Corporation. That is, if every thing else is the same, the banks with lower capital ratios would be charged higher insurance premiums under RBIP. One possible explanation for this result may be that investors do

not necessarily directly relate the capital ratio of the banks to the insurance premium it pats. Or rather, since banks with lower capital ratios tend to be larger ones, investors might believe that lower capital-ratio banks have better potential to diversify asset risk and more ability to evade the burden of RBIP.

6. Either fixed effects or random effects model would be appropriate for the analysis of panel data sets such as this study because they contain multiple observations on the same individuals. We have also included time fixed effects to control for changes in average level of risk common to all banks in the sample and estimated a random effects model to control for time-invariant bank-specific factors relating to risk. The results for this estimation are available from the authors.

REFERENCES

Allen, P. R., & Wilhelm, W. J. (1988). The Impact of the 1980 Depository Institutions Deregulations and Monetary Control Act on Market Value and Risk. *Journal of Money, Credit, and Banking*, *20*, 364–380.

Benston, G. J, Eisenbeis, R. A., Horvitz, P. M., Kane, E. J., & Kaufman, G. G. (1986). *Perspectives on Safe and Sound Banking: Past, Present, and Future*. Cambridge, Mass.: MIT Press.

Bhandari, L. C. (1988). Debt/Equity Ratio and Expected Common Stock Returns: Empirical Evidence. *Journal of Finance*, *43*, 507–528.

Cook, D. O., & Spellman, L. J. (1991). Federal Financing Guarantees and the Occasional Market Pricing of Default Risk. *Journal of Banking and Finance*, *15*, 1113–1130.

Cook, D. O., & Spellman, L. J. (1994). Repudiation Risk and Restitution Costs: Toward Understanding Premiums on Insured Deposits. *Journal of Money, Credit, and Banking*, *26*, 439–459.

Cook, D. O., & Spellman, L. J. (1996). Firm and Guarantor Risk, Risk Contagion, and the Interfirm Spread Among Insured Depsoits. *Journal of Financial and Quantitative Analysis*, *31*, 265–231.

Fama, E. F. (1985). What's Different about Banks. *Journal of Monetary Economics*, *15*, 29–39.

James, C. (1987). Some Evidence of the Uniqueness of Bank Loans. *Journal of Financial Economics*, *19*, 217–235.

Kolari, J., Mahajan, A., & Saunders, E. (1988). The Effect of Changes in Reserve Requirements on Bank Stock Prices. *Journal of Banking and Finance*, *12*, 184–198.

O'Hara, M., & Shaw, W. (1990). Deposit Insurance and wealth Effects: The Value of Being "Too Big to Fail". *Journal of Finance*, *45*, 1587–1600.

Osborne, D. K., & Zaher, T. S. (1992). Reserve Requirements, Bank Share Prices, and the Uniqueness of Bank Loans. *Journal of Banking and Finance*, *16*, 799–812.

Sundaram, S., Rangan, N., & Davidson, W. N. (1992). The Market Valuation Effects of the Financial Institutuions Reform, Recovery and Enforcement Act of 1989. *Journal of Banking and Finance*, *16*, 1097–1122.

6. ARE GOING-CONCERN AUDIT OPINIONS A SELF-FULFILLING PROPHECY?

Charlotte Pryor and Joseph V. Terza

ABSTRACT

*This paper investigates the existence of the purported self-fulfilling prophecy effect of going-concern audit opinions. Whether the self-fulfilling prophecy effect exists is an empirical question that has not been resolved in part, at least, because it is difficult to test. We estimate a logistic regression model to assess whether going-concern opinions (*gcos*) increase the probability of bankruptcy. However, factors that are correlated with bankruptcy may "cause"* gcos*. If that is the case, the* gco *variable will be endogenous and the estimate of its effect will be biased. We control for the potential endogeneity of the opinion in two ways. Our bankruptcy regression model includes additional bankruptcy related variables that are believed to influence the opinion. If all bankruptcy related factors that are correlated with the opinion can be included in the model, the endogeneity bias can be eliminated. Any relation between the opinion variable and the bankruptcy outcome must, then, be related to the opinion itself rather than to bankruptcy related factors that lead auditors to issue* gcos *(because those factors would be controlled by inclusion in the model). To assess whether endogeneity related bias is successfully eliminated by the addition of significant correlated variables, a two-stage technique suggested by Terza (2001) is used. This procedure*

Advances in Quantitative Analysis of Finance and Accounting, Volume 10, pages 89–116.

ISBN: 0-7623-0969-5

also provides endogeneity consistent parameter estimates when significant correlated variables are omitted. The results suggest that, ceteris paribus, the presence of a going-concern opinion directly increases the probability of bankruptcy, and the larger the firm the more it increases.

1. INTRODUCTION

If accounting information (including audit opinions) provides value, that implies that the information is useful for decision making. By influencing decisions, accounting information can affect that which it measures. The purported self-fulfilling prophecy effect of going-concern audit opinions provides a potential example. There is evidence that at least some auditors' opinion decisions are influenced by their belief that issuing a going-concern opinion may create a self-fulfilling prophecy (e.g. Bell, 1991; Kida, 1980; Mutchler, 1984). The AICPA Commission on Auditors' Responsibilities (1978) supported elimination of going-concern audit reports in part, at least, because of the presumed existence of the self-fulfilling prophecy effect. The Commission argued that a going-concern opinion (*gco*) is often considered by a firm's creditors as a reason, in addition to the underlying circumstances that gave rise to the opinion, for refusing to grant credit to the firm. Nonetheless, the AICPA issued Statement on Auditing Standards (SAS) No. 59 "The Auditor's Consideration of an Entity's Ability to Continue as a Going Concern" in 1988 in response to concerns raised by some highly publicized bankruptcies of companies that had not received a *gco*.[1] The presumption that going-concern opinions create a self-fulfilling prophecy (*sfp*) is not universally accepted, however. It has been argued that the self-fulfilling prophecy effect is a myth because many firms which receive *gco*s do not become bankrupt (Altman, 1982; Boritz, 1991). Whether *gco*s create self-fulfilling prophecies (*sfp*) and, if so, under what circumstances they do, is an empirical question that has not been resolved.

The authors identified 330 Compustat listed firms that received first-time going-concern audit opinions for fiscal years ending December 31, 1989 through 1993. Of these, 56 (17%) entered bankruptcy prior to receiving a subsequent audit opinion. The remaining 274 had not entered bankruptcy prior to issuing the annual report for the following fiscal year. During the sample period, approximately 1.6% of financially distressed Compustat listed firms that did not receive a *gco* entered bankruptcy. However, the existence of a higher rate of bankruptcy among first-time *gco* firms than among financially distressed non-*gco* firms is not sufficient to conclude that the opinion creates a *sfp*. Auditors may have seen indications of impending bankruptcy which influenced them to issue a *gco*. In other words, it may be that factors correlated with bankruptcy "cause" *gco*s rather than that *gco*s "cause" bankruptcy. If that is the case, and a *gco* indicator variable is regressed on bankruptcy, the *gco* variable will be endogenous. If variables are omitted that have a significant correlation with the outcome and which are also correlated with *gco*s, the opinion indicator (dummy) variable will be correlated with the regression error term. As is well-known, such endogeneity leads to biased regression estimates (see Greene, 1997, Section 6.7.8).

Endogeneity bias would be eliminated if sampled firms were randomized with respect to *gco* status and then tested for subsequent bankruptcy; obviously, such an approach is not possible. Survey (non-randomized) data must be used and an appropriate econometric technique must be chosen to deal with the potential endogeneity of the opinion variable. Hopwood et al. (1989) used a regression approach to measure the power of audit opinions to explain the probability of bankruptcy. They did not attempt to distinguish the influence of *gco*s on bankruptcy from the influence of bankruptcy related unobservables on *gcos*. In contrast, the purpose of this study is to discern whether there is a separate and distinct *sfp* effect. Two steps are taken to accomplish this goal. First, bankruptcy related variables that are known, or suspected, to influence auditors' opinion decisions are included as covariates with an opinion variable in a logistic regression of the probability of bankruptcy. If all significant covariates can be included in the regression model, then the endogeneity bias can be eliminated and any relation between the opinion variable and the bankruptcy outcome must be related to the opinion itself rather than to bankruptcy related factors that lead auditors to issue *gco*s (because those factors would be controlled by inclusion in the model).[2]

Second, a two-stage technique suggested by Terza (2001) is used to test for the existence of and to control for any remaining endogeneity if significant correlated variables have been omitted. If the test results indicate that the model omits factors related to bankruptcy that are also significant determinants of going-concern opinions (the opinion variable is endogenous), then an endogeneity consistent *gco* coefficient can be obtained via the two-stage method to provide an unbiased estimate of the opinion's effect. The statistical significance of the direct effect of *gco*s on the likelihood of subsequent bankruptcy can be tested via the conventional *t*-statistic for the coefficient of the *gco* dummy – the *t*-stat of the two-stage estimate if the *gco* dummy is found to be endogenous; the *t*-stat of the conventional logistic regression estimate if (and only if) the *gco* dummy is exogenous.

The model used in this study includes bankruptcy related variables believed to influence auditor going-concern opinion decisions (such as default status).

Results of the endogeneity test suggest that the opinion variable is exogenous in this model. There is a significant and positive relation between first-time going-concern opinions and subsequent bankruptcy after controlling for the influence of bankruptcy related factors on the opinion. We, therefore, conclude that the results provide evidence in support of the existence of a self-fulfilling prophecy effect. The results also show that the interaction between company size and *gco*s has a significant, positive effect on the likelihood of bankruptcy. The remainder of the paper is organized as follows. Section 2 discusses the research design and methodology. Section 3 provides the results. The conclusions and implications of the study are summarized in the final section.

2. RESEARCH DESIGN AND METHODOLOGY

This section begins with a review of the literature on the self-fulfilling prophecy effect. The econometric model and method used to test for, and estimate, the *sfp* effect are then discussed in detail.

The Self-fulfilling Prophecy Effect

Mutchler (1984) reports that three of the audit partners she interviewed stated that they were familiar with cases in which a *gco* had caused a firm to fail. Informal discussions with auditors indicate that many believe that the decision to issue a *gco* is preceded by careful consideration of the potential effect on the company. Nevertheless, fewer than half of the partners interviewed by Mutchler agreed that *gco*s were a self-fulfilling prophecy. Boritz (1991) refers to the *sfp* effect as a "myth" citing that none of 213 Canadian firms that received going-concern audit "disclosures" actually went bankrupt (although 92 were placed in receivership, liquidated, de-listed, or otherwise unfavorably resolved). Many U.S. firms do not enter bankruptcy after receiving a going-concern audit opinion; in a recent study only 28% of firms with *gco*s entered bankruptcy some time after the initial opinion, frequently after receiving the opinion for multiple years (Nogler, 1995). The fact that many firms that receive a *gco* do not fail is not sufficient evidence to conclude that the *sfp* effect does not exist. If the average probability of bankruptcy across firms that receive a *gco* increases as a direct result of the opinion, that would provide evidence that a self-fulfilling prophecy effect exists. Further, some firms may be affected more than others. If the occurrence of the effect varies among firms, it would be useful to know which specific firm characteristics affect susceptibility to the *sfp* effect.

There is a negative relation between *gco*s and firm survival (George et al., 1996). Although this result is consistent with the existence of a *sfp*, as the researchers recognized, their research method (a proportional hazards approach) could not separate the relative influence of the opinion on survival from the influence of failure related evidence on the opinion. Louwers et al. (1995) purports to show that the *sfp* effect does not exist on the basis of a discrete-time survival analysis. However, their study was limited to firms that received a *gco* and is, consequently, a study of the survival rates of firms given that they have received the opinion. The study could not assess whether firms that receive a *gco* are more likely to fail than those which do not. As noted by Citron and Taffler (1992), the self-fulfilling prophecy theory is difficult to test. The researcher cannot determine what would have happened to firms that received *gco*s had they not received that opinion, nor is it possible to randomly select which firms will receive a *gco* in a controlled experiment. Because of this, one must find an appropriate statistical technique that affords results that can be interpreted *as if* the data were experimentally generated (i.e. randomized with respect to *gco* status).

Equal rates of bankruptcy for a sample of going-concern and non-going-concern firms matched on the basis of financial status, year, industry, and size lead Citron and Taffler (1992) to conclude that the *sfp* effect does not exist. Unfortunately, they did not describe how the matched firms were selected nor did they provide the data needed to evaluate the success of the matching process.[3] In any case, matched-pair analysis may not solve the research problem because any bankruptcy related factor that is used by the auditor when issuing a *gco* that is not adequately matched results in latent (uncontrolled) correlation between bankruptcy and the opinion. This will lead to bias in attributing a difference-of-means to the *sfp* effect because part of the observed difference will actually be due to unmatched factors that relate to bankruptcy and that also influence *gco*s. A similar problem holds for regression-based analyses. The incremental power of *gco*s to explain the likelihood of bankruptcy reported by Hopwood et al. (1989) includes the influence of omitted factors related to impending bankruptcy on the opinion and any possible effect the opinion may have on bankruptcy. Because they were interested in forecasting only, no correction for endogeneity was needed. In contrast, this study seeks to discern whether *gco*s exert a separate and distinct effect on the probability that firms will enter bankruptcy. To determine whether the *sfp* effect exists, we must control for the influence of bankruptcy related factors on auditor opinion decisions.

Econometric Model and Estimation Strategy

To investigate whether the *sfp* effect exists, the bankrupt versus non-bankrupt outcome measure must be confined to events that occur subsequent to the release of the audit opinion. Accordingly, firms that were in bankruptcy or that had announced intentions to enter bankruptcy at the time the audit report was released are excluded. Also, the term "*sfp* effect" implies that the opinion is a proximate cause of firm failure. Therefore, it is not appropriate to include firm failure after two or more years of receiving repeated *gco*s in a test of the existence of the *sfp* effect. Therefore, the study considers the outcomes for firms that had received an initial *gco* versus the outcomes for financially distressed firms that had not received a *gco* for at least three consecutive years.

Two steps are taken to control for the potential influence of bankruptcy related variables on the auditor's opinion. Variables are included in the bankruptcy model that are indicative of impending bankruptcy and that are known (or believed) to influence auditors' going-concern opinions. In addition, an econometric method is used that tests whether the opinion variable is endogenous, and if it is, that controls for the influence of any omitted correlated variables. To accomplish these two objectives, a joint model of bankruptcy and the going-concern opinion decision was developed and estimated using a version of the econometric technique proposed by Terza (2001). The model estimation technique assumes that the process determining the issuance of a *gco* can be cast in a binary logit framework where a *gco* is issued (GC = 1) if and only if

$$z\alpha + \nu > 0,$$

where z is a row vector of observable *gco* determinants, α is the column vector of logit coefficients, and ν is the logistically distributed random variable representing relevant but omitted *gco* determinants. It follows that conditional on the vector of exogenous determinants z, the probability of a *gco* is:

$$\Pr\{GC = 1 \mid z\} = \Lambda(z\alpha) \tag{1}$$

where $\Lambda(\cdot)$ denotes the logistic distribution function. Conditional on the row vector of observable bankruptcy determinants (x) [which includes the going concern dummy variable (GC)], and ν (the omitted *gco* determinants), the probability of bankruptcy is:

$$\Pr\{BR = 1 \mid x, \nu\} = \Lambda(x\beta + \theta\nu) \tag{2}$$

where BR is the binary variable that has a value of 1 if the firm enters bankruptcy and 0 otherwise, β is the column vector of logistic regression coefficients, and θ is the coefficient of the omitted *gco* determinants.

The logistic specification was chosen because firms for which GC = 1 *or* BR = 1, or both, are relatively infrequent in the population, so that choice-based sampling must be implemented. Andersen (1972) shows that the bias which results from using a choice-based sample is confined to the intercept term in the logistic regression case. Further, the form of this bias is known and can be corrected via an adjustment (γ) to the intercept term where

$$\gamma = -\ln p,$$

$$p = p_2/p_1,$$

and p_2 is the proportion of the population included in the sample for which the dependent variable of interest is present (e.g. 100% of *gco* firms) and p_1 is the proportion that is sampled from the population in which the dependent variable is not present (~ 7.5% of Compustat listed, distressed, non-*gco* firms).[4] The two-stage technique introduced by Terza (2001) is implemented as follows. In the first stage, the *gco* logistic regression model defined in Eq. (1) is estimated via the conventional maximum likelihood method. A consistent (large-sample unbiased) estimate of α is thus obtained. In the second stage, β and θ, the parameters of the bankruptcy regression Eq. (2), are consistently estimated by applying the nonlinear least squares method to the bankruptcy model conditional on the estimates of the first stage parameters (including the adjustment [γ]). Details of the method are provided in the appendix.

The estimate of θ provides the means to test whether there are variables omitted from the model that are common to both *gco*s and bankruptcy. For example, if the estimate of θ is significant and positive, then it can be inferred that bankruptcy related variables that are also *gco* determinants have been omitted from the model. If, however, θ is not significantly different from zero, then, there is no evidence that any bankruptcy related factors that have been omitted from the model are also related to *gco*s (the model successfully controls for the influence of bankruptcy related factors on auditors' opinion decisions). Note, also, that if $\theta = 0$, the bankruptcy model defined in (2) reduces to the logistic regression model

$$\Pr\{BR = 1 \mid x\} = \Lambda(x\beta).$$

In this case, inferences about the existence of the *sfp* effect could be drawn from the *gco* coefficient in the conventional logistic regression of the bankruptcy model. Note that this conclusion applies only to the specific bankruptcy model tested. If the GC variable is exogenous in the model used in this study, it does not follow that the *gco* variable is exogenous in another bankruptcy model with different variables. The conventional asymptotic *t*-statistic for θ (i.e. under the null hypothesis that $\theta = 0$) in the nonlinear least squares estimation of (2) can be used to test for the endogeneity of the *gco* dummy.

The estimation strategy has two components. First, estimate the model by the two-stage method and test for the endogeneity of GC (by testing H_0: $\theta = 0$). Second, if GC is endogenous (H_0 is rejected), use the second-stage coefficient estimates of GC and its interactions as measures of the *sfp* effect, and test its significance using conventional *t*-tests and joint likelihood ratio tests. If GC is exogenous in this bankruptcy model, estimate the model by conventional logistic regression and, similar to the endogeneity case, draw inferences about the *sfp* effect from the estimates of the coefficients of the *gco* variables. The variables used in the bankruptcy and going-concern models are described in the next section.

Model Variables

If a bankruptcy model could be constructed that incorporates all of the significant related variables that auditors use in making going-concern audit opinion decisions, a *gco* indicator variable included in the model would be an exogenous variable. Any relation between the opinion variable and the bankrupt/non-bankrupt outcome could then be attributed to the opinion itself. Accordingly, the first step to investigate the self-fulfilling prophecy effect is to identify the bankruptcy related factors that are also related to auditors' going-concern decisions.

Bankruptcy Related Variables

Empirical research has identified liquidity, leverage, and profitability as key indicators of bankruptcy (Zmijewski, 1984). Liquidity and leverage have also been identified as determinants of bankruptcy because insolvency in a cash flow sense can place creditors in the position of forcing a firm into bankruptcy. Economic theory posits that profitability is also a bankruptcy determinant. Financially distressed firms which are relatively less (more) profitable have greater (lower) value in liquidation than as continuing entities (Bulow & Shoven, 1978). Bulow and Shoven also demonstrate that term-length of debt is a bankruptcy determinant. As the term length of debt shortens, the joint claim of the firm's bankers and equity holders under bankruptcy increases in value relative to their claim under continuation. When the joint claim of a firm's bank lenders and equity holders is greater in liquidation than in continuation of the firm, the banks withdraw their support and the firm enters bankruptcy. Accordingly, the following financial ratios are expected to be key factors that are related to bankruptcy: CURRAT (current ratio – a liquidity proxy);

LTDBTTA (Long-term Debt/Total Assets – a proxy for leverage); NITA (Net Income/Total Assets – a profitability proxy); and LTDBTTL (Long-term Debt/Total Liabilities – a proxy for term-length of debt).

When a firm defaults on debt payments or covenants, that event allows creditors to call the debt, an action that can force the firm into bankruptcy. An indicator variable (DDFLT) is set equal to one if a firm has defaulted on debt payments, or violated the terms of its debt covenants and the violation has either not been waived or waived for a limited period of time (less than one year). A few studies have reported a negative relation between firm size and bankruptcy (Ohlson, 1980; Pastena & Ruland, 1986). Using total assets has produced similar results to those obtained using market value of common stock as a measure of firm size (Freeman, 1987; Bamber, 1986). "Book value of total assets . . . [may be] a more stable measure of a firm's size than its market value of common shares outstanding." (Bamber, 1986, p. 45). Firm size (measured as the natural log of the book value of assets) may be related to bankruptcy and also influence the opinion decision.

Troubled firms attempt to continue in existence either by renegotiating their debt structure privately or by filing for bankruptcy in order to reorganize their debt while under court protection from creditors. Gilson et al. (1990) suggests that because public-debt holders are more numerous and dispersed than private lenders, it may be harder to conclude debt renegotiations that enable a firm to avoid bankruptcy. Firms may be more likely to enter bankruptcy when the proportion of their debt financing obtained from public sources is large relative to the proportion obtained from private sources. The variable PUBDEBT (Publicly Held Debt/Total Liabilities) measures the proportion of a firm's liabilities that are publicly held.

Going-concern Opinion Variables

Consistent with auditing standards, financial ratios intended to provide a measure of financial distress are among the factors that are useful in predicting auditors' going-concern opinion decisions (Mutchler, 1985). Some CPA firms are known to use financial distress prediction models (for example, Altman's [1968] Z-score) to identify client firms that may not be able to continue in existence (Carmichael et al., 1995). Accordingly, the bankruptcy related financial ratios discussed in the previous section are also expected to be related to *gco*s. Auditors may rely heavily on debt default as an indicator of impending bankruptcy (Chen & Church, 1992).[5] Therefore, the bankruptcy related default status variable (DDFLT) is also expected to influence *gco*s.

Some investigators report that client firm size is negatively related to receipt of a *gco* (McKeown et al., 1991; Mutchler et al., 1997). Auditors appear to be *less* likely to issue a *gco* to a large company than to a smaller one with similar financial indications of distress. Auditors may hesitate to issue a *gco* to large client companies due to the potential economic impact on the audit firm if the client dismisses the auditor as a result of the unfavorable opinion or for some other reason. Firm size may also be related to the probability of failure as assessed by the auditor. Therefore, firm size (In assets) may be related to auditors' economic incentives as well as to auditors' assessments of the probability that a client will fail. DeAngelo (1981) posits that fear of losing an audit client should not affect large, Big 6 audit firms as much as smaller, non-Big 6 firms because the loss of any one client should have relatively less effect on the economic base of large audit firms.[6] Thus, she argues that Big 6 firms provide a higher quality audit product. An indicator variable set equal to one if the auditor is one of the Big 6 firms is intended to capture the possible differences in economic incentives and quality provided by large audit firms. An interactive variable, SIZE $*$ BIG6, is posited to reflect any difference in the relation between *gco*s and size for Big 6 versus non-Big 6 auditors.

Companies that receive *gco*s may experience longer time periods between the fiscal year end and the audit report date than those receiving clean opinions if audit procedures are extended or if protracted discussions between the auditor and firm management occur. The number of days between the close of the fiscal year and the audit report date (ARLAG) is, therefore, expected to be related to *gco* decisions (McKeown et al., 1991).

Self-fulfilling Prophecy Effect Variables

The *sfp* effect is investigated by using a multi-step approach. In the first step, a bankruptcy model is developed that includes the significant related factors that auditors use to make their opinion decisions. The bankruptcy model includes an indicator variable (GC) set equal to one for firms that received an initial going-concern audit opinion and equal to zero if the opinion did not indicate a going-concern issue for at least three consecutive years. Audit opinions are defined as initial *gco*s if the opinion follows at least three consecutive years in which a *gco* was not received. In addition to the opinion variable, the model includes the bankruptcy related variables described above. These include the financial ratios, default status, and firm size variables that should also be related to auditors' going-concern opinion decisions. By including default status and firm size as well as the key financial ratios related to bankruptcy in the model, the possibility that the GC indicator variable may be exogenous in the model is increased. It is not necessary that all variables that are related to bankruptcy, nor that all variables that are related to auditors' opinion decisions be included in the bankruptcy model. The opinion variable will be exogenous if the significant factors that are related to impending bankruptcy and that are also used by auditors to decide when to issue a going-concern opinion are included.

The strength of any *sfp* effect may vary among firms. This possibility has not been investigated previously and there is little theory to guide such an investigation. Discussions with bank lenders coupled with a review of economics literature on the role of public (outside) versus private (inside) debt suggests that the type of debt a firm carries may affect whether creditors' actions are influenced by a *gco*. Bank lenders generally have access to more detailed and more timely information about the companies to which they extend loans than other creditors (Diamond, 1991). Publicly traded bonds have been characterized as outside debt, in contrast to bank debt, because bondholders must rely, primarily, on information that is publicly available (Fama, 1985; Rajan, 1992). Therefore, public-debt holders may be more likely than bank lenders (and other private lenders) to perceive the receipt of a *gco* as an informative event. The larger the proportion of a firm's creditors that perceive a *gco* to be informative, then the more likely it may be that the cumulative effect of their actions in response to a going-concern opinion could result in the firm entering bankruptcy. Thus, a variable to capture the possible interactive effect between *gco*s and the proportion of firms' total liabilities that are comprised of publicly held debt (GC ∗ PUBDEBT) is added to the bankruptcy model.

If creditors and investors are aware that auditors may be biased against issuing a *gco* to large companies (and/or if they believe that, all else equal, large companies are more likely to survive financial distress without resorting to bankruptcy), when a large company does receive a going-concern opinion it is more likely that creditors and investors will be surprised by the opinion. If the opinion is unexpected, it could provide information to financial statement users that causes them to take actions (such as withholding refinancing opportunities) that affect the firm. Therefore, a variable for the interactive effect of *gco*s and size (GC ∗ SIZE) is added to the bankruptcy model to capture the possibility that firm size affects the relation between *gco*s and bankruptcy.

Bankruptcy related variables that are also correlated with *gco*s may be omitted from the model despite efforts to identify and include these variables. Therefore, a joint model of the opinion decision and bankruptcy is estimated using the two-stage method discussed previously. The opinion variables described above are used to construct the required *gco* model. Summarizing the above discussion, the variables included in each model are as follows:

$$\Pr\{\mathrm{GC} = 1 \mid z\} = \Lambda(z\alpha)$$

$$z\alpha = \alpha_0 + \alpha_1\text{DDFLT} + \alpha_2\text{CURRAT} + \alpha_3\text{LTDBTTA} + \alpha_4\text{NITA} + \alpha_5\text{LTDBTTL} + \alpha_6\text{SIZE} + \alpha_7\text{BIG6} + \alpha_8(\text{SIZE} * \text{BIG6}) + \alpha_9\text{ARLAG} \quad (3)$$

and

$$\Pr\{\text{BR} = 1 \mid x, \nu\} = \Lambda(x\beta + \theta\nu)$$

$$x\beta = \beta_0 + \beta_1\text{DDFLT} + \beta_2\text{CURRAT} + \beta_3\text{LTDBTTA} + \beta_4\text{NITA} + \beta_5\text{LTDBTTL} + \beta_6\text{SIZE} + \beta_7\text{PUBDEBT} + \beta_8\text{GC} + \beta_9(\text{GC} * \text{PUBDEBT}) + \beta_{10}(\text{GC} * \text{SIZE}) \quad (4)$$

where (expected sign in parentheses)

BR = 1 if the firm entered bankruptcy after the audit report's release and prior to the next year's annual report
DDFLT = 1 if the firm is in default on debt, 0 otherwise (+)
CURRAT = current ratio (−)
LTDBTTA = the ratio of long-term debt to total assets (+)
NITA = the ratio of net income to total assets (−)
LTDBTTL = the ratio of long-term debt to total liabilities (−)
SIZE = ln of assets – median sample ln of assets (−)
BIG6 = 1 if the auditor is one of the Big 6 audit firms, 0 otherwise (+)
SIZE * BIG6 = SIZE for firms that have a Big 6 auditor, 0 otherwise (+)
ARLAG = the number of days between the end of the fiscal year and the auditor's report date (+)
PUBDEBT = the ratio of public debt to total liabilities (+)
GC = 1 if the firm received an initial gco, 0 otherwise (+)
GC * PUBDEBT = PUBDEBT for firms that have received a gco, 0 otherwise (+),
and GC * SIZE = SIZE for firms that have received a gco, 0 otherwise (+)

The existence of the *sfp* effect is investigated by estimating whether the *gco* indicator variable coefficient (β_8) in Eq. (4) is positive and significant, and by examining the significance of the joint contribution of all three *gco* variables (GC, GC * SIZE, and GC * PUBDEBT) to the probability of bankruptcy (as evidenced by the likelihood ratio statistic for the full model versus a model that is identical except for the omission of the going-concern variables). The importance of PUBDEBT and SIZE as firm specific characteristics that may influence the presence of the *sfp* effect is evaluated by estimating whether the coefficients β_9 and β_{10} are positive and significant. Interpretation of the SIZE variable coefficient (β_6) depends on the significance of the interaction term

(GC * SIZE). The interaction term measures the incremental effect of *gco*s on the relation between firm size and the probability of bankruptcy. If there is no interactive effect (GC * SIZE is not significant), then the SIZE variable coefficient (β_6) estimates the relation between size and the probability of bankruptcy for all sample firms. However, if there is a significant incremental effect (β_{10} is significant), then the relation between size and bankruptcy is different for companies that received a *gco* than it is for non-*gco* companies. In that case, the sum ($\beta_6 + \beta_{10}$) provides an estimate of the relation between size and bankruptcy for firms that received a *gco* and β_6 estimates the relation between size and bankruptcy for firms that did not receive a *gco*.

Note that, like all indicator variables, β_8 is an "intercept shifter" (it measures the relation between going-concern opinions and bankruptcy at the origin). The inclusion of the GC * Size interactive term allows the relation between *gco*s and bankruptcy to differ according to firm size. If, β_{10} is significant, as expected, then the opinion variable coefficient (β_8) estimates the relation between *gco*s and bankruptcy only at the point where company size equals zero (the origin). There are, of course, no companies with a size of zero; therefore, an adjustment must be made to the Size variable for the estimate of β_8 to be meaningful. Accordingly, the median size of the sample companies is used to adjust the Size variable (Size = ln assets minus the sample median ln assets). As a result of this adjustment, β_8 estimates the relation between *gco*s and bankruptcy for sample-median sizedfirms.[7] The following section discusses the sample used to conduct the investigation.

Sample Design

The sample data were obtained for the time period from December 31, 1989 through December 31, 1993 to ensure that the audit reports for all observations are issued under the same standard (SAS No. 59). Financial firms and utilities are excluded from the sample; the relation between financial ratios and bankruptcy is not expected to be comparable for these firms. Hopwood et al. (1994) demonstrates the importance of partitioning on the basis of financial distress; accordingly, the sample consists solely of financially distressed firms. A company is considered financially distressed if it meets one or more of the following:

(1) it reports negative working capital in the sample year;
(2) it reports negative net income before interest and taxes in the sample year or any of the preceding two years;
(3) it reports negative retained earnings for the second year prior to the sample year; or

(4) it reports a bottom line loss in the sample year or any of the preceding two years.

Consistent with prior research (Hopwood et al., 1994; Foster et al., 1998) we seek to exclude firms that do not exhibit signs of financial distress. Some firms enter bankruptcy strictly for strategic purposes (to ward off impending lawsuits or some similar purpose) and these firms typically appear to be in sound financial condition. (For example, Hopwood et al., 1994, obtained a sample of 16 firms that were bankrupt despite not meeting any of the distress criteria used in this study.) An important purpose of the distress criteria is to ensure that the sample does not include such cases of strategic bankruptcy; the criteria, therefore, serve to screen out firms that are clearly in good financial health. The sample of non-bankrupt firms should be subject to the same screens as the bankrupt firms; otherwise, the proportion that did not receive a *gco* may be biased. Further, prior research has shown that auditors do not issue *gco*s to companies that don't show some signs of financial distress. Kida (1980) and Mutchler (1985) note that auditors' going-concern opinion decisions involve a two-stage process. First, the auditor identifies whether a client firm should get a second look for going-concern issues and only then does the auditor gather evidence to make the opinion decision. The distress criteria are also designed to screen out firms that auditors would not "look at twice." If the company has a loss the auditor will pause and think about that company more deeply than one that does not have a loss.

The Compact Disclosure database was used to identify firms with *gco*s. Of the firms so identified, those that had received a first-time *gco* for a fiscal year ending during the period 12/31/89 through 12/31/93 and that were also available on Compustat are included (number of *gco* firms = 330).[8] The *Bankruptcy Yearbook and Almanac* (McHugh, 1991–1995) was used to identify bankrupt firms (*br*firms). Specifically, Compustat listed bankrupt firms for which data were available to determine whether the last audit opinion issued prior to bankruptcy was either a first-time *gco* or a non-*gco* are included (number of *br* firms = 128). As was the case for the *gco* firms, the dataset of *br* firms compiled is actually a census of the *br* firms that satisfy the data availability requirements.[9] Fifty-six of the 330 *gco* firms are also included among the 128 *br* firms (we refer to these as *gco*/*br* firms). The combined population of *gco* and *br* firms can be categorized as follows: *gco*/*br* firms (number = 56); *gco* firms that did not become bankrupt before issuance of a subsequent audit report (*gco*/non-*br* firms, number = 274); and firms that became bankrupt but that did not receive a *gco* prior to entering bankruptcy (non-*gco*/*br* firms, number = 72).

The estimation strategy requires that logistic regressions be estimated for both the GC model (conventional) and BR models (conventional and two-stage). To do this, random samples of non-*gco* firms and of non-*br* firms are required to estimate the GC and BR models. To reduce the costs of collecting the requisite data, a stratified random sampling approach is used that yields representative random samples for the non-*gco* and non-*br* categories without requiring the selection of two completely separate, random control samples. First, a random sample of 128 non-*gco*/non-*br* firms was drawn. The non-*gco* control sample for the GC model estimation is composed of the random sample of 128 non-*gco*/non-*br* firms combined with a sample of size $n^* = 2$ drawn at random from the population of 72 non-*gco*/*br* firms. A sample size of 2 is derived as follows. Approximately 1.6% of the stressed non-*gco* firms listed on Compustat entered bankruptcy during the sample period. Therefore, the desired sample size n^* is the nearest lower integer value to the solution of $N^* = 0.016 \times (128 + N^*)$ with respect to N^*. Likewise, the non-*br* control sample for the BR model estimation is composed of the random sample of 128 non-*gco*/non-*br* firms plus a random sample of size $n^* = 8$ drawn from the population of 274 *gco*/non-*br* firms.[10] Thus, the size of the full sample for the GC model is 460 (330 *gco* firms and 130 non-*gco* control firms) and for the BR model is 264 (128 *br* firms and 136 non-*br* control firms).

For *br* firms, the independent variable values are obtained from the financial statements for the last fiscal year prior to the date of bankruptcy and for *gco* firms, the variable values are obtained from the financials for the year in which the company received an initial *gco*. The variable values for non-*br*/non-*gco* firms are obtained from the financial statements for the randomly chosen sample year. Default status (DDFLT) and the proportion of publicly held debt (PUBDEBT) are obtained from the firms' financial statement debt footnotes.[11] Debt issues which are described as "debentures" or which discuss the terms of the "indenture"; which refer to repurchases of the securities on the open market; or which describe the public offering of the security are categorized as public debt. Debt issues which are described as being held by banks, insurance companies, or related parties; which are referred to as private placements; which include reference to interest rates at the lender's prime rate; or which are described as promissory notes, installment or term loans, or capital leases are categorized as non-public debt.

3. RESULTS

Following the estimation strategy previously described, the two-stage method was used to estimate the bankruptcy model. Each stage uses a different sample

Table 1. Sample Composition.

Panel A:

BR Model Sample			
Bankrupt firms	n = 128		
a gco/br		44%	n = 56
b non-gco/br		56%	n = 72
Non-Bankrupt, distressed firms	n = 136		
c gco/non-br		6%	n = 8
d non-gco/non-br		94%	n = 128

a gco/br firms – firms that entered bankruptcy after a first-time going-concern audit report was issued and prior to the release of the following year's annual report,

b non-*gco/br* firms – firms that entered bankruptcy after receiving at least 3 consecutive years without receiving a gco (including the last year immediately preceding bankruptcy),

*c gco/*non-br firms – randomly chosen firms from among those that met the financial distress criteria, that had not entered bankruptcy prior to the following year's audit report and had received a first-time going-concern opinion,

d non-*gco/*non-*br* firms – randomly chosen firms from among COMPUSTAT firms that meet financial distress criteria, that had not entered bankruptcy and had not received a going-concern opinion for at least 3 consecutive years.

Panel B:

GC Model Sample			
First-time gco firms	n = 330		
a gco/br		17%	n = 56
*e gco/*non-*br*		83%	n = 274
Non-*gco*, distressed firms	n = 130		
f non-gco/br		1.5%	n = 2
d non-*gco/*non-*br*		98.5%	n = 128

a gco/br firms – firms that entered bankruptcy after a first-time going-concern audit report was issued and prior to the release of the following year's annual report,

*e gco/*non-*br* firms – firms that met the financial distress criteria, that had not entered bankruptcy prior to the following year's audit report and had received a first-time going-concern opinion,

f non-*gco/br* – randomly chosen firms from among those that entered bankruptcy after receiving at least 3 consecutive years without receiving a going-concern opinion (including the last year immediately preceding bankruptcy),

d non-*gco/*non-*br* firms – randomly chosen from among COMPUSTAT firms that meet financial distress criteria, had not received a going-concern opinion for at least 3 consecutive years, and had not entered bankruptcy.

(n = 460 in the first stage [330 *gco* firms and 130 non-*gco* firms] and n = 264 in the second [128 *br* firms and 136 non-*br* firms]). Although the set of variables used in each stage is not identical, both contain the financial ratios, firm size, and default status. Because the sampling procedure randomly selected a small number of non-*gco*/*br* firms (two) included in the non-*gco* control sample (used in the first stage) and a small number of *gco*/non-*br* firms (eight) included in the non-*br* control sample (used in the second stage), selection of these randomly determined non-*gco*/*br* and *gco*/non-*br* firms was repeated 100 times. Mean values for the model parameter estimates derived from the repeated samples are estimated to evaluate the robustness of the study's results to the random selection of the non-*gco*/*br* and *gco*/non-*br* firms. The discussion which follows presents the results obtained using the original sample which is representative of the mean results.[12]

Results of estimating the *gco* logistic regression are presented in Table 2. The pseudo R-square (Harrell, 1983) is approximately 56% and the Wald $\underline{X}^2$ statistic is 105.085 with 9 degrees of freedom (significant with $p < 0.005$) indicating that this model specification has significant explanatory power.[13] The results are comparable to those reported in prior studies; however, although the SIZE variable parameter is negative, it is not significant.[14]

We estimated the bankruptcy model parameters conditional on the estimates of the *gco* parameters ($\hat{\alpha}$) given in Table 2 via the nonlinear least squares method. We then tested for the endogeneity of the GC variable using the *t*-statistic corresponding to the estimate of θ. As can be seen in the last row of Table 3, θ is statistically insignificant, as is the Hausman test (Hausman, 1978) statistic (4.480).[15] These results suggest that there are no significant variables omitted from our bankruptcy model that are also related to going-concern opinions; thus, there is no evidence that the conventional logistic regression yields biased estimates of the parameters of the bankruptcy model. For this reason we can evaluate the logistic regression results given in Table 4 for the conventional logistic estimation of this specific bankruptcy model.

The model pseudo R-square is approximately 25% and the Wald $\underline{X}^2$ statistic is 47.667 with 10 degrees of freedom (significant with $p < 0.005$). The signs and significance of the financial ratio variables are comparable to those of other studies which included the same ratios (e.g. Hopwood et al., 1989). In addition, as expected by Bulow and Shoven (1978), long-term debt/total assets is positive and significant and long-term debt to total liabilities is negative and significant (both at $p < 0.005$). Default status is positive but it is not significant. The proportion of public debt is negatively related to bankruptcy, not positively related as expected (Gilson et al., 1990).[16]

Table 2. Conventional Logistic Regression Estimates of the Going-Concern Model.

$$z\alpha = \alpha_0 + \alpha_1 DDFLT + \alpha_2 CURRAT + \alpha_3 LTDBTTA + \alpha_4 NITA + \alpha_5 LTDBTTL + \alpha_6 SIZE + \alpha_7 BIG6 + \alpha_8 (SIZE^* BIG6) + \alpha_9 ARLAG$$

Variable	Coefficient*	Std. Error	T-Stat
Constant	–2.544	0.768	–3.312***
DDFLT[a]	2.509	0.489	5.128***
CURRAT[b]	–0.237	0.137	–1.731*
LTDBTTA[c]	7.678	1.961	3.915***
NITA[d]	–6.418	1.117	–5.746***
LTDBTTL[e]	–6.863	1.641	–4.182***
SIZE (median-adjusted)[f]	–0.223	0.212	–1.053
BIG6[g]	0.078	0.509	0.153
SIZE(median-adjusted)* BIG6	0.008	0.233	0.033
ARLAG[h]	0.039	0.008	4.784***

[a] 1 if the firm is in default on debt or in violation of debt covenants, 0 otherwise
[b] current assets to current liabilities
[c] long-term debt to total assets
[d] net income to total assets
[e] long-term debt to total liabilities
[f] ln assets less median ln assets
[g] 1 if the auditor is one of the Big-Six audit firms, 0 otherwise
[h] the number of days from the last day of the fiscal year to the audit report date
* Parameter estimates for simple logit estimation of the going-concern opinion model
$n = 460$
WALD $\underline{X}^2 = 105.085$ with 9 d.f. $p < 0.005$
Pseudo $R^2 = 0.56$
LR statistic $= 324.636$ with 9 d.f. $p < 0.005$
* $p < 0.05$
** $p < 0.01$
*** $p < 0.005$.

The GC variable coefficient (β_8) is positive and significant. Because we have evaluated the relation between first-time *gco*s and the occurrence of bankruptcy subsequent to the audit opinion (and prior to release of the next audit report), and because we find no evidence that the results are driven by the effect of bankruptcy related factors on the auditors' opinions (there is no evidence that any bankruptcy variables that are also correlated with *gco*s have been omitted), the logit estimate of the GC coefficient can be understood as an estimate of the self-fulfilling prophecy effect for sample-median sized firms. We can apply this interpretation to the logit results for this particular bankruptcy model only because we specifically tested for the possible influence of omitted correlated variables.

The interactive variable coefficient for GC $*$ SIZE (β_{10}) is also positive and significant; the probability of bankruptcy following receipt of a *gco* increases with increasing firm size. The variable for the interaction of *gco*s with the proportion of public debt is not statistically significant. The likelihood ratio statistic for the model which includes all three GC variables (Eq. (4)) versus an otherwise identical model without the GC variables (GC, GC $*$ PUBDEBT, and GC $*$ SIZE) is significant at $p < 0.05$ (20.724 with three degrees of freedom).[17]

4. SUMMARY, LIMITATIONS, AND CONCLUSIONS

In an article aimed at commercial bank lenders, Menon and Schwartz (1986) warn that auditors are reluctant to issue going-concern opinions because of their belief that *gco*s create a self-fulfilling prophecy. If audit opinions provide value to financial statement users, then it is to be expected that they will affect outcomes at least some of the time. This study investigates the existence of the *sfp* effect by specifically testing and controlling for the possibility that omitted bankruptcy related factors could have an effect on prior going-concern opinions. This study is also the first to investigate the possibility that the *sfp* effect may not apply equally to all firms. The results suggest that, *ceteris paribus,* going-concern opinions increase the probability of bankruptcy and the larger the firm, the more it increases.

The insignificance of the endogeneity test factor, θ (Table 3) suggests that all the significant bankruptcy related factors that influence auditors' opinion decisions have been included in the bankruptcy model. This implies that the opinion does not provide additional information about the likelihood of impending bankruptcy beyond that which is provided by the other included variables (if the opinion did provide information about non-included bankruptcy related factors, θ should be significant). Still, the probability of bankruptcy increases after firms receive a *gco*. Perhaps audit report readers respond to a *gco* because they believe that it provides evidence of private information held by the auditor when, in actuality, such private auditor information may not be highly correlated with bankruptcy, on average. Alternatively, the insignificance of θ could be due to a lack of power. There could be additional bankruptcy related variables that also relate to auditor going-concern opinion decisions which have been omitted from the model and the estimation procedure lacked the power to detect this. If so, the opinion variables will be endogenous despite the lack of power of the estimation procedure to provide evidence of this endogeneity. However, recall that the two-stage procedure produces endogeneity consistent parameter estimates, and note that similar results are obtained when the endogeneity consistent two-stage procedure is used (Table 3). Therefore, the results are robust to both possibilities:

Table 3. Two-Stage Logistic Regression Estimates of the Bankruptcy Model.

$$x\beta + \theta\nu = \beta_0 + \beta_1 DDFLT + \beta_2 CURRAT + \beta_3 LTDBTTA + \beta_4 NITA + \beta_5 LTDBTTL + \beta_6 SIZE + \beta_7 PUBDEBT + \beta_8 GC + \beta_9 (GC * PUBDEBT) + \beta_{10}(GC * SIZE) + \theta\nu$$

Variable	Coefficient*	Std. Error	T-Stat
Constant	0.373	0.519	0.718
DDFLT[a]	0.688	0.628	1.096
CURRAT[b]	–0.529	0.218	–2.421**
LTDBTTA[c]	8.170	2.514	3.250***
NITA[d]	–2.995	1.460	–2.051*
LTDBTTL[e]	–5.499	2.027	–2.713***
SIZE (median-adjusted)[f]	–0.030	0.099	–0.302
PUBDEBT[g]	–3.193	1.316	–2.426
GC[h]	2.924	1.350	2.166*
GC * PUBDEBT	–0.178	2.132	–0.083
GC * SIZE (median-adjusted)	1.416	0.568	2.491**
θ[i]	0.068	0.179	0.379

[a] 1 if the firm is in default on debt or in violation of debt covenants, 0 otherwise
[b] current assets to current liabilities
[c] long-term debt to total assets
[d] net income to total assets
[e] long-term debt to total liabilities
[f] ln assets less median ln assets
[g] total publicly held debt to total liabilities
[h] 1 if the firm received an initial going-concern opinion, 0 otherwise
[i] unobservables parameter
* Two-stage parameter estimates
$n = 264$
WALD $\underline{X}^2 = 38.765$ with 11 d.f. $p < 0.005$
* $p < 0.05$
** $p < 0.01$
*** $p < 0.005$.

Table 4. Conventional Logistic Regression Estimates of the Bankruptcy Model.

$$x\beta = \beta_0 + \beta_1 DDFLT + \beta_2 CURRAT + \beta_3 LTDBTTA + \beta_4 NITA + \beta_5 LTDBTTL + \beta_6 SIZE + \beta_7 PUBDEBT + \beta_8 GC + \beta_9 (GC * PUBDEBT) + \beta_{10}(GC * SIZE)$$

Variable	Coefficient*	Std. Error	T-Stat
Constant	–0.178	0.419	–0.426
DDFLT[a]	0.459	0.505	0.910
CURRAT[b]	–0.248	0.142	–1.748*
LTDBTTA[c]	6.306	1.885	3.345***
NITA[d]	–2.654	1.139	–2.329**
LTDBTTL[e]	–4.180	1.589	–2.631***
SIZE (median-adjusted)[f]	0.027	0.089	0.298
PUBDEBT[g]	–2.548	1.146	–2.224
GC[h]	1.985	0.749	2.650***
GC * PUBDEBT	2.100	3.046	0.689
GC * SIZE (median-adjusted)	0.740	0.297	2.489**

[a] 1 if the firm is in default on debt or in violation of debt covenants, 0 otherwise
[b] current assets to current liabilities
[c] long-term debt to total assets
[d] net income to total assets
[e] long-term debt to total liabilities
[f] ln assets less median ln assets
[g] total publicly held debt to total liabilities
[h] 1 if the firm received an initial going-concern opinion, 0 otherwise
* Parameter estimates for simple logit estimation of the bankruptcy model
$n = 264$
WALD $X^2 = 47.667$ with 10 d.f. $p < 0.005$
Pseudo $R^2 = 0.25$
LR statistic = 111.546 with 10 d.f. $p < 0.005$
* $p < 0.05$
** $p < 0.01$
*** $p < 0.005$.

(1) that the opinion variables are exogenousas a result of including all the significant bankruptcy related factors that influence auditors' opinions in the bankruptcy model (Table 4 results); or
(2) that the opinion variables are endogenous because the potential bankruptcy outcome influences the opinion via factors not considered in the model (Table 3 results).

The finding that the effect of *gco*s on bankruptcy increases as firm size increases is consistent with evidence that the larger the firm, the closer it must be to bankruptcy before the auditor will issue a *gco*. Thus, a going-concern opinion may be less expected for large firms in financial distress than for small ones with otherwise similar indications of trouble as measured by financial ratios and default status. If the opinion is more likely to be a surprise when a large firm receives it, it may have a greater effect on financial statement readers whose resulting actions increase the likelihood that the firm will, indeed, fail.

Despite the expected differences between "outside" (public) debt and "inside" debt, no evidence was found to suggest that the proportion of debt that is publicly traded has any interaction with the effect of *gco*s on the probability of bankruptcy. Several limitations could account for the inability to find evidence of this expected interaction. Debt footnotes are quite variable in the amount of detailed information they provide; therefore, publicly traded debt issues may not have been properly identified in all cases. Because the possibility of misidentification of public debt may include both non-public debt classified as public and publicly held debt classified as non-public, the direction of any potential bias resulting from the misidentification of public debt is indeterminate.

The results obtained are consistent with the idea that going-concern opinions constitute a self-fulfilling prophecy by raising the average probability that recipient firms will fail. This effect is intensified as firm size increases. This is, perhaps, not surprising. By definition, information that is not used to affect decisions has little value. Information is of value precisely because it is used to influence the choices made by those who receive the information. Therefore, if accounting information has value, it must influence decisions and thus it can affect that which it measures. The evidence this study provides that is consistent with the existence of the self-fulfilling prophecy effect is evidence that accounting information has value. The finding is important because there has been only limited empirical evidence that going-concern audit opinions can create a self-fulfilling prophecy. It should be recognized that the results may differ if a different definition of financial distress is used.

This study is unable to shed light on the specific mechanisms by which the opinion affects users' decisions. Future research should focus on understanding the mechanisms by which the *sfp* effect occurs. It is likely that there are unidentified factors that significantly influence the effect that *gco*s have on the probability of firm failure. For example, suppliers' (customers') decisions may be influenced when a customer (vendor) receives a *gco*. Suppliers may react to the opinion by refusing to provide goods on customary trade terms and customers may decide not to purchase a company's products. Such reactions may depend on the type of firm or the firm's major products. For example, firms that market durable goods and/or products for which continuing support relationships are crucial, may experience a greater loss of customers as a result of receiving a *gco* than companies which sell single use products. Additional research using a broad range of methodologies, such as case studies and behavioral research, should be pursued to gain the insights needed to identify additional firm specific characteristics that relate to the impact of a going-concern opinion on the probability that a firm will subsequently enter bankruptcy.

NOTES

1. SAS No. 59 requires that auditors actively consider (as part of every audit engagement) the need to include an expression of doubt about an entity's ability to continue as a going concern.

2. Although bankruptcy is not synonymous with firm failure it is often used as a proxy for failure because it is a clearly defined event that results in significant costs for investors and creditors and often does signal the ultimate demise of the firm.

3. The matched firms should be randomly chosen from among the pool of firms that meet the matching criteria. Otherwise, the researcher could inadvertently select sample firms with an incidence of the variable of interest that is not representative of the population of matching firms.

4. See Maddala, 1991, pp. 792–793 for details.

5. A study by Mutchler et al. (1997) explores the issue further by considering various types of default.

6. Among Big 8/6 firms, increasing client size reduces the likelihood that a *gco* will be issued to a greater extent if the audit firm's partner compensation plan emphasizes local office profits ("small-pool" firms) than if the compensation plan emphasizes worldwide firm profits ("large-pool" firms) (Carcello et al., 2000).

7. The median sized firm was $30,960,000 and the sample mean was $25,870,000.

8. Firms with opinions coded as going-concern were retrieved and the full text of the audit report was read for a sufficient number of years to identify first-time going-concern opinions. Firms that had received *gcos* for two or more years preceding bankruptcy were omitted. However, if the first *gco* was received during the period covered by the study, but was received several years prior to bankruptcy, the firm was included as a *gco*/non-*br* firm. Such firms were categorized as non-bankrupt observations because bankruptcy did not occur prior to issuance of a subsequent audit report following the company's first *gco*. The following sources were used to obtain the full text of the audit reports: Compact Disclosure; NAARS; SEC-On-Line; and the SEC File microfiche database.

9. Compact Disclosure was examined for all sample firms not listed in the *Yearbook* to ensure that they had not entered bankruptcy prior to issuance of a subsequent year's financial statements. This step identified two additional bankruptcies not included in the

Yearbook. Bankrupt firms that did not have all the requisite years' audit report texts needed to determine their prior opinion type were omitted.

10. The sample size is derived as follows: approximately 6% of the COMPUSTAT population of stressed, non-*br* firms are also *gco* firms; therefore, the desired sample size n* is the nearest lower integer value to the solution of $N^* = 0.06 \times (128 + N^*)$ with respect to N*.

11. The sample selection procedure resulted in the inclusion of many small public firms traded over-the-counter in regional markets. Among these were companies whose sole sources of debt financing were from private (sometimes related) parties. Often such firms did not have credit lines available through any bank (nor any publicly held debt). The absence of default, therefore, does not mean that the company had continuing lines of credit available.

12. The mean values for the simple logistic regression estimates of the opinion and bankruptcy models and the two-stage bankruptcy model estimation (based on 100 replications of the sampling procedure) are similar to those reported in the tables.

13. The Pseudo R^2 is calculated by subtracting two times the number of variables in the model ($2 * p$) from the model Chi-Square (Likelihood Ratio statistic) and dividing the result by –2 times the log likelihood of the model with an intercept term only. The Wald test evaluates whether the model parameters are jointly different from zero. The test statistic is asymptotically distributed $\underline{X}^2$ with degrees of freedom equal to the number of parameters (Kennedy, 1993). The Wald test statistic is presented as an aid in evaluating model fit because the logit pseudo R-Square statistic is not available for the endogeneity consistent, two-stage bankruptcy model estimation.

14. Multicolinearity among the independent variables could explain the lack of significance of the size variable. BIG6 and SIZE are correlated at 0.364 in the GC sample and NITA and SIZE are correlated at 0.386 in both samples. In addition, the debt variables LTDBTTL and LTDBTTA are correlated at 0.609 for the GC sample and exhibit a mean weighted correlation of 0.879 in the BR sample (although both of these variables are significant in both the GC model (Table 2) and the BR models (Tables 3 and 4)). PUBDEBT exhibits a mean weighted correlation with LTDBTTL at 0.334, with LTDBTTA at 0.384, and with SIZE at 0.413 in the BR sample. (Because the proportions of each combination of opinion type and bankruptcy condition were different in each sample, weights were used to adjust the proportions of each combination in the BR sample to match those proportions in the GC estimation sample prior to obtaining the correlation matrix. Correlations were obtained for each of the 100 sample repetitions to obtain mean weighted variable correlations.)

15. The Hausman statistic evaluates the equality of the simple logit parameter estimates and the two-stage parameter estimates. The statistic is distributed $\underline{X}^2$ with 11 degrees of freedom (the number of parameters common to both models).

16. A large proportion of public-debt holders may hold amounts that are not material to them individually. They may, therefore, be less motivated to take actions that result in a firm entering bankruptcy than private investors, despite theincentives that public-debt holders are expected to possess as discussed by Gilson et al. (1990). The authors wish to thank a reviewer for this insight.

17. The likelihood ratio test statistic (distributed $\underline{X}^2$ with three degrees of freedom) is calculated as: –2 times the log likelihood for the model without the going-concern opinion variables less –2 times the log likelihood for the full model.

ACKNOWLEDGMENTS

The authors wish to thank Jane Mutchler, Mark Dirsmith, and Jim McKeown, for their valuable assistance. We also wish to acknowledge Joseph Carcello, Charles Cullinan, Dana Hermanson, Roger Martin, Steve Rock, Tim Rupert, Pete Wilson, participants at the AAA's Auditing Section mid-year meeting, the Boston Accounting Research Colloquium and the research workshop at the University of New Hampshire, and an anonymous reviewer for helpful comments on an earlier version of this paper.

REFERENCES

Altman, E. (1968). Financial Ratios, Discriminant Analysis and the Prediction of Corporate Bankruptcy. *Journal of Finance*, *23* (September), 589–609.

Altman, E. (1982). Accounting Implications of Failure Prediction Models. *Journal of Accounting, Auditing, and Finance*, *6* (Fall), 4–19.

AICPA (1978). *The Commission on Auditors' Responsibilities: Report, Conclusions, and Recommendations*. American Institute of Certified Public Accountants.

AICPA (1988). *The Auditor's Consideration of an Entity's Ability to Continue as a Going Concern, SAS no. 59*. New York: American Institute of Certified Public Accountants.

Andersen, J. (1972). Separate Sample Logistic Discrimination. *Biometrika*, *59*, 19–35.

Bamber, L. (1986). The Information Content of Annual Earnings Releases: a Trading Volume Approach. *Journal of Accounting Research*, *24* (Spring), 40–56.

Bell, T. B. (1991). Discussion of: Towards an Explanation of Auditor Failure to Modify the Audit Opinions of Bankrupt Companies. *Auditing: A Journal of Practice and Theory*, *10* (Supplement), 14–20.

Boritz, J. E. (1991). *The 'Going Concern' Assumption: Accounting and Auditing Implications*. Canadian Institute of Chartered Accountants.

Bulow, J., & Shoven, J. (1978). The Bankruptcy Decision. *Bell Journal of Economics*, *9* (Autumn), 437–456.

Carcello, J. V., Hermanson, D. R., & Huss, H. F. (2000). Going-concern Opinions: the Effects of Partner Compensation Plans and Client Size. *Auditing: A Journal of Practice and Theory*, *19* (Spring), 67–77.

Carmichael, D. R., Messier, W. F., Jr., Mutchler, J. F., Pany, K., & Sullivan, J. B. (1995). Communications with Users. In: T. Bell & A. M. Wright (Eds), *Auditing Practice, Research, and Education: A Productive Collaboration* (pp. 144–173). New York: American Institute of Certified Public Accountants.

Chen, K. C., & Church, B. K. (1992). Default on Debt Obligations and the Issuance of Going-Concern Opinions. *Auditing: A Journal of Practice and Theory*, *11* (Fall), 30–49.

Citron, D., & Taffler, R. (1992). The Audit Report Under Going Concern Uncertainties: An Empirical Analysis. *Accounting and Business Research*, *22* (Autumn), 337–345.

DeAngelo, L. E. (1981). Auditor Size and Audit Quality. *Journal of Accounting & Economics*, *3* (December), 183–199.

Diamond, D. (1991). Monitoring and Reputation: The Choice Between Bank Loans and Directly Placed Debt. *Journal of Political Economy*, *99* (August), 689–721.

Fama, E. (1985). What's Different About Banks? *Journal of Monetary Economics*, *15* (January), 29–39.

Freeman, R. (1987). The Association Between Accounting Earnings and Security Returns for Large and Small Firms. *Journal of Accounting and Economics*, *9* (July), 195–228.

Foster, B. P., Ward, T. J., & Woodroof, J. (1998). An Analysis of the Usefulness of Debt Defaults and Going Concern Opinions in Bankruptcy Risk Assessment. *Journal of Accounting, Auditing, and Finance*, *13* (Summer), 351–371.

Gilson, S., John, K., & Lang, L. (1990). Troubled Debt Restructurings: An Empirical Study of Private Reorganization of Firms in Default. *Journal of Financial Economics*, *27* (October), 315–353.

George, C., Spiceland, J. D., & George, S. (1996). A Longitudinal Study of the Going-Concern Audit Decision and Survival Time. *Advances in Quantitative Analysis of Finance and Accounting*, *4*, 77–103.

Greene, W. H. (1997). *Econometric Analysis* (3rd ed.). MacMillan.

Harrell, F., Jr. (1983). The Logist Procedure. In: S. P. Joyner (Ed.), *SUGI Supplementary Library Users Guide* (pp. 181–202). SAS Institute, Inc.

Hausman, J. A. (1978). Specification Tests in Econometrics. *Econometrica*, *46* (November), 1251–1271.

Hopwood, W., McKeown, J., & Mutchler, J. (1989). A Test of the Incremental Explanatory Power of Opinions Qualified for Consistency and Uncertainty. *The Accounting Review*, *64* (January), 28–48.

Hopwood, W., McKeown, J., & Mutchler, J. (1994). A Reexamination of Auditor vs. Model Accuracy within the Context of the Going-Concern Opinion Decision. *Contemporary Accounting Research*, *10* (Spring), 409–431.

Kennedy, P. (1993). *A Guide to Econometrics*. Cambridge: The MIT Press.

Kida, T. (1980). An Investigation Into Auditor's Continuity and Related Qualification Judgments. *Journal of Accounting Research*, *18* (Autumn), 506–523.

Louwers, T. J., Messina, F. M., & Richard, M. D. (1995). The Auditor's Going Concern Modification as a Self-Fulfilling Prophecy: A Discrete-Time Survival Analysis. Working Paper, University of Houston, Houston, TX.

Maddala, G. S. (1991). A Perspective on the Use of Limited-Dependent and Qualitative Variables Models in Accounting Research. *The Accounting Review*, *66* (October), 788–807.

McHugh, C. M. (1991–1995). *Bankruptcy Yearbook and Almanac*. New Generation Research, Inc.

McKeown, J., Mutchler, J., & Hopwood, W. (1991). Towards an Explanation of Auditor Failure to Modify the Audit Opinions of Bankrupt Companies. *Auditing: A Journal of Practice and Theory*, *10* (Supplement), 1–13.

Menon, K., & Schwartz, K. (1986). The Auditor's Report for Companies Facing Bankruptcy. *The Journal of Commercial Bank Lending*, *68* (January), 42–52.

Mutchler, J. F. (1984). Auditors' Perceptions of the Going-Concern Opinion Decision. *Auditing: A Journal of Practice and Theory*, *3* (Spring), 17–30.

Mutchler, J. F. (1985). A Multivariate Analysis of the Auditor's Going-Concern Opinion Decision. *Journal of Accounting Research*, *23* (Autumn), 668–682.

Mutchler, J. F., Hopwood, W., & McKeown, J. (1997). The Influence of Contrary Information and Mitigating Factors on Audit Opinion Decisions on Bankrupt Companies. *Journal of Accounting Research*, *35* (Autumn), 295–310.

Nogler, G. E. (1995). The Resolution of Auditor Going Concern Opinions. *Auditing: A Journal of Practice and Theory*, *14* (Fall), 54–73.

Ohlson, J. (1980). Financial Ratios and the Probabilistic Prediction of Bankruptcy. *Journal of Accounting Research*, *18* (Spring), 109–131.
Pastena, V., & Ruland, W. (1986). The Merger/Bankruptcy Alternative. *The Accounting Review*, *61* (April), 288–301.
Rajan, R. (1992). Insiders and Outsiders: The Choice Between Informed andArm's-Length Debt. *Journal of Finance*, *47* (September), 1367–1400.
Terza, J. V. (2001). Parametric Nonlinear Regression with Endogneous Switching. Working Paper, Department of Economics, Penn State University, University Park, PA.
Zmijewski, M. (1984). Methodological Issues Related to the Estimation of Financial Distress Prediction Models. *Journal of Accounting Research*, *22* (Supplement), 59–82.

APPENDIX

The process determining the issuance of a *gco* is cast in the simple binary logit framework as

$$GC = \begin{cases} 1 \text{ if and only if a } gco \text{ is issued} \\ 0 \text{ otherwise} \end{cases}$$

where a *gco* is issued if and only if

$$z\alpha + \nu > 0,$$

z is a row vector of observable *gco* determinants, α is the conformable column vector of logit coefficients, and υ is the logistically distributed random variable representing relevant but omitted *gco* determinants. It follows that conditional on the vector of exogenous determinants z, the probability of a *gco* is

$$\Pr\{GC = 1 \mid z\} = \Lambda(z\alpha) \quad (1)$$

where $\Lambda(\cdot)$ denotes the logistic distribution function. We also assume that conditional on the row vector of observable bankruptcy determinants (x) [which includes the going concern dummy variable (GC)], and υ (the omitted *gco* determinants), the probability of bankruptcy is

$$\Pr\{BR = 1 \mid x, \nu\} = \Lambda(x\beta + \theta\nu) \quad (2)$$

where BR is the binary variable that has a value of 1 if the firm falls into bankruptcy and 0 otherwise, β is the column vector of logistic regression coefficients, and θ is the coefficient of the omitted *gco* determinants.

It can be shown that the assumptions underlying Eqs (1) and (2) imply (see Terza 2001 for details)

$$E[BR \mid w, GC] = GC \frac{\int_{-z\alpha}^{\infty} \Lambda(x\beta + \theta\nu)\lambda(\nu)\, d\nu}{\Lambda(z\alpha)} + (1 - GC) \frac{\int_{-\infty}^{-z\alpha} \Lambda(x\beta + \theta\nu)\lambda(\nu)\, d\nu}{1 - \Lambda(z\alpha)} \quad \text{(a)}$$

where

$$\lambda(\cdot) = \Lambda(\cdot)[1 - \Lambda(\cdot)]$$

is the logistic probability density function, and w is the vector of all exogenous variables in the model (i.e. the union of z and x not including GC). Consistent parameters of the bankruptcy equation can be estimated by applying the nonlinear least squares method to

$$BR = h(w, GC, \beta, \theta, \hat{\alpha}) + e \quad \text{(b)}$$

where

$$h(w, GC, \beta, \theta, \hat{\alpha}) = GC \frac{\int_{-z\hat{\alpha}}^{\infty} \Lambda(x\beta + \theta\nu)\lambda(\nu)\, d\nu}{\Lambda(z\hat{\alpha})} + (1 - GC) \frac{\int_{-\infty}^{-z\hat{\alpha}} \Lambda(x\beta + \theta\nu)\lambda(\nu)\, d\nu}{1 - \Lambda(z\hat{\alpha})},$$

and $\hat{\alpha}$ represents the consistent (large sample unbiased) estimate of α obtained in the first stage. The estimated gco model parameters ($\hat{\alpha}$) include the choice based sample bias adjustment to the intercept term (γ).

7. BOUNDS FOR OPTION PRICES AND THE EXPECTED PAYOFFS WITH SKEWNESS AND KURTOSIS

Cheng-few Lee, Peter Zhang and Alice C. Lee

ABSTRACT

The purpose of this paper is to incorporate both skewness and kurtosis explicitly through extending Zhang (1994) to provide bounds for the prices of and expected payoffs for options, given the first two moments and skewness and kurtosis. The rest of this paper is organized as follows. Section 2 distributions of terminal stock prices with given expected price, standard deviation, skewness, and kurtosis under the assumption that the underlying asset price is continuously distributed. Similar to the results given in (1), the bounds derived in this paper depend on the information of the cumulative distribution of the underlying asset. However, it is shown in Section 2 that for each set of moments, there always exists one semi-parametric upper bound which is independent of the information of any distribution of the underlying asset. This semi-parametric upper bound has the same property as that in the case of the first two moments in Zhang (1994), that is, it is always greater than or equal to the distribution dependent bounds.

1. INTRODUCTION

Though the study of the bounds of option prices starts as early as 1973 with Merton (1973), the earliest paper that concentrates on bounds of option prices is Perrakis and Ryan (1984). Perrakis (1986) improves their bounds under the

Advances in Quantitative Analysis of Finance and Accounting, Volume 10, pages 117–138.

ISBN: 0-7623-0969-5

assumption that return distributions have a finite range and also provides a multiple-period model for bounding American puts. In general, these bounds require more information than the Black and Scholes (1973) pricing model, but they do not rely on the continuous time risk-free hedge used by Black and Scholes. There are other approaches to find bounds of option prices. Ritchken (1985) develops the linear programming approach with constraints on time preferences, risk aversion, and state probabilities; Levy (1985) uses a stochastic dominance (SD) approach to find the upper bounds. Perrakis and Ryan (1986) show that bounds developed by their early approach are identical to Levy's stochastic dominance bounds and also to Ritchken's linear programming bounds. For a more detailed review of the literature, see Zhang (1994).

These studies depend on the distributions of the prices or returns of the underlying assets. Lo (1987) pioneers the semi-parametric approach and obtains upper bounds for the expected payoffs of European options. He then obtains the upper bounds for the European option prices by discounting the upper bounds of the expected payoffs at the risk-neutral rate of return. Using an alternative approach, Zhang (1994) sharpens Lo's upper bounds with the additional assumption that the underlying asset price is continuously distributed. These upper bounds for the expected payoffs of the call and put options are given by

$$\bar{R}_{2c} = [1 - F(K)][\mu(t) - K] + \sigma(t)\sqrt{F(K)[I - F(K)]}, \text{ and} \tag{1a}$$

$$\bar{R}_{2p} = \bar{R}_{2c} - \mu(t) + K \tag{1b}$$

where $\bar{R}_{2c}$ and $\bar{R}_{2p}$ are the upper bounds for the expected payoffs of the European call and put options respectively; F(K) is the value of the cumulative distribution function of any distribution at the strike price K; and $\mu(t)$ and $\sigma(t)$ are the mean and standard deviation of the underlying asset price, respectively.

It is shown in Zhang (1994) that Eqs (1a) and (1b) are always sharper than Lo's upper bounds over all possible distributions with the same first two moments except for one distribution with which Eq. (1) becomes the same as Lo's bounds. In other words, Lo's bounds are the maximum value of Eq. (1a) over all possible distributions with the same first two moments and this maximum value is obtained at one continuous distribution. Though the increased sharpness in Eq. (1) is obtained using additional information about the distribution of the underlying assets. F(K), the maximization of Eq. (1a) with respect to F(.) yields the same semi-parametric least upper bounds which depend only on the given first two moments.

All the above studies are motivated either directly or indirectly by the modem option pricing theory which, in general, neglects skewness and kurtosis of the distribution of the underlying assets. These studies have certain limitations because they depend largely on the first two moments of the distribution of the price or the return of the underlying asset. The first two moments can, traditionally believed (see Samuelson, 1970), capture most characteristics of a distribution. However, recent studies (see Francis, 1975; Kraus & Litzenberger, 1976; Kane, 1982; Lee & Wu, 1985; Bollerslev, 1986; Werth & Rubinstein, 1996; Stutzer, 1996) show that skewness and kurtosis may still have important effects on the portfolio choices and on the expected payoffs of options.

The purpose of this paper is to incorporate both skewness and kurtosis explicitly through extending Zhang (1994) to provide bounds for the prices of and expected payoffs for options, given the first two moments and skewness and kurtosis. The rest of this paper is organized as follows. Section 2 provides the upper bounds for the expected payoffs for both call and put options over all possible distributions of terminal stock prices with given expected price, standard deviation, skewness, and kurtosis under the assumption that the underlying asset price is continuously distributed. Similar to the results given in Eq. (1), the bounds derived in this paper depend on the information of the cumulative distribution of the underlying asset. However, it is shown in Section 2 that for each set of moments, there always exists one semi-parametric upper bound which is independent of the information of any distribution of the underlying asset. This semi-parametric upper bound has the same property as that in the case of the first two moments in Zhang (1994), that is, it is always greater than or equal to the distribution dependent bounds.

Section 3 translates the bounds of the expected payoffs of options into bounds for option prices through discounting the bounds of the expected payoffs at the lower bound of the expected rate of return of options. We use Grundy's (1991) lower bounds of the expected rates of returns of options instead of the risk neutrality valuation relationship used by Lo. In order to test the effectiveness of our bounds, in Section 4 we consider the application of the risk- neutral-valuation relationship in our problem to compare our bounds with those of others. Section 5 provides some simulation results using given values for the parameters. Section 6 concludes the paper.

2. THE UPPER AND LOWER BOUNDS OF EXPECTED PAYOFFS

In this section, we derive upper and lower bounds for the expected payoffs of both call and put options. Let C(t) be the current price of a call option with strike price K on a stock with current price S(t) expiring at date T. The current expectation of the terminal payoff of the call is given by $R_C(t) = E_t[\max[\tilde{S}(T) - K, 0]]$, where $E_t(\cdot)$ is the conditional expectation operator at current time t and $T > t$. Our objective is to find out the least upper bound and the greatest lower bound for $R_C(t)$ over all the possible distributions with the given mean, variance, skewness, and kurtosis. The problem can be described formally as follows,[1]

$$\bar{R}_C(t) = \text{Max} \int_0^{\infty} \max[\tilde{S}(T) - K, 0]\, dF[\tilde{S}(T)] \tag{2}$$

$$\int_0^{\infty} dF[\tilde{S}(T)] = 1 \tag{3}$$

$$\int_0^{\infty} \tilde{S}(T)\, dF[\tilde{S}(T)] = \mu(t) \tag{4}$$

$$\int_0^{\infty} [\tilde{S}(T)]^2\, dF[\tilde{S}(T)] = \mu^2(t) + \sigma^2(t) \tag{5}$$

$$\int_0^{\infty} [\tilde{S}(T)]^3\, dF[\tilde{S}(T)] = M_3(t) \tag{6}$$

$$\int_0^{\infty} [\tilde{S}(T)]^4\, dF[\tilde{S}(T)] = M_4(t) \tag{7}$$

where $F[\tilde{S}(T)]$ is any cumulative distribution function of the terminal stock price $\tilde{S}(T)$ with $0 \le F(0) < F[\tilde{S}(T)] < 1 = F(+\infty) \forall \tilde{S}(T) > 0$, M_3 and M_4 are the third and fourth non-central moments of the price of the underlying asset.

The second, third, and fourth moments given by Eqs (5), (6), and (7) can also be expressed in the following central moments

$$\int_0^{\infty} [\tilde{S}(T) - \mu(t)]^2\, dF[\tilde{S}(T)] = \sigma^2(t) \tag{5}$$

$$\int_0^{\infty} [\tilde{S}(T) - \mu(t)]^3\, dF[\tilde{S}(T)] = K\sigma^3(t), \text{ and} \tag{6}$$

$$\int_0^{\infty} [\tilde{S}(T) - \mu(t)]^4\, dF[\tilde{S}(T)] = \eta\sigma^4(t) \tag{7}$$

where K and η represent skewness and kurtosis of the distribution of the asset price.

The central moments given in Eqs (6) and (7) can be expressed in terms of the noncentral moments given in Eqs (5)–(7) as follows

$$\int_0^\infty [\tilde{S}(T) - \mu(t)]^3 \, dF[\tilde{S}(T)] = M_3 - 3\sigma^2(t)\mu(t) - 4\mu^3(t), \text{ and}$$

$$\int_0^\infty [\tilde{S}(T) - \mu(t)]^4 \, dF[\tilde{S}(T)] = M_4 - 4M_3\mu(t) - + 6\sigma^2(t)\mu^2(t) + 7\mu^4(t).$$

The five conditions Eqs (3)–(7) constitute a moment problem, or a Stieltjes problem,[2] with the first five moments. It is clear that Eq. (2) will not exist if there does not exist any distribution Finance satisfying Eqs (3) through (7), and it is a trivial case if there exists only one distribution F satisfying Eqs (3) through (7), because there is only one expected value corresponding to this unique distribution. So the maximum expected payoff Eq. (2) is meaningful only when the solution to the Stieltjes problem given by Eqs (3) to (7) is not unique. The existence of non-unique distributions satisfying Eqs (3)–(7) can be shown similarly as in Zhang (1994). The existence and uniqueness of the least upper bound and the greatest lower bound of Eq. (2) can also be shown as in Zhang (1994).

The Upper and lower bounds of the expected payoffs of a put, $R_p(t) = E_t\{\max[K - \tilde{S}(T), 0]\}$ can be derived in a similar way. These bounds, however, can also be obtained more conveniently by using the following identity

$$\max[K - \tilde{S}(T), 0] = \max[K - \tilde{S}(T), 0] + \tilde{S}(T) - K \tag{8}$$

Attempts have been made to find close from solutions to the problem Eqs (2)–(7) as in Zhang (1994) in the case of the first two moments. Our problem involves solving quartic equations. Though the quartic equations are solvable by radicals, there are no convenient mathematical expressions for these roots.[3] Therefore, in general, we need to use computer programs to solve quartic equations involved, except of the rare case of $\mu(t) = K$. The results are presented below.

Proposition 1: If $\mu = K$ and the asset price is continuously distributed, then upper bounds of $R_C(t)$ and $R_p(t)$ subject to constraints Eqs (3)–(7) over all possible distributions with the known first four moments are given by

$$\bar{R}_{4c1} = \sigma\left(\frac{\eta F^3(K)}{a}\right)^{1/4},$$

and

$$\bar{R}_{4p1} = \tilde{R}_{4c1} - \mu = K,$$

where

$$a = 1 + \left(\frac{F(K)}{1 - F(K)}\right)^3 > 1,$$

and

F(K) is the value of the cumulative function at the strike price K.

Proof: See Appendix. Q.E.D.

Corollary 1.1: $\bar{R}_{c1}$ has the maximum $\frac{1}{2}\sigma\eta^{1/4}$ at F(K) = 1/2.

Proof: Taking derivative of $\bar{R}_{c1}$ given in Proposition 1 with respect to F(K) yields

$$\frac{\partial \bar{R}_{c1}}{\partial F(K)} = \frac{3s^2(1-s)^2[(1-s^2)+s^2](1-2s)}{(1-3s+s^2)^2} \tag{9}$$

where s = F(K), 0 < s < 1.

It can be shown that the denominator of the right hand side of Eq. (9), $(1-3s+s^2)^2$ is always greater than 1/16 > 0. Thus Eq. (9) is greater than zero for s < 1/2, zero for s = 1/2, and smaller than zero for s > 1/2. Therefore, $\bar{R}_{c1}$ has maximum at s = F(K) = 1/2. Substituting s = 1/2 into $\bar{R}_{c1}$ yield $\frac{1}{2}\sigma\eta^{1/4}$. Q.E.D.

The bounds given in Proposition 1 depend on the cumulative distribution function F(.). Corollary 1.1 is similar to Theorem 7 in Zhang (1994) which proves the semi-parametric upper bound of $\bar{R}_{4c}(t)$. The semi-parametric bound, $\frac{1}{2}\sigma\eta^{1/4}$, does not depend on the specific distribution function F(.) and is always greater than any distribution-dependent-bound $\tilde{R}_{4c}(t)$ with the exception of one distribution F(K) = 1/2 with which $\bar{R}_{4c1}(t) = \frac{1}{2}\sigma\eta^{1/4}$. These results are intuitive in the sense that with some information about the cumulative function F(K), the upper bounds become tighter.

Proposition 2: If $\mu > K$ and the asset price is continuously distributed, then upper bounds of $R_c(t)$ and $R_p(t)$ subject to constraints Eqs (3)–(7) with the known first four moments are given by

$$\bar{R}_{4c2} = x_4(\mu - K), \tag{10}$$

and

$$\bar{R}_{4p2} = \tilde{R}_{4c2}(t) - \mu + K, \tag{11}$$

where x_4 is the largest real root of the quartic equation

$$ax^4 - 4x^3 + 6x^2 - 4x + b = 0$$

where

$$b = 1 - \phi F^3(K),$$

and

$$\phi = \frac{\eta\sigma^4}{(\mu - K)^4} + \frac{4K\sigma^3}{(\mu - K)^3} + \frac{6\sigma^4}{(\mu - K)^2} + 1$$

and a is the same as Proposition 1; and the lower bounds for $R_c(t)$ and $R_p(t)$ subject to the same constraints are

$$R_{-4c2} = Max[x_1(\mu - K), 0],$$

and

$$R_{-4p2} = R_{-4c2} - \mu + K,$$

where x_2 is the smallest real root of the above quartic equation.

Proof: See Appendix. Q.E.D.

Corollary 2.1: For the quartic equation given in Proposition 2, there always exists at least one pair of real roots.

Proof: This can be shown following the proof of Theorem 9 on page 114 in Birkhoff and Lane (1953). Q.E.D.

Corollary 2.1 shows the existence of the real roots for the quartic equation involved, therefore it also shows the existence of the bounds given in the above Proposition. The following corollary provides some comparative static results.

Corollary 2.2

$$\frac{\partial \bar{R}_{4c2}}{\partial \mu} = x_4 - 4w\left\{\frac{\eta\sigma^4}{(\mu - K)^5} + \frac{3K\sigma^3}{(\mu - K)^4} + \frac{3\sigma^2}{(\mu - K)^5}\right\}, \frac{\partial \bar{R}_{4c2}}{\partial K} = -\frac{\partial \bar{R}_{4c2}}{\partial \mu}.$$

$$\frac{\partial \bar{R}_{4c2}}{\partial \sigma} = 4w\left\{\frac{\eta\sigma^3}{(\mu - K)^4} + \frac{K\sigma^2}{(\mu - K)^3} + \frac{3\sigma}{(\mu - K)^2}\right\}, \frac{\partial \bar{R}_{4c2}}{\partial K} = \frac{4w\sigma^3}{(\mu - K)^4} > 0,$$

and

$$\frac{\partial \bar{R}_{4c2}}{\partial \eta} = \frac{w\sigma^4}{(\mu - K)^4},$$

$$\frac{\partial R_{-4c2}}{\partial \mu} = x_1 - 2w_1\left\{\frac{\eta\sigma^4}{(\mu - K)^5} + \frac{3K\sigma^3}{(\mu - K)^4} + \frac{3\sigma^2}{(\mu - K)^5}\right\}, \frac{\partial R_{-4c2}}{\partial K} = -\frac{\partial R_{-4c2}}{\partial \mu}$$

$$\frac{\partial R_{-4c2}}{\partial \sigma} = 4w\left\{\frac{\eta\sigma^3}{(\mu - K)^4} + \frac{K\sigma^2}{(\mu - K)^3} + \frac{3\sigma}{(\mu - K)^2}\right\}, \frac{\partial R_{-4c2}}{\partial K} = \frac{4w\sigma^3}{(\mu - K)^4} > 0,$$

and

$$\frac{\partial R_{-4c2}}{\partial \eta} = \frac{w\sigma^4}{(\mu - K)^4}$$

where

$$w = F^3(K)/[4(ax^3 - 3x_4^2 + 3x^4 - 1)] > 0$$

and

$$w_1 = F^3(K)/[4(ax^3 - 3x_4^2 + 3x^4 - 1)] < 0.$$

Proof: Immediate *from* taking derivatives to both sides of Eq. (10) and using quartic equation involved, the positiveness of w and w_1 can be seen from the proof of Proposition 2. Q.E.D.

Corollary 2.2 states that whereas the upper bounds $\bar{R}_{4c2}$ may either increase or decrease with the first moment μ and the strike price K, it is always strictly increasing with the skewness and kurtosis parameters κ and η. For positively or slightly negatively skewed asset, the upper bound $\bar{R}_{4c2}$ is always increasing with the second moment. The lower bounds R_{-4c2} and the upper bounds $\bar{R}_{4c2}$ are always changing at the opposite directions with respect to the second moment σ, skewness κ, and kurtosis η.

Proposition 3: If $\mu < K$ and the asset price is continuously distributed, then upper bounds of $R_c(t)$ and $R_p(t)$ subject to constraints Eqs (3)–(7) over all possible distributions with the known first four moments are given by

$$\bar{R}_{4c3} = y_4(K - \mu), \tag{12}$$

and

$$\bar{R}_{4p3} = \bar{R}_{4c3} - \mu + K, \tag{13}$$

where y_4 is the largest root of the quartic equation

$$ay^4 + 4y^3 + 6y^2 + 4y + b = 0, \text{ and}$$

where a and b are the same as in Propositions 1 and 2.

Proof: See Appendix. Q.E.D.

Because there are no general close form solutions to x_4 or y_4, we have to use computer programs to solve the quartic equations for x_4 and y_4. The two quartic equations in Propositions 2 and 3 are standard polynomial equations which can be solved conveniently for x_4 or y_4 in any computer systems or personal computers. Thus, the bounds are easily obtainable for given parameters of η, κ, σ, K and F(K).

The bounds given in Propositions 2 and 3 depend on the specific cumulative function F(.), these bounds have different values for different functions F(.). Though we can not obtain a close form solution to x_4 as an implicit function of F(K) determined by the quartic equation ax4 $ax^4 - 4x^3 + 6x^2 - 4x + b = 0$, $x_4 = x_4(F(X))$. Similar to Corollary 1.1, we have the following results.

Proposition 4: If $u > K$, then the necessary and sufficient condition that there exists one unique semi-parametric upper bound for $\bar{R}_{4c2}$ is $\phi > 0$ and this unique semi-parametric upper bound is given by

$$\bar{R}_{4c2sp} = [1 - G(\mu, \sigma, \text{K}, \eta, K)]\{\eta\sigma^4 + 4\kappa\sigma^3(\mu - K) + 6\sigma^4(\mu - K)^2 + (\mu - K)^4\}^{1/4},$$

which is always greater than $\bar{R}_{4c2}$ given in Proposition 2 over all possible distributions F(K) except one distribution

$$F(K) = s = G(\mu, \sigma, \kappa, \eta, K)$$

is determined by

$$a(1-s)^4(1-b) - 4(1-s)^3(1-b)^{3/4}s^{3/4} + 6(1-s)^2(1-b)^{1/2}s^{3/2} - 4(1-s)(1-b)^{1/4}s^{9/4} + bs^3 = 0 \tag{14}$$

and the corresponding semi-parametric upper bound for the put option is given by

$$\bar{R}_{4p2sp} = \bar{R}_{4c2sp} - \mu + K.$$

Proof: See Appendix. Q.E.D.

Proposition 5: If $\mu < K$, then the necessary and sufficient condition that there exists one unique semi-parametric upper bound for $\bar{R}_{4p3}$ is $\phi > 0$ and that this unique semi-parametric upper bound is given by

$$\bar{R}_{4p3p} = [1 - H(\mu, \sigma, \kappa, \eta, K)]\{\eta\sigma^4 - 4\kappa\sigma^3(\mu - K) + 6\sigma^2(\mu - K)^2 + (\mu - K)^{1/4}\},$$

which is always greater than $\bar{R}_{4c3}$ given in Proposition 3 over all possible distributions F(K) except one distribution

$$F(K) = s = H(\mu, \sigma, \kappa, \eta, K)$$

with which $\bar{R}_{4c3sp}$ is the same as $\bar{R}_{4c3}$, the distribution $H(\mu, \sigma, \kappa, \eta, K)$ is determined by

$$a(1 - s)^4(1 - b) - 4(1 - s)^3(1 - b)^{3/4}s^{3/4} + 6(1 - s)^2(1 - b)^{1/2}s^{3/2} - 4(1 - s)(1 - b)^{1/4}s^{9/4} + bs^3 = 0$$

and the corresponding semi parametric upper bound for the put option is given by

$$\bar{R}_{4p3sp} = \bar{R}_{4c3sp} - \mu + K.$$

Proof: Similar to the proof of Proposition 4. Q.E.D.

The semi-parametric upper bounds given in Proposition 4 (Proposition 5) $\bar{R}_{4c2sp}$ and $\bar{R}_{4p2sp}$ ($\bar{R}_{4c3sp}$ and $\bar{R}_{4p3sp}$) do not depend on any specific distribution function F(.) and are always greater than any corresponding distribution-dependent bounds *R4c2* with the exception of one distribution $F(K) = G(\mu, \sigma, \kappa, \eta, K)$ $F(K) = H(\mu, \sigma, \kappa, \eta, K)$) with which $\bar{R}_{4c2sp} = \bar{R}_{4c2}$ and $\bar{R}_{4p2sp} = \bar{R}_{4p2}$($\bar{R}_{4c2sp} = \bar{R}_{4c2}$ and $\bar{R}_{4p3sp} = \bar{R}_{4p3}$). In general, it is difficult to solve either Eqs (14) or (15) for the critical distribution G(.) (H(.)) which yields the semi-parametric bounds. However, an alternative convenient and practical way to find the critical distribution is to calculate the values of $\bar{R}_{4c2}$ for different values of F(K) and then the F(K) that yields the greatest $\bar{R}_{4c2}$ is the critical distribution and the greatest $\bar{R}_{4c2}$ is equal to the semi-parametric upper bound.

3. BOUNDS FOR OPTION PRICES

The bounds obtained in the previous section are bounds for the expected payoffs of options. In order to translate them into bounds for options prices, we need to find some appropriate discounting rates. Fortunately, Grundy (1991) provides such rates.

Proposition 6: (Grundy (1991)). Consider the true and risk-neutral distributions corresponding to the following diffusion processes

$$ds_t = \mu(S_t, t)S_t\, dt + \delta(S_t, t)S_t\, dz_t, \tag{16}$$

and

$$ds_t'' = r(t)S_t'' dt + \delta(S_t, t)S_t'' dz_t,$$

where z_t is the standard Gauss-Weiner process. If interest rates are non-stochastic[4] and $\mu(.) \geq r(t)$, $\forall t$, then the expected return on the call over its life is at least one plus risk-free rate over the j same time period.

Proof: See Proposition 5 of Grundy (1991). Q.E.D.

Proposition 7: (Grundy (1991)). If the conditions of Proposition 6 are satisfied and $\partial C/\partial t < 0$, then the expected return on a call over its life is at least the mean gross return of the underlying stock over the same time period.

Proof: See Proposition 6 of Grundy (1991). Q.E.D.

Propositions 6 and 7 provide the least expected rates of returns on the call option. With these rates, we can translate our upper bounds of expected payoffs of call options into upper bounds for option prices for the following reason:

$$\text{The Call Price C} = \frac{\text{Expected Payoff}}{1 + \text{Expected Return on Call}}$$

$$\leq \frac{\text{Upper Bound of Expected Payoff}}{1 + \text{Expected Return on Call}}$$

$$\leq \frac{\text{Upper Bound of Expected Payoff}}{\text{Lower Bound on } (1 + \text{Expected Return on Call})}$$

Let ς denote the lower bound on the expected rate of return from the call option[4] over its life (if the conditions of Proposition 6 are satisfied, then ς = risk-free rate over the life of the call option, and if the conditions of Proposition 7 are satisfied, then ς = the expected return of the underlying stock). The upper bounds of the call and the put options are easily obtained as $\bar{R}_{4ci}/(1+\varsigma)$, and $\bar{R}_{4pi}/(1+\varsigma)$, i = 1, 2, and 3, respectively.

4. THE EFFECTIVENESS OF THE BOUNDS

In order to test the effectiveness of our bounds, we compare in this section, our bounds with the option prices of Cox and Ross (1976) and Schroder (1989) in the general Constant Elasticity Volatility (CEV) model. Lo (1987) argues that bounds of option prices exist in general using the bounds of the expected payoffs and the Risk Neutral Valuation Relationship (RNVR) and points out the empirical difficulty in using the RNVR to obtain bounds of option prices. In this section, we use the general CEV model to obtain the bounds of the risk-neutral distribution, then discount these bounds at the risk-neutral rate of return and obtain the bounds for option prices.

The use of the RNVR is problematic in the two-moment case as Lo points out, because it requires the same information to obtain the two-moment-bounds when the Black-Scholes prices can also be obtained, thus the two-moment-bounds are not very useful under the RNVR. However, in the four-moment case, the use of the RNVR provides valid bounds as results of the first four moments whereas neither the Black-Scholes model nor the Cox-Ross model considers skewness and Kurtosis explicity. In other words, when the first four moments are considered explicitly, whereas the Black-Scholes and the Cox-Ross models fail to hold, these our bounds are still valid even under RNVR. In the general CEV model, the stock price is assumed to be governed by the diffusion process[5]

$$dS = \mu S\, dt + \delta S^{\beta/2}\, dz,$$

where β is the elasticity parameter and z is the standard Weiner process. If $\beta = 2$, this process is identical to the lognormal process as is assumed in the well-known Black-Scholes model. We will try to find bounds for options with $\beta < 2$ and $\beta > 2$.

In the risk-neutral world, the upper bounds for the call and put options are defined as follows

$$\hat{C}(S(t), t) = e^{-\tau T} \int_0^\infty \max[\tilde{S}(T) - K, 0]\, dF''[S(T)], \tag{17a}$$

and

$$\hat{P}(S(t), t) = e^{-\tau T} \int_0^\infty [K - \tilde{S}(T), 0]\, dF''[S(T)], \tag{17b}$$

where F″ [S(T)] is the risk-neutral distribution function.

A: The CEV Model For $\beta > 2$

Cox (1975) shows that, for a CEV process with $\beta < 2$, the density function of S(T) conditional on the current stock price S_t in a risk-neutral world is

$$f(S(T)) = (2 - \beta)\alpha^{1/(2-\beta)}[\xi w^{1-2\beta}]^{1/(4-2\beta)}\, e^{-\xi - w} I_{1/(2-\beta)}(2\sqrt{\xi w}). \tag{18}$$

where

$$\alpha = \frac{2\mu}{\delta^2(2-\beta)(e^{(2-\beta)\mu\tau}-1)},$$
$$\xi = \alpha S_t^{2-\beta} e^{(2-\beta)\mu\tau},$$
$$w = \alpha S_T^{2-\beta},$$

and $\tau = T - t$ and $I_q(.)$ is the modified Bessel function of the first kind of order q.

With the density function given in Eq. (18), we can obtain the value of the cumulative function at K as follows[6]

$$F(K; \nu, \lambda) = \sum_{j=0}^{\infty} \left(\frac{(\lambda/2)^j}{j!} \right) \cdot P_\tau[\chi^2_{2\nu+2} \leq K],$$

where $P_\tau[\chi^2_{2\nu+2} \leq K]$ is the cumulative distribution function of the central χ^2 distribution $\upsilon = 2 + 2/(2-\beta)$; and $\lambda = 2\xi$. $F(K; \upsilon, \lambda)$ can be considered as a mixture of the central χ^2 distribution and the Poisson distribution.

Cox and Ross (1976) obtain exact pricing formulas for European call options and Schroder (1989) simplifies these formulas in terms of the noncentral χ^2 cumulative functions

$$C = S_t Q[2y; 1 + 2/(2-\beta), 2\xi] - Ke - \tau\tau\{1 - Q[2\xi; 1 + 2/(2-\beta), 2y]\}, \quad (20)$$

where $y = \alpha K^{2-\beta}$; $Q[s; \upsilon, \lambda]$ is the complementary distribution function of the noncentral χ^2 distribution with $\upsilon = 2 + 2/(2-\beta)$ degrees of freedom, noncentral parameter $\lambda = 2\xi$, and lower integrated limit s, and $Q[s; \upsilon, \lambda] = 1 - F[s; \upsilon, \lambda]$.

Using the density function given in Eq. (18), the noncentral moments of the stock price can be expressed

$$M_i = S_t^i e^{i\mu\tau} \lambda^{-(i-1)/(2-\beta)} E(Y^{(i-1)/(2-\beta)}; \upsilon, \lambda) \quad (21)$$

where i = 1, 2, 3, 4, . . . , $E(Y^{(i-1)/(2-\beta)}; \upsilon, \lambda)$ is the $(i-1)/(2-\beta)$-th moment of the noncentral χ^2 distribution with $\upsilon = 2 + 2/(2-\beta)$ degrees of freedom and noncentral parameter $\lambda = 2\xi$.

The noncentral moments of the noncentral χ^2 distribution $E(Y^{(i-1)/(2-\beta)}; \upsilon, \lambda)$ can be calculated using the moment generating function of the distribution[7,8]

$$M(\theta; \nu, \lambda) = (1-2\theta)^{-\nu/2} \exp\left(\frac{\lambda\theta}{1-2\theta} \right)$$

With the noncentral moments given in Eq. (21), we can express the necessary moment parameters as follows (for simplicity, we drop the degree of freedom and noncentral parameters in the noncentral moment expressions)

$$\mu(t) = S(t)\, e^{\mu\tau}, \tag{22a}$$

$$\sigma(t) = S(t)\, e^{\mu\lambda}(\lambda^{-1/(2-\beta)})E(Y^{1/(2-\beta)} - 1)^{1/2}, \tag{22b}$$

$$\kappa = \frac{\lambda^{-2/(2-\beta)}E(Y^{2/(2-\beta)}) - 3\lambda^{-1/(2-\beta)}E(Y^{1/(2-\beta)}) - 1}{(\lambda^{-2/(2-\beta)}E(Y^{-2/(2-\beta)}) - 1)^{3/2}}, \tag{22c}$$

$$\eta = \frac{\lambda^{-3/(2-\beta)}E(Y^{3/(2-\beta)} - 4\lambda^{-2/(2-\beta)}E(Y^{2/(2-\beta)}) + 6\lambda^{-2/(2-\beta)}E(Y^{1/(2-\beta)}) + 1}{(\lambda^{-2/(2-\beta)}E(Y^{-2/(2-\beta)}) - 1)^{2}}. \tag{22d}$$

For any given parameter $\beta < 2$, we can calculate the noncentral moments $E(Y^{(i-1)/(2-\beta)}; \upsilon, \lambda)$. For example,

$$\beta = 1,\ \upsilon = 2 + 2/(2 - \beta) = 4,$$

$$\lambda = 4\mu S_t\, e^{\mu\tau}/[\delta^2(e^{\mu\tau} - 1)], \tag{23a}$$

and

$$E(Y; \upsilon, \lambda) = \upsilon + \lambda, \tag{23b}$$

$$E(Y^2; \upsilon, \lambda) = (\upsilon + \lambda)^2 + 2(\upsilon + 2\lambda), \tag{23c}$$

$$E(Y^3; \upsilon, \lambda) = (\upsilon\_\lambda)^3 + 6(\upsilon + \lambda)(\upsilon + 2\lambda) + 8(\upsilon + 3\lambda),$$

$$E(Y^4; \upsilon, \lambda) = (\upsilon + \lambda)^4 + 12(\upsilon + \lambda)(\upsilon + 2\lambda) + 12(\upsilon + 3\lambda)^2 + 32(\upsilon + 3\lambda)(\upsilon + \lambda) + 48(\upsilon + 4\lambda). \tag{23d}$$

Using Propositions 1, 2, and 3, Eqs (17), and (22), we obtain the bounds for the call and the put options prices as follows

$$\hat{C}(S(t), t) = x_4[S(t) - Ke^{-\tau\tau}],\ \textit{if } S(t)\, e^{\mu\tau} > K, \tag{24a}$$

$$= S(t)\left(\frac{\eta N^3(-d_2)}{a}\right)^{1/4}(e^{\delta^2\tau} - 1)^{1/2},\ \textit{if } S(t)\, e^{\mu\tau} = K, \tag{24b}$$

$$= y_4[Ke^{-\tau\tau} - S(t)],\ \textit{if } S(t)\, e^{\mu\tau} < K, \tag{24c}$$

and

$$\hat{P}(S(t), t) = \hat{C}(S(t), t) - S(t) + Ke^{-\tau\tau} \tag{25}$$

B: The CEV Model For $\beta > 2$

Emanuel and MacBeth (1982) shows that, for a CEV process with $\beta < 2$, the density function of S(T) conditional on the current stock price S_1 in a risk-neutral world $f(S(T)) = (\beta - 2)\alpha^{1/(2-\beta)}[\xi w^{1-2\beta}]^{1/(4-2\beta)}\ e^{-\xi-w}I_{1/(\beta-2)}(2\sqrt{\xi w})$ where α, ξ and w are the same as defined before.

It can be shown that using the same parameters α, ξ and w as in the case of $\beta < 2$, the value of the European call option can be expressed as follow[9]

$$C = S_t\{1 - Q[2\xi; 2/(\beta - 2), 2y]\} - K^{e^{-r\tau}}Q[2y; 2 + 2/(\beta - 2), 2\xi], \quad (26)$$

where $y = \alpha K^{2-\beta}$ and $Q[s; \upsilon, \lambda]$ is the same complementary distribution function as given in Eq. (20).

Following the similar procedure and using the above density function given by Emanual and MacBeth, we can derive the necessary noncentral moments for the asset price

$$M_i = S_t^i\, e^{i\mu\tau}\lambda^{i/(\beta-2)}E(Y^{i/(2-\beta)}; \nu_2, \lambda), \quad (27)$$

where i = 1, 2, 3, 4, . . . ,$E(Y^{i/(2-\beta)}; \nu_2, \lambda)$ is the $i/(2-\beta)$-th moment of the noncentral χ^2 distribution with $\upsilon_2 = 2 + 2/(\beta - 2)$ degrees of freedom and noncentral parameter $\lambda = 2\xi$.

With the noncentral moments given in Eq. (26), we can express the necessary moment parameters as follows (again we drop the degree of freedom and noncentral parameters for simplicity)

$$\mu(t) = S(t)\, e^{\mu\tau}\lambda^{1/(\beta-2)}E(Y^{1/(2-\beta)}), \quad (28a)$$

$$\sigma(t) = S(t)\, e^{\mu\tau}\lambda^{-1(\beta-2)}(E(Y^{2/(2-\beta)}) - [E(Y^{2/(2-\beta)}]^2)^{1/2}, \quad (28b)$$

$$\kappa = \frac{E(Y^{3/(2-\beta)}) - 3E(Y^{2/(2-\beta)})E(Y^{1/(2-\beta)}) - 3[E(Y^{1/(2-\beta)})]^3}{(E(Y^{2/(2-\beta)}) - E(Y^{1/(2-\beta)})]^2)^{3/2}}, \quad (28c)$$

$$\eta = \frac{E(Y^{4/(2-\beta)}) - 4E(Y^{3/(2-\beta)})E(Y^{1/(2-\beta)}) + 6E(Y^{2/(2-\beta)})[E(Y^{1/(2-\beta)})]^2 + [E(Y^{1/(2-\beta)})]^4}{(E(Y^{2/(2-\beta)}) - [E(Y^{1/(2-\beta)}]^2)^{3/2}}. \quad (28d)$$

The bounds for the call and the put option prices can be obtained similarly as in Eqs (24) and (25) in the case of $\beta < 2$.

5. SOME SIMULATION RESULTS

The effectiveness of the bounds derived in Eqs (24a)–(24c) can be obtained through comparing Eq. (24) with the Cox-Ross (1976) and Schroder (1989) option pricing formula given in Eq. (20). However, the effectiveness is not easily observable. Because of the complexity of the option pricing formula given in Eq. (20) and of the bounds formula given in Eq. (24), we can hardly obtain any comparative statistics results to compare the bounds with the option prices using Eq. (20). In this section, we try to show the effectiveness through simulation using some given parameters for $\beta = 1$ and 1.5.

When $\beta = 1$, the general CEV Stochastic process becomes $dS = \mu S\, dt + \delta S^{1/2}\, dz$, which is studied by Cox and Ross (1976). When $\beta = 1.5$, the general CEV stochastic process becomes $dS = \mu S\, dt + \delta S^{1/4}\, dz$.

The option pricing formulas given in Eqs (20) and (26) look simple, they are actually not easy to be used because it is difficult, in general, to obtain the values of the cumulative distribution function of the noncentral χ^2 distribution. Table 1 provides the values of the degrees of freedom, $\upsilon = 2 + 2/(2 - \beta)$; noncentral parameter, $\lambda = 2\xi$; the values of the Cox-Ross and Schroder option prices, C_{CR}; the Black-Scholes option prices, C_{BS}; and our bounds $\hat{C}$, given the current stock price $S_t = \$50$, the diffusion parameter $\delta = 0.10$, the time to maturity τ = three months = 1/4 year, and the risk-free rate of return = 10%. For these parameters chosen, the noncentral parameter A is rather large for both $\beta = 1$ and 1.5. Because the noncentral χ^2 distribution is approaching the normal distribution as λ is approaching infinity,[10] we could use the normal

Table 1. Effectiveness of the Upper Bounds Through Simulations.

Current Stock Price $S(t) = \$50$, Diffusion parameter $\delta = 0.10$, time to maturity $\tau = T = t = 1/4$ Year, and risk-free rate of return = 10%

$\beta = 1$ $\upsilon = 4$ $\alpha = 790.0416$ $\varepsilon = 40502.08$ $\lambda = \varepsilon = 81004.16$

K	$2y$	C_{CR}	C_{CB}	$\hat{C}$	$\hat{C} - C_{CR}$	$\hat{C} - C_{BS}$
20	31601.66	30.49380	30.16597	30.49394	0.000138	0.327970
25	39502.08	25.61725	25.20746	25.61760	0.000348	0.410140
30	47402.49	20.74070	20.24896	20.74165	0.000954	0.574956
35	55302.91	15.86415	15.29045	15.86540	0.001253	0.574956
40	63203.32	10.98760	10.33194	10.98870	0.001098	0.656762
45	71103.74	6.111053	5.380447	6.111665	0.000611	0.731218
50	79004.16	1.207076	1.158981	2.066423	0.859346	0.907442

$\beta = 1.5$ $\upsilon = 6$ $\alpha = 3184.041$ $\varepsilon = 22769.13$ $\lambda = 2\varepsilon = 45538.26$

K	$2y$	C_{CR}	C_{CB}	$\hat{C}$	$\hat{C} - C_{CR}$	$\hat{C} - C_{BS}$
20	28443.15	30.49380	30.16597	30.49394	0.000138	0.327970
25	31800.41	25.61725	25.20746	25.61760	0.000348	0.410140
30	34835.60	20.74070	20.24896	20.74165	0.000954	0.492696
35	37626.75	15.86415	15.29045	15.86540	0.001253	0.574956
40	40 40224	10.98760	10.33194	10.98870	0.001098	0.656762
45	42664.72	6.111054	5.380447	6.111665	0.000610	0.731218
50	44972.57	1.284176	1.158981	1.357954	0.073777	0.198973

approximation to calculate the values of the distribution function of the noncentral χ^2 distribution.

First of all, we calculated the parameters, a, ~ for the density function given in Eq. (18), using $\alpha = -2\mu\{\delta^2(2-\beta)(e^{(2-\beta)\mu\tau}-1\}$ and $\xi = \alpha\{S_t^{2-\beta}\, e^{(2-\beta)\mu\tau}$. Next we calculated the two parameters υ and λ for the noncentral χ^2 distribution using $\upsilon = 2 + 2/(2-\beta)$ and $\lambda = 2\xi$. Then we calculated the integration limit for the distribution function of Eq. (20), $2y = 2\alpha K^{2-\beta}$. With the values of the degrees of freedom, noncentral parameter λ, and 2y, we could stardize 2y using

$$(\chi'^2 - \nu - \lambda)/[2(\nu + 2\lambda)])^{1/2} = (2y - \nu - \lambda)/[2(\nu + 2\lambda)]^{1/2} = z_1.$$

Thus, $Q(2y; \upsilon, \lambda) \equiv N(-z_1)$ when $\lambda \rightarrow +\infty$, υ remaining fixed. $Q(2\xi; \upsilon, 2y)$ is similarly calculated as $\equiv N(z_2)$, where $z_2 = (2\xi - \upsilon - 2y)/[2(\upsilon + 4y)]^{1/2}$. With $Q(2y; \upsilon, y)$ and $Q(2\xi; \upsilon, 2y)$, we calculated the option prices using Eq. (20).

With the two parameters for the noncentral χ^2 distribution, $\upsilon = 2 + 2/(2-\beta)$and $\lambda(2\xi\varepsilon$, we calculated the necessary moment parameters for our bounds using Eqs (22a)–(22d). In the case of $\beta = 1$, the first three moments for the noncentral χ^2 distribution, $E(Y; \upsilon, \lambda)$, $E(Y^2; \upsilon, \lambda)$, and $E(Y^3; \upsilon, \lambda)$ are given in Eqs (23a)–(23c). However, in the case of $\beta = 1.5$, we need the 2nd, the 4th, and the 6th moment for the noncentral χ^2 distribution, $E(Y^2; \upsilon, \lambda)$, $E(Y^4; \upsilon, \lambda)$, $E(Y^6; \upsilon, \lambda)$. The 2nd and the 4th moments are given in Eqs (23b) and (23d), however the 6th moment has to be derived using the moment generating function. The expression $E(Y^6; \upsilon, \lambda)$ is too long to be listed here and we put it at the end of the Appendix. With these moment parameters, we could obtain the parameters of the quartic equation. Solving the quartic equation by trials and errors and using Eq. (24a), we obtained our bounds values $\hat{C}$.

Table 1 shows that the bounds are rather tight for the parameters chosen. From our calculation, we have learned that although we have to solve the quartic equation to obtain the bounds, solving the quartic equation may be even easier than to calculate the values of the distribution functions of the noncentral χ^2. For the CEV model, it is not convenient to obtain the necessary moment parameters as we see from the expression of $E(Y^6; \upsilon, \lambda)$, however, for most empirical studies, these moment parameters can be estimated using market data. Therefore, our model may have provided a convenient way to calculate the option prices.

6. CONCLUSIONS

We have obtained upper bounds for the option prices and the expected payoffs of options, given the first four moments of the distribution of the price of the underlying asset. When the cumulative distribution of the price of the underlying asset is known, tight bounds are derived, and when the cumulative distribution is not known, semi-parametric bounds can be obtained as the maximum of the tight bounds which depend on the cumulative distributions. The contribution of this paper lies in the fact that it provides one way to provide effective bounds for the expected payoffs and the prices of options when skewness and kurtosis are considered explicitly.

NOTES

1. Grundy (1991) obtains upper bounds for the expected payoffs of the European call options given an nth moment ($N \geq 1$) of the gross return distribution. Grundy's results are interesting, yet he only considers the two parameter distributions but not distributions with skewness and kurtosis.

2. A moment problem studies the existence and the derivation of distributions when n (n = l, 2, 3, . . .) moments are given. The stochastic variables can be either positive or negative. A Stieltjes problem is a special moment problem the variable of which is within [0,00]. For definitions and detailed studies, see Shohat and Tamarkin (1943), Achyeser (1965), or Krein and Nudelman (1977).

3. See Birkhoff and Lane (1953).

4. Snow (1991) provides lower bounds for discount factors when the risk-neutral rate *of* return is stochastic, yet his results are not directly applicable to our problem. However, it may be interesting to entice further studies following similar directions.

5. Bergman et al. (1996) have used this model to investigate the comparative statics of volatility change.

6. See Johnson and Kotz (1970), p. 132 for the cumulative distribution function of the noncentral X 2 distribution.

7. See Johnson and Kotz (1970), p. 134 for the moment generating function of the noncentral *X* 2 distribution.

8. If(I − 1)/(2 − ~) is not an integer, then we can not use the moment generating function to obtain the moments and we have to use the numerical integration.

9. This expression is the same as Eq. (20) as it is indicated in footnote 2 of Schroder (1989). The reason that we use this fonnula is to avoid the negativeness of the parameter of degrees of freedom $2 - 2/(\beta - 2)))$ for some $(\beta > 2)^2$. The formula can be readily obtained by using the identity $Q(2y; 2 - 2/(\beta - 2), 2\xi) + Q(2\xi; 2/(\beta - 2), 2y) = 1$.

10. See Johnson and Kotz (1970), p. 135. The standardized variable {(X2 − '\) − A)/ [2('\) + 2*A*)]1/2} tends to normality as A − + 00, '\) remaining fixed and X2 being the noncentral X2 variable. 22 i.

REFERENCES

Achyeser, N. I. (1965). *The Classical Moment Problem and Some Related Topics in Analysis.* Fizmatgiz, Moscow, 1961; English translation, Hafner, New York.

Bergman, Y. Z., Grundy, B. D., & Wiener, Z. (1996). General properties of option prices. *Journal of Finance*, *51*(5), 1573–1610.

Birkhoff, G., & Lane, S. M. (1953). *A Survey of Modem Algebra* (Rev. ed., pp. 112–115). New York: The Macmillan Company.

Black, F., & Scholes, M. (1973). The Pricing of Options and Corpoarte Liabilities. *Journal of Political Economy, 81*, 637–654.

Bollerslev, T. (1986). Generalized Autoregressive Conditional Heteroscedasticity. *Journal of Econometrics, 31*, 307–327.

Campbell, J. Y., Lo, A. W., & Mackinlay, A. C. (1997). *The Econometrics of Financial Markets.* Princeton University Press.

Cox, J. (1975). Notes on Option Pricing I: Constant Elasticity of Variance Diffusion. Unpublished note. Stanford University, Graduate School of Business.

Cox, J., & Ross, S. A. (1976). The Valuation of Options for Alternative Stochastic Processes. *Journal of Financial Economics, 3* (January–March), 145–166.

Emanual, D. C., & MacBeth, J. D. (1982). Further Results on the Constant Elasticity of Variance Call Option Pricing Model. *Journal of Financial and Quantitative Analysis, 17* (November), 533–554.

Francis, J. (1975). Skewness and Investor Decision. *Journal of Financial and Quantitative Analysis*, 163–172.

Grundy, B. (1991). Option Prices and the Underlying Assets Return Distribution. *Journal of Finance, 46*(3), 1045–1069.

Jackwerth, J. C., & Rubinstein, M. (1996). *Recovering Probability Distributions from Option Prices, 51*(5), 1611–1632.

Johnson, N. L., & Kotz, S. (1970). *Distribution in Statistics: Continuous Univariate Distributions* (Vol. 2). Boston: Houghton Miffin Company.

Kane, A., (1982). Skewness Preference and Portfolio Choice. *Journal of Financial and Quantitative Analysis*, 15–25.

Kraus, A., & Litzenberger, R. (1976). Skewness Preference and The Valuation of Risk Assets. *Journal of Finance*, 1085–1100.

Krein, M. G., & Nudelman, A. A. (1977). The Markov Moments Problem and Extremal Problems (Vol. 50). Translation of Mathematical Monographs, American Mathematical Society, Providence, Rhode Island.

Lee, C. F., & Wu, C. (1985). The Impacts of Kurtosis on Risk Stationarity: Some Empirical Evidence. *Financial Review, 20*(4), 867–874.

Levy, H. (1985). Upper and Lower Bounds of Put and Call Option Values: Stochastic Dominance Approach. *Journal of Finance, 40*, 1197–1271.

Lo, A. W. (1987). Semi-parametric Upper Bounds For Options Prices And Expected Payoffs. *Journal of Financial Economics, 19*, 373–387.

Merton, R. (1973). The Theory of Rational Option Pricing. *The Bell Journal of Economics and Management Science, 4*, 141–183.

Perrakis, S. (1986). Option Bounds in Discrete Time: Extension and the Pricing of American Put. *The Journal of Business, 59*, 119–141.

Perrakis, S., & Ryan, P. J. (1984). Options Pricing Bounds in Discrete Time. *Journal of Finance, 39*, 519–525.

Perrakis, S., & Ryan, P. J. (1986). Options Pricing Bounds: A Comparative Analysis, Synthesis and Extensions. Working Paper, Faculty of Administration, University of Ottawa.

Ritchken, P. H. (1985). On Option Pricing Bounds. *Journal of Finance, 40*, 1219–1233.

Samuelson, P. A. (1970). The Fundamental Approximation Theorem of Portfolio Analysis in Terms of Means, Variances, and Higher Moments. *Review of Economic Studies, 37*.

Schroder, M. (1989). Computing the Constant Elasticity of Variance Option Pricing Formula. *Journal of Finance*, (March), 211–219.

Shohat, J. A., & Tamarkin, J. D. (1943). *The Problem of Moments, Mathematical Surveys* (No. II). New York: American Mathematical Society.

Stutzer M. (1996). A Simple Nonparametric Approach to Derivative Security Valuation. *Journal of Finance*, *51*(5), 1633–1652.

Snow, K. N. (1991). Diagnosing Asset Pricing Models Using the Distribution of Asset Returns. *Journal of Finance*, *XLVI*(3), 955–983.

Widder, D. V. (1961). *Advanced Calculus* (2nd ed.). Prentice-Hall Inc.

Zhang, P. g. (1992). Bounds for Option Prices and Expected Payoffs. *Review of Quantitative Finance and Accounting*, *4*(2), 179–198.

APPENDIX

Proofs of Propositions 1–3: If any distribution function F(x) is continuous, then there is a one to one correspondence between $0 \leq x < +\infty$ and $0 \leq F(x) < 1$, and the inverse function of $F(x)$ exists uniquely. Let $x = F^{1}(x) = x(F)$ and $s = F(x)$. The five moments (3)–(7) become

$$\int_0^1 1dF = 1, \int_0^1 x\, dF = \mu, \int_0^1 (x-\mu)^2\, dF = \sigma^2, \int_0^1 (x-\mu)^3\, dF = k\sigma^3,$$

and

$$\int_0^1 (x-\mu)^4\, dF = \eta\sigma^4, \tag{AI}$$

Let $Q(x) = Max(x - K, 0)$. $Q(x)$ is a continuous function of x. Using Schwarz inequality [See Widder (1961, p. 364), we get

$$\left(\int_\beta^\alpha Q(x)\, dF = \right)^2 \leq \left\{\int_\beta^\alpha [Q(x)]^2\, dF\right\}\left\{\int_\beta^\alpha 1^2\, dF\right\} = (\alpha - \beta)\int_\beta^\alpha [Q(x)]^2\, dF, \tag{A2}$$

where α and β are arbitrary real numbers satisfying $\alpha \geq \beta$.

Using Eq. (A2) we get the following inequality

$$(R_C)^2 = \left\{\int_S^1 Max(x-K, 0)\, dF\right\}^2 dF \leq (1-s)\int_S^1 (x-K)^2\, dF, \tag{A3}$$

Squaring both sides of Eq. (A3) and using Eq. (A2) again yield

$$(R_C)^4 \leq (1-s)^3 \int_S^1 (x-K)^4 \, dF,$$

or

$$\frac{(R_C)^4}{(1-s)^3} \leq \int_2^1 (x-K)^4 \, dF, \tag{A4}$$

Similarly, we get the inequality for the expected payoff of the put as follows

$$\frac{(R_p)^4}{s^3} \leq \int_S^1 (x-K)^4 \, dF, \tag{A5}$$

Adding both sides of Eqs (A4) and (A5) using Eq. (AI) yields

$$\frac{(R_p)^4}{(1-s)^3} + \frac{(R_p)^4}{s^3} \leq \int_0^1 (x-K)^4 \, dF = \int_0^1 [(x-\mu)+(\mu-K)^4 \, dF, \tag{A6}$$

Expending Eq. (A6) and using Eq. (AI) yields $(R)4$ $(R)4$

$$\frac{(R_p)^4}{(1-s)^3} + \frac{(R_p)^4}{s^3} \leq \eta\sigma^4 + 4k\sigma^3(\mu-K) + 6\sigma^2(\mu-K)^2 + (\mu-K)^4. \tag{A7}$$

Taking expectation to both sides of Eq. (A8) yields

$$R_p = R_c - (\mu - K). \tag{A8}$$

Multiplying $s^3 > 0 > 0$ to both sides of Eq. (A7) and substituting Eq. (A8) into Eq. (A7) yield the following inequality

$$a(R_c)^4 - 4(\mu-K)(R_c)^4 + 4(\mu-K)^2(R_c)^2 - 4(\mu-K)^3 R_c(\mu-K)^4$$
$$\leq s^3[\eta\sigma^4 + 4k\sigma^3(\mu-K) + 6\sigma^2(\mu-K)^2 + (\mu-K)^4]. \tag{A9}$$

when $\mu = K$, Eq. (A9) becomes $a(R_c)^4 \leq \eta s^3 \sigma^4$, which yields Proposition 1 immediately. When $\mu > K$, multiplying both sides of (A9) by $1/(\mu-K)^4$ and letting $x = R_c/(\mu-K)$ yield

$$ax^4 - 4x^3 + 6x^2 - 4x + b \leq 0. \tag{A10}$$

When $\mu < K$, multiplying both sides of Eq. (A9) by $1/(K-\mu)^4$ and letting $x = R_c/(K-\mu)$ yield

$$ay^4 + 4y^3 + 6y^2 - 4y + b \leq 0. \tag{A11}$$

As $a > 1 \forall F(K)$ the polynomial $ax^4 - 4x^3 + 6x^2 - 4x + b$ must have positive derivative at the largest root x_4. Therefore in order for $ax^4 - 4x^3 + 6x^2 - 4x + b$ to be nonpositive, x must be smaller than x_4, or x_4 is the maximum x satisfying Eq. (A10). The same argument can be made to Eq. (A11).

Proof of Proposition 4: Let $P(x) = ax^4 - 4x^3 + 6x^2 - 4x + b$. As x_4 is the largest root of $P(x) = 0$ and $a > 1 \forall F(K) > 0$, the polynomial P(x) must be positively sloped at x_4, thus

$$P'(x_4) = 4(ax_4^3 - 3x_4^2 + 3x_4 - 1) > 0. \tag{A12}$$

Let $x_4 = \alpha(s)$ stand for the implicit function determined by $P(x_4) = 0$ and take derivative to both sides of $P(x_4) = 0$ with respect to s yields

$$\frac{\partial \alpha(s)}{\partial s} = \frac{3s^2}{P'(x_4)} \left[\phi - \left(\frac{x_4}{1 - s} \right)^4 \right]. \tag{A13}$$

Letting the right hand side *of* Eq. (A13) equal zero yields

$$\alpha(s) = (1 - s)\phi^{1/4}. \tag{A14}$$

Taking derivative to both sides *of* Eq. (A13) using Eq. (A14) yield

$$\frac{\partial^2 \alpha(s)}{\partial s^2} = -\frac{12s^2\phi}{(1 - s)P'(x_4)}. \tag{A15}$$

Equation (A15) implies that the necessary and sufficient condition for $x_4 = \alpha(s)$ to have a maximum ($\bar{R}_{4c2}$ reaches maximum simultaneously as $x_4 = \alpha(s)$ reaches maximum) is $\phi > 0$. For positively skewed asset prices, $\kappa > 0$, and $\kappa > 0$ is sufficient for $\phi > 0$ but not necessary. When $\phi > 0$, the negativeness *of* Eq. (A15) shows that $x_4 = \alpha(s)$ reaches its maximum at the s that is determined by Eq. (A14). Equation (A14) is a function *of* s = F(K), it determines s as a function *of* ϕ, therefore, the optimal s + F(K) which yields the maximum x_4 can be written as $F(K) = G(\mu, \delta, \eta, K)$.

$$\begin{aligned} E(Y^4; \nu, \lambda) = &(\nu + \lambda)^6 18(\nu + \lambda)^4(\nu + 2\lambda) + 4(\nu + \lambda)^3[16(\nu + 3\lambda) + 3(\nu + 2\lambda)] \\ &+ (\nu + \lambda)^2[432(\nu + 4\lambda) + 96(\nu + 3\lambda) + 12(\nu + 2\lambda) + 48(\nu + 2\lambda)^2] \\ &+ 640[(\nu + 3\lambda)^2 + (\nu + 2\lambda)^2] + 1440(\nu + \lambda)(\nu + 4\lambda) \\ &+ 288(\nu + \lambda)(\nu + 2\lambda)(\nu + 3\lambda) + 48(\nu + \lambda)(\nu + 3\lambda) \\ &+ 2304(\nu + \lambda)(\nu + 5\lambda) + 288(\nu + 2\lambda)(\nu + 3\lambda) + 288(\nu + \lambda)(\nu + 4\lambda) \\ &+ 72(\nu + \lambda)(\nu + 2\lambda)^2 + 3840(\nu + 6\lambda). \end{aligned}$$

8. CAPITAL BUDGETING IN CONTINUOUS TIME, COMPLETE MARKET ECONOMY

Ren-Raw Chen and Cheng-few Lee

ABSTRACT

There have been many uses of the option pricing theory in corporate finance areas. These "real options" affect greatly how corporate managers make their financing, investment, and dividend policy decisions. In this paper, we study the real options in capital budgeting decisions. In particular, we use the option pricing theory to compute risk-adjusted discount rate and certainty equivalent cash flows. We demonstrate that a great deal of option pricing theory can be applied to computing certainty equivalent cash flows.

1. INTRODUCTION

There have been many uses for the option pricing theory in corporate finance areas.[1] These "real options" affect greatly how corporate managers make their financing, investment, and dividend policy decisions. In this paper, we study the real options in capital budgeting decisions. In particular, we use the option pricing theory to compute certainty equivalent cash flows. Then we use the theory to compute the popular transition matrix. We demonstrate that a great

Advances in Quantitative Analysis of Finance and Accounting, Volume 10, pages 139–155.

ISBN: 0-7623-0969-5

deal of option pricing models (e.g. Geske (1979)) can be applied to computing certainty equivalent cash flows.

Capital budgeting has long been one of most the important issues faced by managerial accountants and financial economists. Capital budgeting techniques help decision makers pick out most attractive investment opportunities. They balance the benefits and costs associated with a particular investment plan and allocate the firm's capital optimally. The traditional capital budgeting methods adopt the idea of cost-benefit analysis under the concept of time value of money, i.e. the present value of futures benefits generated by the project should exceed the cost. Formally, the net present value (NPV) should be positive for a project to be profitable:

$$\mathrm{NPV} = \sum_{i=1}^{m} E\left[\exp\left(-\int_0^T k(u)\,du\right)X(T_i)\right] - \sum_{j=0}^{n} P(T_j)C(T_j) \qquad (1)$$

where $X(T_i)$ is the (uncertain) cash income occurred at T_i, k is an instantaneous risk-adjusted rate defined by Cox, Ingersoll and Ross (1985a), $C(T_j)$ is the (certain) cash cost occurred at time T_j, and $P(T_j)$ is the discount factor for certainty cash flows, which is also the price of a \$1-face value zero coupon bond (Cox, Ingersoll & Ross, 1985b).

Equation (1) explicitly considers two risks: the interest rate risk (that k is random) and the cash flow risk (that X is random). Equation (1) is the risk-adjusted discount rate method in capital budgeting. However, in this paper, we use the certainty equivalent method under which the option pricing theory is more applicable.

If the markets are dynamically complete (as defined by Duffie & Hwang, 1985), or equivalently, the markets allow for continuous trading, then there exists an equivalent probability measure where all assets, after being deflated by the risk free rate, are martingales. Formally, we can re-write Eq. (1) as:

$$\mathrm{NPV} = \sum_{i=1}^{m} \hat{E}\left[\exp\left(-\int_0^T r(u)\,du\right)X(T_i)\right] - \sum_{j=0}^{n} P(T_j)C(T_j) \qquad (2)$$

where $\hat{E}[\,.\,]$ is the risk-neutralized expected value and r is the instantaneous risk free rate. The difference between Eqs (1) and (2) is the discount rate inside the expectation (details in Cox, Ingersoll & Ross (1985a)). Applying the forward measure result see Jamshidian (1987); Chen and Huang (2002), we can further re-write Eq. (2) as:

$$\text{NPV} = \sum_{i=1}^{m} P(T_i)\tilde{E}^{T_i}[X(T_i)] - \sum_{j=0}^{n} P(T_j)C(T_j) \tag{3}$$

where $\tilde{E}^{T_i}[X(T_i)]$ is the forward expected value that computes the forward price for the cash flow $X(T_i)$. Note that, as Chen and Huang (2002) point out, the forward measure is maturity dependent, as opposed to the risk-neutralized measure that is maturity-independent.

2. CAPITAL BUDGETING UNDER UNCERTAINTY – THE CONTINGENT CLAIM APPROACH

The first study[2] in capital budgeting with the contingent claim theory was done by Banz and Miller (1978) where they used the state-preference model laid out in Breeden and Litzenberger (1978). Banz and Miller use the option theory to compute certainty equivalent cash flow values. They show that a multi-period capital budgeting problem can be solved by combining the state-preference model and the Black-Scholes formula. What we show in this section is that with the Cox-Ross methodology (1976), the capital budgeting problem can be solved by simply the Black-Scholes formula. Mixing the state-preference model with the Black-Scholes formula may generate some difficulties in carrying out capital budgeting calculations, when the analysis is applied to multiple periods.

Let the stochastic process of some state variable, $S(t)$, and the instantaneous interest rate, $r(t)$, satisfy the following stochastic differential equations:

$$\begin{cases} \dfrac{dS(t)}{S(t)} = \mu\, dt + \sigma\, dW_S(t) \\ dr(t) = \alpha(\theta - r)dt + \gamma\, dW_r(t) \end{cases} \tag{4}$$

where $dW_S(t)\, dW_r(t) = \rho\, dt$. In Eq. (4) we adopt the log normal process for the underlying state variable and Ornstein-Uhlenbeck process for the instantaneous interest rate. All the Greek letters, μ, σ, α, θ, and γ are constants. To obtain the risk-neutralized processes, we define:

$$\begin{aligned} d\hat{W}_S(t) &= dW_S(t) + \frac{\mu - r}{\sigma}\, dt \\ d\hat{W}_r(t) &= dW_r(t) + q\, dt \end{aligned} \tag{5}$$

These changes of measure are defined in Cox, Ingersoll, and Ross (1985a) and Vasicek (1977) respectively. The first change of measure assumes that S is a traded asset and the second change of measure assumes log utility. The resulting processes are:

$$\begin{cases} \dfrac{dS(t)}{S(t)} = r\,dt + \sigma\,d\hat{W}_S(t) \\ dr(t) = \alpha\left(\theta - r - \dfrac{\gamma q}{\alpha}\right)dt + \gamma\,d\hat{W}_r(t) \end{cases} \tag{6}$$

Lastly, the forward measure is defined as:

$$\begin{cases} \dfrac{dS(t)}{S(t)} = \left(r - \rho\sigma\gamma\dfrac{P_r(T)}{P(T)}\right)dt + \sigma\,d\tilde{W}_S(t) \\ dr(t) = \left(\alpha\theta - \alpha r - \gamma q - \gamma^2\dfrac{P_r(T)}{P(T)}\right)dt + \gamma\,d\tilde{W}_r(t) \end{cases} \tag{6}$$

where $P_r(T) = \partial P(T)/\partial r$. A contingent claim value can be computed as:

$$C(0) = \hat{E}\left[\exp\left(-\int_0^T r(u)\,du\right)C(T)\right] = P(T)\tilde{E}[C(T)] \tag{7}$$

where

$$P(T) = e^{-r_0F(T) - G(T)}$$

$$F(T) = \frac{1 - e^{-\alpha T}}{\alpha}$$

$$G(T) = \left(\theta - \frac{\gamma q}{\alpha} - \frac{\gamma^2}{2\alpha^2}\right)(T - F(T)) + \frac{\gamma^2 F(T)^2}{4\alpha}$$

In the above equation, r_0 is the initial interest rate.

A. One Period, Two States

First, let us assume that a project will pay C^G when $S(T) > K$ (a good economy) and C^B $S(T) < K$ (a bad economy). The present value of this cash flow can then be easily computed:

$$\begin{aligned} C(0) &= P(T)(\tilde{E}[1_{S(T)>K})C^G + \tilde{E}[1_{S(T)<K}]C^B) \\ &= P(T)(C^G N(d) + C^B(1 - N(d))) \end{aligned} \tag{8}$$

where 1[.] is an indicator function and

$$d = \frac{\ln(S(0)/K) + rT + V/2}{\sqrt{V}}$$

$$V = \int_0^T \sigma^2 - \rho\sigma\gamma \frac{P_r(u)}{P(u)} + \left(\gamma \frac{P_r(u)}{P(u)}\right)^2 du$$

The closed form solution can be found in Rabinovitch (1989).

B. n periods, m States

In a multi-period, multi-state case, we have both *m* (states) and *n* (periods) and the formula will look like:

$$\mathrm{PV} = \sum_{j=1}^{n} P(T_j)\left(\sum_{i=1}^{m} \tilde{E}[1_{S(T_j) > K_{i,j}})C_{i,j} + \tilde{E}[1_{S(T_j) < K_{i,j}}]C_{i,j})\right.$$

$$= \sum_{j=1}^{n} P(T_j)\left(\sum_{i=1}^{m} C_{i,j}(N(d_{i,j}) - N(d_{i+1,j}))\right) \tag{9}$$

where

$$d_{i,j} = \frac{\ln S(0) - \ln K_{i,j} + rT_j - V_j}{\sqrt{V_j}}$$

$$V_j = \int_0^{T_j} \sigma - 2\rho\sigma\gamma \frac{P_r(u)}{P(u)} + \left(\gamma \frac{P_r(u)}{P(u)}\right)^2 du$$

$$N(d_{1,j}) = 1$$

$$N(d_{m,j}) = 0$$

Banz and Miller (1978) use the state preference framework to consider such a multi-period problem. They abandon the assumption that the stochastic process for *M* is applied to the whole time period through out and adopt a different approach in which more than one stochastic process is considered. Following the example set up in the previous section, we classify the economy into two states as described in Fig. 1.

It can be easily seen from Fig. 1 that to get to the bad state in time 2 from the good state in time 0 needs $p_{11}p_{12} + p_{12}p_{22}$. The other state in time 2 can be

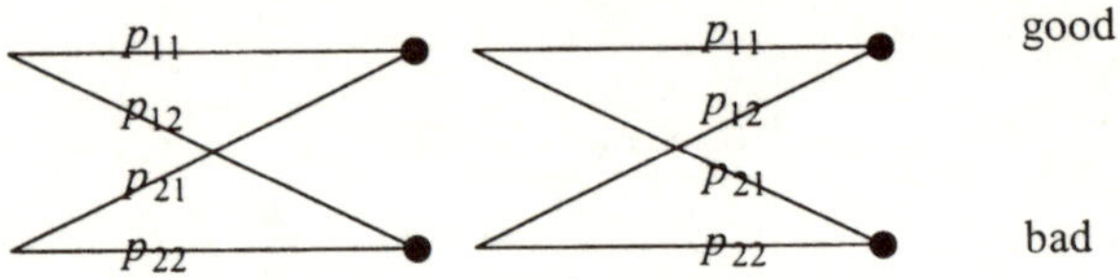

Fig. 1. Transition Probabilities.

achieved in a similar fashion. The two states at time 2 can be reached from the bad state in time 0 in the same way. In sum, we have the following 4 results:

$$\begin{array}{cc} & T_2 \\ & \begin{array}{cc} \quad good & \quad\quad bad \end{array} \\ t \begin{array}{c} good \\ bad \end{array} & \begin{bmatrix} p_{11}p_{11}+p_{12}p_{21} & p_{11}p_{12}+p_{12}p_{22} \\ p_{21}p_{11}+p_{22}p_{21} & p_{21}p_{12}+p_{22}p_{22} \end{bmatrix} \end{array}$$

This is equivalent to:

$$\begin{bmatrix} p_{11} & p_{12} \\ p_{21} & p_{22} \end{bmatrix}\begin{bmatrix} p_{11} & p_{12} \\ p_{21} & p_{22} \end{bmatrix} = \begin{bmatrix} p_{11} & p_{12} \\ p_{21} & p_{22} \end{bmatrix}^2$$

Generalizing this to n periods, we have the matrix for all $j < n$.

$$\begin{bmatrix} p_{11} & p_{12} \\ p_{21} & p_{22} \end{bmatrix}^j$$

where the subscript j represents the transition matrix from period j–1 to period j. Note that $[\cdot]_j$ and $[\cdot]_k$ are different and thus $[\cdot]_j \neq [\cdot]^j$. Also note that for a given period (say, between time 0 and time 1) the assumption about the stochastic movement about the economy (measured by the market index) can still be valid. Although the conditional distributions about the next period's economy from both good and bad can still be both log-normal, they differ in mean and variance.

This model is inconsistent with the use of $N(d)$ in continuous time. This is because for the second period, the value of $N(d)$ depends on the level of a continuously determined $S(T_1)$ and hence cannot be same for all the states whose stock value falls below the strike. While is it possible to stay within the Banz-Miller framework, we feel that it is more straightforward to stay within the Black-Scholes setting.

A more realistic assumption for the cash flows is to allow cash flows to be continuous function of the state variable. In situations of continuous states,

$$\mathrm{PV} = \sum_{j=1}^{n} P(t, T_j)\tilde{E}_t[C(T_j)] \tag{10}$$

where C_j is a function of the underlying state variable $S(T_j)$. Many cash flows have the call-style payoff due to the fact that the firm can choose to forego the investment opportunity if it is not worth pursuing. In such a case, the existing results in the option literature is readily usable. There is one important extension one can proceed – allowing stochastic interest rates and the state variable being non-traded, which we leave for future research.

4. EQUILIBRIUM PRICING

One drawback of the above model is the assumption of continuous rebalancing. The cash flows that arrive in discrete points in time are not continuously transactable. One can perhaps argue that many account receivables are factorized to cash and more and more contingent assets are securitized. But liquidity is always a concern and these securitized contingent cash flows usually suffer an significant discount due to the liquidity problem. At any rate, simply assuming the possibility of risk neutral pricing is not correct. In a recent paper, Chen, Palmon, and Wald (2002) show that risk premium for non-continuous trading is both statistically and economically significant in S&P 500 index options. Chen and Palmon (2002) hence propose the following equilibrium methodology. For any contingent cash flow, the discounted present value is given by Eq. (1). Under constant interest rates, Eq. (1) becomes:

$$C_j(0) = e^{-kT}E[C_j(T)] \tag{11}$$

where

$$e^{kT} = e^{rT} + \beta[E[S(T)/S(0)] - e^{rT}] \tag{12}$$

and

$$\beta = \frac{\mathrm{cov}[S(T)/S(0),\, C(T)/C(0)]}{\mathrm{var}(S(T)/S(0))} \tag{13}$$

Note that β depends upon the current value of the cash flow, $C(0)$, by Eqs (12) but the cash flow in turn depends on β. Hence, Eqs (10)–(12) have to be solved recursively for all the variables simultaneously.

The equilibrium pricing methodology in Chen and Palmon (2002) and Chen, Palmon and Wald (2002) provide similar results as the risk neutral methodology. For example, the put-call parity holds within the methodology. Note that the beta definition under the CAPM:

$$\beta_C = \frac{\frac{S(0)}{C(0)}\operatorname{cov}[R, \max\{R - K^*, 0\}}{\operatorname{var}[R]}$$
$$\beta_P = \frac{\frac{S(0)}{P(0)}\operatorname{cov}[R, \max\{K^* - R, 0\}}{\operatorname{var}[R]} \tag{14}$$

where

$$R = \frac{S(T)}{S(0)}$$

$$K^* = \frac{K}{S(0)}$$

Hence,

$$\frac{C(0)}{S)(0)}\beta_C - \frac{P(0)}{S(0)}\beta_P = \frac{\operatorname{cov}[R, R - K^*]}{\operatorname{var}[R]} = 1$$
$$C(0)\beta_C - P(0)\beta_P = S(0) \tag{15}$$

Using CAPM, we get:

$$P(0)(k_P - R) = (C(0)\beta_C - S(0))(k - R)$$
$$= C((0)(k_C - R) - S(0)(k - R) \tag{16}$$

Re-arranging terms:

$$R(C(0) - P(0) - S(0)) = C(0)k_C - P(0)k_P - S(0)k$$
$$= \max(S(T) - K, 0\} - \max(K - S(T), 0\} - S(T)$$
$$= K \tag{17}$$

This proves the put-call parity:

$$\frac{1}{k_C}E[\max\{S(T)-K,0\}]-\frac{1}{k_P}E[\max\{K-S(T),0\}=S(0)-\frac{K}{R} \quad (18)$$

The binomial implementation of the model is also straightforward. In a Bernulli distribution where X is 0 or 1, the mean is p and variance is pq. If X is 1 or –1, then the mean and variance are $2p-1$ (or $p-q$) and $4pq$. If X is a or $-a$, then they become $a(p-q)$ and $4a^2pq$.

In the binomial model,

$$a=\ln u$$

$$\hat{p}=(R-\hat{d})/(\hat{u}-\hat{d}) \quad (19)$$

Hence the mean is $\ln\hat{u}(2\hat{p}-1)$ and the variance is $4(\ln\hat{u})^2\hat{p}\hat{q}=4\sigma^2\Delta t\hat{p}\hat{q}$. In the equilibrium, the objective probability is given as p. The variance is $4(\ln u)^2pq$. In order to match the volatility of the binomial model, we set: $4(\ln u)^2pq=4\sigma^2(\Delta t)\hat{p}\hat{q}$. Hence, $u=\exp(\sigma\sqrt{\Delta t\hat{p}\hat{q}/pq})$. It is clear that when $p=\hat{p}$, $u=\hat{u}$ and the equilibrium model degenerates to the binomial model.

In a continuous time, the stock price process:

$$S(t)=S(0)e^{(\mu-\sigma^2/2)t+\sigma W(t)}$$

$$=S(0)e^{(r-\sigma^2/2)t+\sigma\hat{W}(t)} \quad (20)$$

The binomial approximation of the risk neutral method is:

$$u=e^{\sigma\sqrt{dt}}$$

$$d=e^{-\sigma\sqrt{dt}}$$

$$R=e^{rdt} \quad (21)$$

$$\hat{p}=\frac{R-d}{u-d}$$

This guarantees that

$$\frac{\hat{E}[S(dt)]}{S(0)}=\hat{p}u+(1-\hat{p})d=R \quad (22)$$

and hence,

$$\hat{E}[\ln S(dt)] = \ln S(0) + \tilde{p} \ln u - (1 - \hat{p}) \ln u$$
$$= \ln S(0) + \ln u(2\hat{p} - 1)$$
$$\text{var}[\ln S(dt)] = \hat{E}[\ln S(dt)^2] - \hat{E}[\ln S(dt)]^2 \tag{23}$$
$$= (\ln u)^2[(2\hat{p} - 1) - (2\hat{p} - 1)^2]$$
$$= (\ln u)^2 4\hat{p}(1 - \hat{p})$$

A parallel argument applied to the real measure gives:

$$u = e^{\sigma\sqrt{dt}}$$
$$d = e^{-\sigma\sqrt{dt}}$$
$$A = e^{\mu\, dt} \tag{24}$$
$$p = \frac{A - d}{u - d}$$

which, by definition, guarantees that

$$\frac{E[S(dt)]}{S(0)} = pu + (1 - p)d = A \tag{25}$$

and,

$$E[\ln S(dt)] = \ln S(0) + p \ln u - (1 - p) \ln u$$
$$= \ln S(0) + \ln u(2p - 1)$$
$$\text{var}[\ln S(dt)] = \hat{E}[\ln S(dt)^2] - \hat{E}[\ln S(dt)]^2 \tag{26}$$
$$= (\ln u)^2[(2p - 1) - (2p - 1)^2]$$
$$= (\ln u)^2 4p(1 - p)$$

We demonstrate the use of the model via a numerical example. The difference of using the equilibrium model can be important. For example, we assume a two period binomial model where up and down are 1.1 and 0.9 respectively. The stock price is \$100 and the risk free rate is 5%. For a call option with \$110 strike (out of money), the current value is \$5.61 (\$5.38 for the put) as shown as follows:

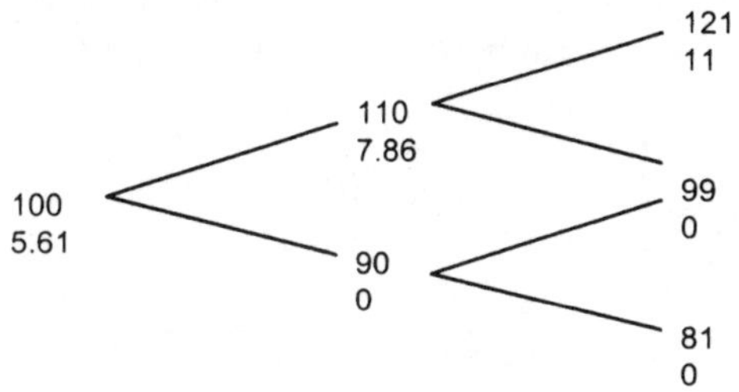

The risk neutral probabilities are 0.75 and 0.25. Now, let us suppose that the actual probabilities are 0.9 and 0.1 instead. With other things held constant, the option price becomes \$5.40 (\$5.18 for the put). The risk-adjusted discount rates are 64.86% for the call and –56.16% for the put. The betas are 8.5456 for the call and –10.3928 for the put.

In a continuous time setting, define:

$$h_1 = \frac{\ln S(0) - \ln K + \left(\mu + \frac{\sigma^2}{2}\right)T}{\sigma\sqrt{T}}$$

$$h_2 = \frac{\ln S(0) - \ln K + \left(\mu - \frac{\sigma^2}{2}\right)T}{\sigma\sqrt{T}} \tag{27}$$

$$h_3 = \frac{\ln S(0) - \ln K + \left(\mu + \frac{3\sigma^2}{2}\right)T}{\sigma\sqrt{T}}$$

Then, the call option formula is:

$$C(0) = e^{-kT}E_t[\max\{S(T) - K, 0\}]$$

$$= e^{-kT}\left[\int_K^\infty S_T\phi(S_T)\, dS(T) - K\int_K^\infty \phi(S(T)\, dS(T)\right] \tag{28}$$

$$= e^{(\mu - k)T}S(0)N(h_1) - e^{-kT}KN(h_2)$$

Note that in the risk neutral setting, all assets earn the risk free rate and hence $k = \mu = r$. In this new setting, both k and μ are risk adjusted. The risk adjusted rate for the option, k, is determined by the CAPM defined above. There is closed form for the log normal model under no-rebalancing. Each component in the beta calculation is as follows. The variance term is:

$$\begin{aligned}\mathrm{var}\left[\frac{S(T)}{S(0)}\right] &= \frac{1}{S(0)^2}\,\mathrm{var}[S(T)] \\ &= \frac{1}{S(0)^2}\,(E[S(T)^2] - (E[S(T)])^2) \\ &= \frac{1}{S(0)^2}\,(S(0)^2\, e^{(2\mu+\sigma^2)T} - S(0)^2\, e^{2\mu T}) \\ &= e^{2\mu T}(e^{\sigma^2 T} - 1)\end{aligned} \tag{29}$$

The covariance term is:

$$\mathrm{cov}\left[\frac{S(T)}{S(0)}, \frac{C(T)}{C(0)}\right] = \frac{1}{S(0)C(0)}\,(E[S(T)C(T)] - E[S(T)]E[C(T)]) \tag{30}$$

in which the expectation of the cross product term can be derived as follows:

$$\begin{aligned}E[S(T)C(T)] &= \int_0^\infty S(T)\max\{S(T) - K, 0\}\phi(S(T))\,dS(T) \\ &= \int_K^\infty S(T)^2\phi(S(T))\,dS(T) - K\int_K^\infty S(T)\phi(S(T))\,dS(T) \\ &= S(0)^2 e^{(2\mu+\sigma^2)T}N(k_3) - KS_t e^{\mu T}N(h_1)\end{aligned} \tag{31}$$

and the expectation of each term is:

$$\begin{aligned}E[S(T)] &= S(0)e^{\mu T} \\ E\{C(T)] &= \int_0^\infty \max\{S(T) - K, 0\}\phi(S(T))\,dS(T) \\ &= S(0)e^{\mu T}N(h_1) - KN(h_2)\end{aligned} \tag{32}$$

Extending the call result to any arbitrary cash flow and feeding it back to the previous section is the goal. For simplicity, we first assume constant interest rates and the inclusion of random interest rates can be done by following the works in the appendix. Let X be the arbitrary cash flow in place of the call payoff. We then have $X(T) \times 1_{S(T)>K}$ instead of the call which is equal to $(S(T) - K) \times 1_{S(T)>K}$ where 1 is the indicator function. To simplify the problem, we let the indicator function be independent of the underlying asset price.

$$\begin{aligned}\sigma_{S,1X} &= E[S_T 1_{t<T} X_T] - E[S_T]E[1_{t<T} X_T] \\ &= pE[S_T X_T] - pE[S_T]E[X_T] \\ &= pS_t \bar{X} e^{\mu(T-t)}(e^{\rho\sigma_1\sigma_2(T-t)} - 1)\end{aligned} \tag{33}$$

and

$$\begin{aligned}\sigma^2_{1X} &= E[(1_{t<T} X_T)^2] - E[1_{t<T} X_T]^2 \\ &= E[1_{t<T} X^2_T] - p^2 \bar{X}^2 \\ &= pE[X^2_T] - p^2 \bar{X}^2 \\ &= p\bar{X}^2 e^{\sigma^2_X} - p^2 \bar{X}^2 \\ &= p\bar{X}^2 (e^{\sigma^2_X} - p)\end{aligned} \tag{34}$$

Hence equating the two, we can solve for $\bar{X}$ as follows:

$$\begin{aligned}e^{\mu(T-t)}(1 - e^{\rho\sigma_1\sigma_2(T-t)}) &= \frac{\bar{X}}{S_t}(e^{\sigma_1\sigma_2(T-t)} - p) \\ \frac{\bar{X}}{S_t} &= \frac{e^{\mu(T-t)}(1 - e^{\mu\sigma_1\sigma_2(T-t)})}{e^{\sigma_2\sigma_2(T-t)} - p}\end{aligned} \tag{35}$$

We, in the appendix establish the necessary results we use here. Linking the results derived in this section to the previous sections, we write (10) as

$$\mathrm{PV} = \sum_{j=1}^{n} P(t, T_j)\tilde{E}_t[X(T_j)] \tag{36}$$

5. CONCLUSION

This paper makes use of the option pricing theory in the evaluation of the capital budgeting cash flows. It is pointed out that the straightforward Black-Scholes methodology is more general and easier than the state space model by Banz and Miller (1978). This paper also provides a present value formula in the environment of stochastic interest rates. It is shown that the state preference model by Banz and Miller (1978) which involves a Markov assumption is hard to implement.

NOTES

1. A review and categorization of this line of research deserves a paper. Recently, Trigeorgis (1996) and Copeland and Antikarov (2001).
2. This may have been the only theoretical study to date.
3. See Arnold (1974), pages 128–134, Section 8.2.

REFERENCES

Arnold, L. (1974). *Stochastic Differential Equations: Theory and Applications*. John Wiley and Sons.

Banz, R., & Miller, M. (1978). Prices for State-Contingent Claims: Some Estimates and Applications. *Journal of Business*, (October).

Black, F., & Scholes, M. (1973). The Pricing of Options and Corporate Liabilities. *Journal of Political Economy*, 637–654.

Breeden, D., & Litzenberger, R. (1978). Prices of State-Contingent Claims Implicit in Option Prices. *Journal of Business*, (October).

Chen, R. (1992). Pricing Stock and Bond Options when the Default-Free Rate is Stochastic: A Comment. *Journal of Financial and Quantitative Analysis*, (September).

Chen, R., & Palmon, O. (2002). An Empirical-Distribution-Based Option Pricing Model: Insights into The Volatility Smile Puzzle. Working paper. Rutgers University.

Chen, R., Palmon, O., & Wald, J. (2002). Equilibrium Option Pricing. Working paper. Rutgers University.

Copeland, T., & Antikarov, V. (2001). *Real Options: A Practitioner's Guide*, Texere, LLC.

Cox, J., Ingersoll, J., & Ross, S. (1985a). An Intertemporal Capital Asset Pricing Model. *Econometrica*, *53*(2).

Cox, J., Ingersoll, J., & Ross, S. (1985b). A Theory of the Term Structure of Interest Rates. *Econometrica*, *53*(2), 385–408.

Cox, J., & Ross, S. (1976). The Valuation of Options for Alternative Stochastic Processes. *Journal of Financial Economics*.

Jamshidian, F. (1987). Pricing of Contingent Claims in One Factor Term Structure model. Working paper. Merrill Lynch Capital Markets.

Lee, C. F., & Finnerty, J. (1990). *Corporate Finance: Theory, Method, and Applications*. HBJ.

Litner, J. (1965). The Valuation of Risk Assets and the Selection of Risky Investments in Stock Portfolios and Capital Budgets. *Review of Economics and Statistics*, (February).

Mossin, J. (1966). Equilibrium in Capital Asset Market. *Econometrica*, (October).

Rabinovitch, R. (1989). Pricing Stock and Bond Options when the Default-Free Rate is Stochastic. *Journal of Financial and Quantitative Analysis*, (December).

Sharpe, W. (1964). Capital Asset Prices: A Theory of Market Equilibrium under Conditions of Risk. *Journal of Finance*, (September).

Sick, G. (1989). Multi-period Risky Project Valuation: A Mean-Covariance Certainty-Equivalent Approach. In: C. F. Lee (Ed.), *Advances of Financial Planning and Forcasting* (Vol. 3, pp. 1–36).

Vasicek, O. (1977). An Equilibrium Characterization of The Term Structure. *Journal of Financial Economics*, 177–188.

Trigeorgis, L. (1996). *Real Options: Managerial Flexibility and Strategy in Resource Allocation*. MIT Press.

APPENDIX

A. Stochastic Interest Rates

In this appendix, we derive the results used in the paper. The Vasicek model for the pure discount bonds is defined in Eq. (7). Taking the partial derivative of the price with respect with the interest rate gives:

$$\frac{\partial P(T)}{\partial r} = P(T)(-F(T)) \tag{A1}$$

and therefore:

$$\frac{P_r(T)}{P(T)} = -F(T) \tag{A2}$$

Hence, the change of measure defined in Eq. (6) can be written as

$$\begin{cases} \dfrac{dS(t)}{S(t)} = (r + \rho\sigma\gamma F(T)\,dt + \sigma\,d\tilde{W}_S(t) \\ dr(t) = (\alpha\theta - \alpha r - \gamma q + \gamma^2 F(T))\,dt + \gamma\,d\tilde{W}_r(t) \end{cases} \tag{A3}$$

Applying the results in Arnold (1974),[3] the future interest rate level can be written as:

$$r(t) = \int_0^t e^{-\alpha(t-s)}(\alpha\theta + F(T-s)\,ds + \gamma\,dW_r(s)) \tag{A4}$$

This leads to a normal distribution with mean and variance as follows:

$$\begin{gathered} \tilde{m}(t) = \tilde{E}[r(t)] = e^{-\alpha t}\left(\int_0^t e^{\alpha u}(\alpha\theta + F(T-u))\,du\right) \\ \tilde{V}(t) = \mathrm{var}[r(t)] = e^{-2\alpha t}\left(\int_0^s e^{2\alpha u}\gamma^2\,du\right) \end{gathered} \tag{A5}$$

Hence, for the discount factor, we have:

$$\int_0^T r(t)\,dt = \int_0^T \int_0^t e^{-\alpha(t-s)}(\alpha\theta + F(T-s)\,ds + \gamma\,dW_r(s))\,dt \tag{A6}$$

which is still normally distributed. Note that the state variable, $S(t)$, has the following solution:

$$S(t) = S(0) \exp\left(\int_0^t [r(u) - \tfrac{1}{2}\sigma^2 + \rho\sigma\gamma F(T-u)]\, du + \int_0^t \sigma\, d\tilde{W}_S(u) \right) \quad \text{(A7)}$$

which clearly contains both sources of randomness. Given that both $\int_0^t r(u)\, du$ and $\int_0^t d\tilde{W}_S(u)$ are normally distributed, it is tedious but straightforward to show that:

$$\begin{aligned}
\tilde{E}[S(T)] &= S(0)\tilde{E}\left[\exp\left(\int_0^T [-\tfrac{1}{2}\sigma^2 + \rho\sigma\gamma F(T-u)]\, du + \int r(u)\, du + \sigma\, d\tilde{W}_S(u) \right) \right] \\
&= S(0)e^{A(T)+\frac{1}{2}B(T)^2} \qquad \text{(A8)} \\
&= S(0)P(T)
\end{aligned}$$

where

$$\begin{aligned}
A(T) &= \tilde{E}\left[\int_0^T [-\tfrac{1}{2}\sigma^2 + \rho\sigma\gamma F(T-u)]\, du + \int_0^T r(u)\, du \right] \\
& \qquad \text{(A9)} \\
B(T) &= \text{var}\left[\int_0^T r(u)\, du + \int_0^T \alpha\, d\tilde{W}_S(u) \right]
\end{aligned}$$

B. Some Useful Results

Covariances:

$$\begin{aligned}
E[S_T X] &= S_t \bar{X} e^{(\mu+\rho\sigma\delta)(T-t)} \\
E[S_T]E[X] &= S_t e^{\mu(T-t)} \bar{X} \qquad \text{(B1)} \\
K[S_T, X] &= S_t \bar{X}(e^{(\mu+\rho\sigma\delta)(T-t)} - e^{\mu(T-t)}) = S_t \bar{X} e^{\mu(T-t)}(e^{\rho\sigma\delta(T-t)} - 1)
\end{aligned}$$

Variances:

$$\begin{aligned}
E[S_T] &= S_t e^{\mu(T-t)} \\
E[S_T^2] &= S_t^2 e^{(2\mu+\sigma^2)(T-t)} \qquad \text{(B2)} \\
V[S_T] &= S_t^2 e^{2\mu(T-t)}(e^{\sigma^2(T-t)} - 1)
\end{aligned}$$

Beta:

$$\beta = \frac{K[S_T, X]}{V[S_T]} = \frac{\bar{X}}{S_t} e^{-\mu(T-t)} \frac{e^{\rho\sigma\delta(T-t)} - 1}{e^{\sigma^2(T-t)} - 1} \tag{B3}$$

The cash flow at the event time t is determined by a trivariate distribution of $\{S_t, X_t, 1_{\{t\}}\}$ which is a change of variable from $\{Z_t, Y_t, J_t\}$. So far there has been no asset pricing model available for such an uncertainty and payoff structure. Therefore, we propose an approximation for the risk adjusted discount rate (capital market line for its non-diversifiability) as follows:

$$k_{0,t} = rt + \frac{\sigma_\eta}{\sigma_s}\left(\frac{E_0[S_t]}{S_0} - rt\right) \tag{B4}$$

where

$$\sigma_\eta^2 = \text{var}\left[\frac{\eta_t}{\eta_0}\right] = \frac{\text{var}[\eta_t]}{\eta_0^2}$$

$$\eta_t = X_t 1_{\{t\}}$$

The above equation needs to be solved iteratively to arrive at the solution. The valuation is done with Monte Carlo.

9. FINANCIAL ANALYSIS, PLANNING AND FORECASTING FOR ANHEUSER-BUSCH COMPANIES, INC.

Jason S. Rich

ABSTRACT

The purpose of this case study is to forecast, through various financial analyses, the future financial position and stock price of Anheuser-Busch Companies, Inc. A basic analysis of the Company's financial ratios and dynamic ratio analyses will be performed to establish the Company's position within the industry. The Company's cost of capital will then be derived using the Capital Asset Pricing Model to determine the required rate of return to shareholders. The sustainable growth rate of the Firm will also be calculated. An option pricing analysis will be conducted to determine if an arbitrage opportunity exists between the current stock price and options on the stock. Finally, we will review the Firm's dividend policy and forecast the Company's financial position over the next five years, including its stock price and dividends per share.

Executive Summary

Anheuser-Busch Companies is one of the largest and most widely recognized names in alcoholic beverages. Known predominately for its Budweiser brand,

Advances in Quantitative Analysis of Finance and Accounting, Volume 10, pages 157–253.

ISBN: 0-7623-0969-5

Anheuser-Busch has managed to grow sales, net income and dividends over the past years, and increase shareholder value. This case study looks to analyze Anheuser-Busch from a financial perspective, concentrating on financial ratios and forecasting models to uncover the true value of the firm. Interestingly enough, closer examination of the company indicates that although investors have been well rewarded for their investment in the "King of Beers", it appears that there is a tremendous amount of untapped potential lying dormant in the financial statements of this company. The following pages contain in-depth analysis on the financial structure of Anheuser-Busch, as well as discussions on the impact of the results of these analyses.

1. BACKGROUND

Anheuser-Busch Companies, Inc. is the holding company for Anheuser-Busch, Incorporated (ABI), a company whose origins date back to 1875. The Company's principal product is beer, produced and distributed by its subsidiary, ABI, in a variety of containers primarily under the brand names Budweiser, Bud Light, Bud Dry, Bud Ice, Bud Ice Light, Michelob, Michelob Amber Bock, Michelob Pale Ale, Michelob Honey Lager, Michelob Hefe-Weizen, Busch, Natural Light, Hurricane Malt Liquor, Safari Amber Lager and Rhumba, among others. ABI's products also include three non-alcohol malt beverages. The Company's beer products are also sold internationally. In addition, the Company is also the parent company to a number of subsidiaries that conduct various other business operations including packaging, entertainment and other. Revenues for the fiscal year ended December 31, 1999 were $11.7 billion, compared with $11.2 billion for the fiscal year ending December 31, 1998.

Worldwide sales of the Company's beer brands aggregated 102.9 million barrels in 1999, as compared with 99.8 million barrels in 1998, and accounted for approximately 82% of the Company's consolidated net sales dollars in 1999, and approximately 80% in 1998 and 1997. Worldwide beer volume is comprised of domestic and international volume. Domestic volume represents Anheuser-Busch brands produced and shipped within the United States. International volume represents Anheuser-Busch brands produced overseas by Company-owned breweries and under license and contract brewing agreements, plus exports from the Company's United States breweries to markets around the world. Total volume includes the Company's pro rata share of the volume of international equity partners, Grupo Modelo, S. A. de C. V. and Companhia Antarctica Paulista (for periods prior to July 1999, when the Company terminated its equity partnership with Companhia Antarctica

Paulista), combined with worldwide Anheuser-Busch brand volume. Total beer volume was 118 million barrels and 111 million barrels in 1999 and 1998, respectively.

Domestic Beer Operations

The Company's principal product is beer, produced and distributed by its subsidiary, ABI, in a variety of containers primarily under the brand names Budweiser, Bud Light, Bud Dry, Bud Ice, Bud Ice Light, Michelob, Michelob Light, Michelob Dry, Michelob Golden Draft, Michelob Golden Draft Light, Michelob Classic Dark, Michelob Black & Tan Lager, Michelob Amber Bock, Michelob Pale Ale, Michelob Honey Lager, Michelob Hefe-Weizen, Busch, Busch Light, Busch Ice, Natural Light, Natural Ice, King Cobra, Red Wolf Lager, ZiegenBock Amber, Hurricane Malt Liquor, Hurricane Ice, Pacific Ridge Ale, Tequiza, Safari Amber Lager, Devon's Shandy and Rhumba. ABI's products also include three non-alcohol malt beverages, O'Doul's, Busch NA and O'Doul's Amber. Domestic beer volume was 95.7 million barrels in 1999, as compared with 92.7 million barrels in 1998.

The Company brews Kirin Light, Kirin Lager and Kirin-Ichiban through a joint venture agreement with Kirin Brewing Company, Ltd. of Japan for sale in the United States. ABI owns a 25% equity interest in Seattle-based Redhook Ale Brewery, Inc. Through this alliance, Redhook products are distributed exclusively by ABI wholesalers in all new United States markets entered by Redhook since 1994. ABI also owns a 31% interest in Portland-based Widmer Brothers Brewing Company. Widmer products are distributed exclusively by ABI wholesalers in all new United States markets entered by Widmer since 1997.

Budweiser, Bud Light, Bud Ice, Bud Ice Light, Michelob, Michelob Light, Michelob Amber Bock, Tequiza, Natural Light, Natural Ice, O'Doul's Amber and O'Doul's are distributed and sold on a nationwide basis. Busch, Busch Light and Michelob Honey Lager are sold in 49 states; King Cobra, Michelob Hefe-Weizen, Bud Dry, Red Wolf Lager and Redhook Ales in 48 states; Michelob Black & Tan Lager in 47 states; Michelob Pale Ale in 46 states; Michelob Classic Dark and Busch NA in 45 states; Hurricane Malt Liquor in 43 states; Michelob Dry in 42 states; Kirin Lager and Kirin-Ichiban in 36 states; Kirin Light in 32 states; Busch Ice in 20 states; Widmer beer products in 18 states; Michelob Golden Draft and Michelob Golden Draft Light in 10 states; Devon's Shandy in five states; Pacific Ridge Ale in two states; Rhumba, Hurricane Ice, Safari Amber Lager and ZiegenBock Amber in one state.

The Company's major competitors in the United States brewing industry during 1999 included Philip Morris, Inc. (through its subsidiary Miller Brewing Co.), Adolph Coors Co. and Pabst Brewery Co.

International Beer Operations

International beer volume was 7.2 million barrels in 1999, compared with 7.1 million barrels in 1998. Anheuser-Busch International, Inc. (ABII), a wholly owned subsidiary of the Company, operates breweries in the United Kingdom and China, negotiates and administers license and contract brewing agreements on behalf of ABI with various foreign brewers, and negotiates and manages equity investments in foreign brewing partners. In addition, ABI's beer products are being sold under import-distribution agreements in more than 80 countries and United States territories and to the United States military and diplomatic corps outside the continental United States.

Packaging Operations

The Company's wholly owned subsidiary, Metal Container Corporation (MCC), manufactures beverage cans at eight plants and beverage can lids at three plants, for sale to ABI and to soft drink customers. Another wholly owned subsidiary of the Company, Anheuser-Busch Recycling Corporation (ABRC), recycles aluminum cans at its plant in Hayward, California, for conversion into new can sheet. The Company's wholly owned subsidiary, Precision Printing and Packaging, Inc. (PPPI), manufactures metalized and paper labels at its plant in Clarksville, Tennessee. Eagle Packaging, Inc. (EPI) was established during 1999 to manufacture and sell crown and closure liners, beginning in 2000. Packaging Business Services, Inc., another wholly owned subsidiary of the Company, provides administrative services and develops existing and new businesses for MCC, ABRC, PPPI and EPI.

Family Entertainment

The Company is active in the family entertainment field, primarily through its wholly owned subsidiary, Busch Entertainment Corporation (BEC), which currently owns, directly and through subsidiaries, nine theme parks. BEC's tenth park, Discovery Cove located in Orlando, Florida, is scheduled to open in summer 2000. BEC operates Busch Gardens theme parks in Tampa, Florida and Williamsburg, Virginia, and SeaWorld theme parks in Orlando, Florida, San Antonio, Texas, Aurora, Ohio, and San Diego, California. BEC operates water park attractions in Tampa, Florida (Adventure Island) and Williamsburg, Virginia (Water Country, USA), and an educational play park for children near Philadelphia, Pennsylvania (Sesame Place). BEC also operates the Baseball City Sports Complex near Orlando, Florida. Through a Spanish affiliate, the Company also owns a 19.9% equity interest in Port Aventura, S. A., which is a theme park near Barcelona, Spain.

Other

Through its wholly owned subsidiary, Busch Properties, Inc. (BPI), the Company is engaged in the business of real estate development. BPI also owns and operates The Kingsmill Resort and Conference Center in Williamsburg, Virginia. Through other wholly owned subsidiaries, the Company owns and operates a marketing communications business (Busch Creative Services Corporation) and a transportation service business (Manufacturers Railway Co.).

2. FINANCIAL STATEMENT ANALYSIS

The financial statement analysis section of this report is comprised of sub-divisions:

(1) financial statements;
(2) ratio analysis; and
(3) the dynamic analysis of financial ratios.

The financial statement section is critical as it serves as the cornerstone for all financial analyses and discussion in this case-study.

The ratio analysis section will analyze seven different financial ratios and discuss the implications of each.

The dynamic ratio analysis section will further analyze and forecast two ratios (current ratio and price earnings ratio) and compare the results to those of PSEG.

(a) *Financial Statements*. The pages containing the Balance Sheet, Income Statement, Cash Flow Statement and Retained Earnings Statement for Anheuser-Busch Companies, Inc. are Tables 1–6 in the Tables section. Please note, the Balance Sheet, Income Statement and Statement of Cash Flows were all obtained from Compustat. The Retained Earnings Statement was adopted from the Company's 10-K filing with the Securities and Exchange Commission.
(b) *Ratio Analysis*. Ratio analysis is an important aspect of company analysis. One of the main benefits of ratio analysis is that it standardizes data,

allowing an individual to compare companies of different sizes on an equal basis. In the analysis of Anheuser-Busch Companies, Inc., seven financial ratios will be calculated. These financial ratios are:

(i) Current Ratio
(ii) Debt to Total Assets Ratio
(iii) Total-Asset Utilization Ratio
(iv) Return on Total Asset Ratio
(v) Payout Ratio
(vi) P/E Ratio (Price – Earnings Ratio)
(vii) Market/Book Ratio

The above ratios will be calculated for the Anheuser-Busch Companies, Inc. for the period 1989 through 1999, and compared to the Alcoholic Beverage Industry ratios over the same time period.

Following the calculation of the seven ratios, dynamic ratio analysis will be performed on the current ratio and the P/E ratio.

Current Ratio

The current ratio is defined a liquidity ratio. Liquidity ratios measure the relative strength of a firm's financial position. The current ratio gives an indication of a firm's ability to meet short-term obligations, as it compares its cash resources (assets) to its cash obligations (liabilities). The current ratio is calculated as follows:

$$\frac{\text{Current Assets}}{\text{Current Liabilities}}$$

The current asset ratios for Anheuser-Busch and the Alcoholic beverage industry are presented in Figs 1 and 2 in the Figure section.

Debt to Total Assets Ratio

The debt to total assets ratio is a leverage ratio. Leverage ratios measure the extent to which a firm has financed its operations with debt. The debt to total assets ratio measures the proportion of debt-financed assets that comprise the firm's financial structure, as it compares its total debt (liability) to its total assets (asset). The debt to total asset ratio is calculated as follows:

$$\frac{\text{Total Debt}}{\text{Total Assets}}$$

It is important to note that "Total Debt", for Anheuser-Bush, is defined as long-term debt and notes payable. The debt to total assets ratios for Anheuser-Busch and the Alcoholic beverage industry are presented in Figs 3 and 4.

Total Asset Utilization Ratio

The total asset utilization ratio is an activity ratio. Activity ratios measure the degree of efficiency to which the firm uses its assets. The total asset utilization ratio gives an indication of the firm's efficiency in generating sales based on its total assets, as it compares net sales to total assets. The total asset utilization ratio is calculated as follows:

$$\frac{\text{Net Sales}}{\text{Total Assets}}$$

The total asset utilization ratios for Anheuser-Busch and the Alcoholic beverage industry are presented in Figs 5 and 6.

Return on Total Assets Ratio

The return on total assets ratio is a profitability ratio. Profitability ratios measure the profitability of the firm's operations. The return on total assets ratio gives an indication of the firm's profitability of the firm's total asset utilization, as it compares net income to total assets. The return on total asset ratio is calculated as follows:

$$\frac{\text{Net Income}}{\text{Total Assets}}$$

The return on total asset ratios for Anheuser-Busch and the Alcoholic beverage industry are presented in Figs 7 and 8.

Payout Ratio

The payout ratio measures the proportion of net income that is paid out in dividends. The payout ratio is an important ratio as each penny paid out in dividends is one lees penny the firm has available to reinvest in its operations. The payout ratio is also an important factor when calculating a firm's sustainable growth rate. The payout ratio is calculated as follows:

$$\frac{\text{Dividends}}{\text{Net Income}}$$

The payout ratios for Anheuser-Busch and the Alcoholic beverage industry are presented in Figs 9 and 10.

P/E Ratio

The P/E ratio (price/earnings ratio) is often used to compare firm valuations. The P/E ratio measures the multiple at which the market is capitalizing the earnings per share of a company. The P/E ratio is calculated as follows:

$$\frac{\text{Market Price per Share}}{\text{Earnings per Share}}$$

The P/E ratios for Anheuser-Busch and the Alcoholic beverage industry are presented in Figs 11 and 12.

Market/Book Ratio

The market/book ratio (or price to book ratio) measures the multiple at which the market is capitalizing the book value per share of the company. The market/book ratio is calculated as follows:

$$\frac{\text{Market Price per Share}}{\text{Book Value per Share*}}$$

* Book value per share is calculated as follows:

$$\frac{\text{Stockholder's Equity}}{\text{Shares Outstanding}}$$

The market/book ratios for Anheuser-Busch and the Alcoholic beverage industry are presented in Figs 13 and 14.

(c) *Dynamic Analysis of Financial Ratios.* The purpose of a dynamic analysis on financial ratios is to improve the comparability of the ratios. In this analysis, the following will be calculated for the current ratio and the Price/Earnings ratio:

- Mean
- Median
- Variance
- Standard Deviation
- Coefficient of Variation
- Skewness
- Coefficient of Skewness
- Kurtosis

The data for these calculations will be obtained from the financial ratio analyses performed on the prior pages.

Dynamic Analysis – Current Ratio and Price/Earnings Ratio

- *Mean* – the mean (X_{bar}) is the average result of a set of data. The mean is calculated by taking the sum of the observations and dividing the total by the number of observations. The formula for the mean is:

$$\sum_{t=1} x_i/n$$

  - The mean is calculated for the current ratio (see Table 7):
  - The mean is calculated for the price/earnings ratio (see Table 8)

- *Median* – the median is a measure of central tendency. It is calculated quite easily by taking the middle observation. In the event there is an even number of samples (as in the case), the average of the two middle observations is taken. When calculating the median for the Anheuser-Busch current asset ratio and price/earnings ratio, the two middle observations occur in years 1994 and 1995. The median is therefore calculated as the average of the two middle observations:

  - Median of the current ratio is calculated in Table 9:
  - Median of the price/earnings ratio is calculated in Table 10:

- *Variance* – the variance (s^2) is a measure of the average squared deviations from the mean. The variance is an effective tool in measuring the risk. The variance is calculated as:

$$\text{Variance} = \sum_{t=1}^{n} \frac{(X_i - \bar{X})^2}{n-1}$$

  It is important to note the divisor of $(n - 1)$, used when calculating the *sample* variance, is different from the divisor of (n) when calculating the *population* variance. This adjustment allows the variance to return a "more precise" answer.

  - The variance of the current ratio is calculated in Table 11:
  - The variance of the price/earnings ratio is calculated in Table 12:

- *Standard Deviation* – the standard deviation (s) is calculated as the *square root* of the variance.
  - The standard deviation of the current ratio for Anheuser-Busch is calculated in Table 13:
  - The standard deviation of the price/earnings ratio is calculated in Table 14.
- *Coefficient of Variation* – the coefficient of variation is the ratio of the standard deviation to the mean. This calculation allows one to compare the variability of data sets that are measured in different units; similar to ratio analysis, this is a formula that standardizes data and allows for comparison across sets of data with dissimilar bases. The coefficient of variation is calculated as follows:

$$CV_x = s/X_{bar}$$

  We recall from our calculations above that:

$$s = \text{standard deviation and } X_{bar} = \text{mean}$$

  - The coefficient of variation of the current ratio of Anheuser-Busch is calculated in Table 15:
  - The coefficient of variation of the price/earnings ratio is calculated in Table 16.:
- *Skewness* – skewness indicates whether or not a distribution is skewed to the left or right of the mean. If there is no skewness, the data is symmetric about the mean. The skewness calculation may be written as follows:

$$\text{Skewness} = \sum_{t=1}^{n} \frac{(X_i - \bar{X})^3}{n}$$

  - The skewness of the current ratio population for Anheuser-Busch is calculated in Table 17:
  - The skewness of the price/earnings ratio populations is calculated in Table 18:
- *Coefficient of Skewness* – the coefficient of skewness allows one to scale the skewness factor and determine if there is positive or negative skewness (or neither), about the mean. The coefficient of skewness is calculated as follows:

$$CS = \frac{\text{Skewness}}{(\text{Standard Deviation})^3}$$

- The coefficient of skewness of the current ratio for both Anheuser-Busch and Company X are calculated in Table 19:
- The coefficient of skewness for the price/earnings ratio of both Anheuser-Busch and Company X are calculated in Table 20:

- *Kurtosis* – kurtosis measures the peakedness of a distribution. The value of the kurtosis measurement is inversely correlated with the frequency of data close to the mean; the more data that are observed close to the mean, the smaller the kurtosis value. Kurtosis is calculated as follows:

$$\text{Kurtosis} = \sum_{t=1}^{n} \frac{(X_i - \bar{X})^4}{n}$$

  - Kurtosis is calculated for the current ratio of both Anheuser-Busch and Company X, see Table 21:
  - Kurtosis is calculated for the price/earnings ratio of both Anheuser-Busch and Company X in Table 22:

- *Dynamic Ratio Analysis – Forecasting*
  An important aspect of dynamic ratio analysis is that it allows one to forecast financial ratios of a company. The current ratio and price/earnings ratio will be forecasted for fiscal year 2000, by regressing the data observed in years 1990 through 1999, see Table 23.
  - Table 24 documents the data used in calculating the regression analysis for the *current ratio*.

  - Table 25 shows the summary output for the calculation of the current ratio regression was obtained from the Microsoft Excel Regression program.
  - From the data presented in Table 25, the 2001 current ratio will be forecasted as follows:

$$Y_t = a_0 + a_1 X_{t-1} + a_2 Y_{t-1}$$

where:

a_0 = intercept coefficient

$a_1 = x_{t-1}$ coefficient

$a_2 = y_{t-1}$ coefficient

X_{t-1} = 1999 Anheuser-Busch current ratio

Y_{t-1} = 1999 Industry Average current ratio

- The forecasted 2000 current ratio is then calculated as follows:

$$CR_{00}(\text{Anheuser-Busch}) = 1.676 - 0.618^*(0.81) + 0.154^*(1.11)$$

$$CR_{00}(\text{Anheuser-Busch}) = 1.3464$$

- Table 26 documents the data used in calculating the regression analysis for the *price/earnings ratio.*
  - Table 27 shows the summary output for the calculation of the price/earnings regression was obtained from the Microsoft Excel Regression program.
  - From the data presented in Table 27, the 2001 price/earnings ratio will be forecasted as follows:

$$Y_t = a_0 + a_1X_{t-1} + a_2Y_{t-1}$$

where:

$$a_0 = \text{intercept coefficient}$$

$$a_1 = x_{t-1} \text{ coefficient}$$

$$a_2 = y_{t-1} \text{ coefficient}$$

$$X_{t-1} = 1999 \text{ Anheuser-Busch price/earnings ratio}$$

$$Y_{t-1} = 1999 \text{ Industry Average price/earnings ratio}$$

  - The forecasted 2000 price/earnings ratio is then calculated as follows:

$$P/E_{00}(\text{Anheuser-Busch}) = 20.3988 + 0.3011^*(18.304) - 0.3855^*(16.904)$$

$$CR_{00}(\text{Anheuser-Busch}) = 19.39$$

Current Ratio: Dynamic Ratio Analysis – Anheuser-Busch vs PSE&G

The dynamic ratio analysis results of Anheuser-Busch are compared to that of PSE&G, for the current ratio (see Table 28).

By comparing the information presented in the chart above, we find that:

- The variance for Anheuser-Busch's current ratio is significantly higher than that of PSE&G, (therefore causing a higher standard deviation).
- The Coefficient of Variation, which allows one to compare the variability of data sets, indicates there is 1.4% variability in the current ratio of PSE&G compared to 0.12% for Anheuser-Busch. This indicates that there will be greater variability in PSE&G's current ratio.

- Skewness for both companies is negative, indicating the data distribution is skewed to the left, or negatively skewed.
- The kurtosis for both companies is relatively small, indicating, indicating the frequency of the data set is close to the mean.
- The 2000 current ratio forecast for Anheuser-Busch is 1.3464, indicating current assets are 1.34 times greater than current liabilities. For PSE&G, however, the forecasted current ratio is 0.6054, indicating current assets are 0.6054 times the size of current liabilities. Based on this information, it would appear Anheuser-Busch is more liquid than PSE&G.

Price/Earnings Ratio: Dynamic Ratio Analysis – Anheuser-Busch vs PSE&G

The dynamic ratio analysis results of Anheuser-Busch are compared to that of PSE&G, for the current ratio and the price/earnings ratio, respectively in Table 29:

By comparing the information presented in the chart above, we find that:

- The variance for Anheuser-Busch's price/earnings ratio is significantly higher than that of PSE&G, (therefore causing a higher standard deviation). Conceptually, this makes sense, as PSE&G has a much more consistent stream of earnings (as it is a utility company), compared to Anheuser-Busch (alcoholic beverage producer).
- The Coefficient of Variation, which allows one to compare the variability of data sets, indicates there is 0.276% variability in the price/earnings ratio of PSE&G compared to 0.31% for Anheuser-Busch. This indicates that there will be greater variability in Anheuser-Busch's price/earnings ratio.
- Skewness for both companies is positive, indicating the data distribution is skewed to the right, or positively skewed.
- The kurtosis for PSE&G is relatively small, indicating, indicating the frequency of the data set is close to the mean. Anheuser-Busch's kurtosis, however, is extremely large, indicating large dispersion in the frequency of the data. This further indicates there is great variability of Anheuser-Busch's price/earnings ratio.

The 2000 current ratio forecast for Anheuser-Busch is 19.39 indicating the stock price for Anheuser-Busch is projected to trade at 19.39 times earnings per share. For PSE&G, however, the forecasted current ratio is 11.93, indicating PSE&G's stock price is expected to trade at 11.93 times earnings.

3. PER SHARE DATA

(a) *Earnings per Share* – Figures 15 and 16 present a graphical and tabular representation of the split-adjusted diluted earnings per share data of Anheuser-Busch over the ten-year period commencing in 1989.
(b) *Dividends per Share* – Figures 17 and 18 present a graphical and tabular representation of the split-adjusted dividend per share data of Anheuser-Busch over the ten-year period commencing in 1989.
(c) *Price per share* – Figures 19 and 20 present a graphical and tabular representation of the split-adjusted price per share data of Anheuser-Busch over the ten-year period commencing in 1989.

4. CAPM APPROACH TO ESTIMATE COST OF CAPITAL

The Capital Asset Pricing Model (CAPM) allows one to calculate both the cost of capital and the relative risk of a project. The significance of calculating a firm's cost of capital lies in that it represents the firm's "cost of funds". By understanding what it's cost of capital is, a firm is able allocate resources to those projects that will provide adequate return relative to the risk that is undertaken.

- *Components of CAPM*

(a) *CAPM* – is defined as follows:

$$E(R_i) = R_f + \beta * [E(R_m) - R_f]$$

where:

$E(R_i)$ = expected rate of return for asset i (or the cost of capital)

R_f = risk-free rate (90-Day T-bill rate)

β = measure of systematic risk (beta) for asset i

$E(R_m)$ = expected return of the market

(b) *Beta* – is defined by the following equation:

$$\beta = \frac{\text{Cov}\,(R_{stock}, R_{market})}{\text{Var}\,(R_{market})}$$

where:

Cov = covariance of return of the stock and the return of the market

R_{stock} = return of the stock

R_{market} = return of the market

Var (R_{market}) = variance of the return of the market

(c) *Covariance* – is further defined as follows:

$$Cov(R_{stock}, R_{market}) = \sum_{t=1}^{n} \frac{(R_{stock\ i} - \bar{R}_{stock})(R_{market\ i} - \bar{R}_{market})}{n-1}$$

where:

$R_{stock\ i}$ = return of the stock for a period i

$\bar{R}_{stock}$ = average return of the stock

$R_{market\ i}$ = return of the market for a period I

$\bar{R}_{market}$ = average return of the market

(d) *Variance* – as calculated on page 18 in the Dynamic Analysis section, is defined as:

$$Variance = \sum_{t=1}^{n} \frac{(X_i - \bar{X})^2}{n-1}$$

• *Calculating Beta*

When calculating Beta, one must first consider the stock (Anheuser-Busch) and the market (S&P 500) in separate terms. To begin the calculation of Beta, it is necessary to calculate the average monthly return of both the stock and the market.

(a) *Calculation of Average Monthly Return* – in calculating the average monthly return, the monthly return is first calculated as follows:

$$\frac{\text{(Price at Close of Period – Price at Open of Period)}}{\text{Price at Open Of Period}}$$

After the monthly returns for each period have been calculated, the average (or mean) of the monthly returns is calculated as follows:

$$\sum \frac{\text{(Monthly Return)}}{\text{Total Number of Periods}}$$

Figure 21 being a time-series graph documents the monthly returns of both Anheuser-Busch and the S&P 500.

Table 30–32 on pages 210–212, contain the five-year data relating to the monthly stock price and index level of Anheuser-Busch and the S&P 500, respectively, as well as the calculations of the average monthly return for each.

(b) *Calculation of Variance* – now that the average monthly returns (mean monthly returns) have been calculated, the variance will be calculated in accordance with the formula presented in sub-section (d) on page 165:

(c) *Calculation of Covariance* – the covariance measures the linear association between two random variables. The covariance between the monthly stock and the market returns will be calculated using the data found in the Calculation of Average Monthly Returns table.

- Now that the variance and covariance have been computed, Beta can be calculated, based on the equation discussed on page 170:

$$\beta = \frac{\text{Cov}\ (R_{\text{stock}}, R_{\text{market}})}{\text{Var}\ (R_{\text{market}})}$$

Recall the following results from above:

$$\text{Cov}\ (R_{\text{stock}}, R_{\text{market}}) = 0.0010$$

$$\text{Var}\ (R_{\text{market}}) = 0.0021$$

$$\beta = 0.0010/0.0021 = 0.4762$$

The calculated Beta of 0.4762 appears reasonable compared to the actual Beta of Anheuser-Busch of 0.4 on July 31, 2000.

- *Calculating CAPM*

  Once Beta has been calculated, one need only obtain the risk-free rate and market risk premium to calculate CAPM

  - *Risk-free rate* – the 90-Day T-Bill Rate will be used to represent the risk-free rate. The 90-Day T-Bill rate was obtained from the Federal Reserve Board of Chicago's website at http://www.frbchi.org/securities/rates.html, as of November 2, 2000. At that time, the 90-Day T-bill was yielding 6.35%.
  - *Market risk premium* – the market risk premium is used rather than separately determining the expected market return. The market risk premium is defined as the difference between the expected market return and the risk-free rate. The market risk premium, historically, has ranged between 8% and 10% (information obtained from Professor Lee's class on 10/9/00). For conservatism, 8.0% will be used.

It is now possible to calculate the cost of capital, using CAPM:

Recall:

$$E(R_i) = R_f + \beta *[E(R_m) - R_f]$$

. . . having defined the following:

$$R_f = 6.35\% \qquad \beta = 0.4762 \qquad [E(R_m) - R_f] = 8.0\%$$

CAPM is solved as follows:

$$E(R_i) = 6.35 + .4762*(8.0)$$

$$E(R_i) = 10.16\%$$

5. OPTION PRICING THEORY

The use of option pricing theory allows an individual to uncover arbitrage opportunities in the price of a security. In this section, we will manually calculate option prices for Anheuser-Busch and then compare the results to those generated by an excel program.

The option pricing model for calculating the call option is defined as follows:

$$C = SN(d_1) - Xe^{-rT}N(d_2)$$

Where:

C = price of the call option

S = current price of the stock

X = exercise price of the option

e = 2.71828 . . .

r = short-term interest rate (T-bill rate) = R_f

T = time to expiration of the option, in years

$N(d_i) = F2(d_i)$ = value of the cumulative standard normal distribution

The information in Table 33, page 213, was obtained from http://www.yahoo.com.

We will be calculating the price of the January 2001 47.5 call and the put options.

In calculating the call option, we have obtained the following information from the table above and http://www.yahooo.com:

$$S = 48.75$$

$$X = 47.5$$

$$r = 6.04\%$$

The risk-free rate (90-day T-bill rate) on December 14, 2000 was obtained from http://www.frbchi.org/securities/rates.html.

Time to expiration is calculated as follows:

Current Day = 12/15/00

Expiration Date = 1/19/01

Total number of days to expiration = 35/365 = 0.0959

The standard deviation of the stock's daily return must also be calculated. For this calculation, we will analyze the stock price of Anheuser-Busch from November 2, 2000 through December 14, 2000. Stock price data was obtained from http://www.yahoo.com. Standard deviation is calculated in Table 34:

Based on the calculations performed above, we see the variance of the stock price over the trailing 30-day period is 0.000345. The standard deviation is calculated as the square root of the variance:

$$(0.000345)^{0.5} = 0.0186$$

The standard deviation of the stock's return over the trailing 30-Day period is 0.0186.

Now that standard deviation has been calculated, we must calculate (d_1).

The formula for (d_i) is:

$$\{[\ln(S/X) + (r + \tfrac{1}{2}*s^2)]T\}/sT^{0.5}$$

Substituting our data into the above formula, we calculate d_1 as follows:

$$\{[\ln(48.875/47.5) + (0.0604 + \tfrac{1}{2}*(0.0186)^2]*0.0959\}/0.0186*(0.0959)^{0.5}$$

We then calculate d_1 as 5.9549

After calculating d_1, we may now calculate d_2 as follows:

$$d_2 = d_1 - s*(T)^{0.5}$$

Substituting our data into the above formula, we calculate d_2 as follows:

$$5.9549 - 0.0186*(0.0959)^{0.5}$$

We then calculate d_2 as 5.9491

Now that all variables have been solved for or provided, we can solve for the price of the call option:

$$C = 47.44*N(5.9549) - 47.5*(2.71828^{-(0.0604*0.0959)})*N(5.9491)$$

The call option price is calculated as $1.6493.

To calculate the put option price, we rearrange the call option pricing formula as follows:

$$P = Xe^{-rt}N(-d_2) - SN(d_1)$$

By taking the variables we calculated for the call option problem, we input the data into the put option formula as follows:

$$P = 47.5e^{-(0.0604)(0.0959)} * N(-5.9491) - 48.875 * N(-5.9549)$$

According to the above model, the put option is priced at 0. However, when using put-call parity, defined as:

$$C + Xe^{-rt} = P + S$$

Based on the above formula, we calculate the put option price to be \$1.375

To check the above calculations for accuracy, the stock and option data is entered into the Excel option pricing model, as obtained from Professor Lee's website at http://rbs.rutgers.edu/ ~ lee (Fig. 22).

There is very little difference between the option values calculated manually to those calculated by the option pricing model. Compared to the actual price of the call and put option, however, there is some variation. This may be attributed to two specific factors: standard deviation of stock price returns and the risk-free rate. In our calculation, the trailing 30-day stock price return was used to calculate standard deviation, whereas the market may take a longer period of history into account in its valuation. Second, the use of the 90-day T-bill as the risk-free rate may differ from that being used by individuals in the market.

6. DIVIDEND POLICY AND FORECASTING

A firm's dividend policy is a significant part of its financial structure. In forecasting Anheuser-Busch's quarterly dividend payment, the following data was gathered, see Table 35.

The dividend per share (DPS and DPS_{t-1}) and earnings per share (EPS) data were obtained from http://www.yahoo.com. To forecast earnings per share in period 40, a multiple regression is run, by regressing the prior period dividends (DPS_{t-1}) and earnings per share in the current period (EPS), against current period dividends (DPS). Table 36 is an output of the regression results.

We note the strength of the regression is quite strong (based on the Multiple R and R Square of 0.990885003 and 0.981853089, respectively), indicating a high "goodness of fit". Now that the strength of the regression has been determined, we are able to construct the forecasting model.

Based on the results from the multiple regression, the following dividend forecasting model is constructed:

$$DPS_t = 0.002656047 + 0.01729273*EPS_t + 0.971233165*DPS_{t-1}$$

To forecast dividends for the 40th period, we enter the following information into the formula:

$DPS_{t-1} = 0.28$ (obtained from the data set)

$EPS_t = 0.56$ (obtained from http://www.yahoo.com)

The data is entered into the equation as follows:

$$DPS_t = 0.002656047 + 0.01729273*(0.56) + 0.971233165*(0.28)$$

The quarterly dividend forecast for the 40th period is \$0.2842. This result appears reasonable in comparison to the historical dividend amounts.

7. FINANCIAL PLANNING AND FORECASTING

Financial planning and forecasting is essential in a firm's decision as to the extent and type of financing it will need to fund operations in the future. The Warren and Shelton model will be used for this exercise. The Warren and Shelton model (or "20 equation model") considers 20 variables (provided by management) as well as a sales growth rate. Before one can begin using the Warren and Shelton model, it is necessary to calculate the sales growth rate. For this exercise, we will be using three different methods to calculate the sales growth rate:

(1) Percentage Change Average Method
(2) Sustainable Growth Rate Method
(3) Sales Regression

(1) *Percentage Change Average Method*
Under this method, the sales growth rate will be calculated by taking the average growth in sales over the trailing twenty-year period, see Table 37

The sales information from 1989–1999 above was obtained from the Anheuser-Busch financial statements found in Section 2, and the sales data from 1980–1989 was obtained from the Company's Income Statement as obtained from the Compustat program. As calculated above, under the Percentage Change Average Method, the annual sales growth rate is 7.26%.

(2) *Sustainable Growth Rate Method*

The sustainable growth rate method considers the equity constraints of the firm. The following is the formula for calculating the firm's sustainable growth rate:

$$S^* = \text{Retention Ratio} * \text{ROE}$$

where:

$$S^* = \text{sustainable growth}$$

$$\text{ROE} = \text{Profit Margin} * \text{Asset Turnover} * \text{Equity Multiplier}$$

We are able to obtain the ratio information from Section 2 – Financial Statements. The other ratios are calculated below. Please note, financial data is averaged to develop a more representative result.

The Average Retention Ratio is calculated as follows, also see Table 38:

$$\text{Average Retention Ratio} = 1 - \text{Average Dividend Payout Ratio}$$

$$\text{Where the Average Dividend Payout Ratio} = \text{Avg DPS/Avg EPS}$$

The Average Retention Rate $= 1 - 0.3219 = 0.6781$

The Average Profit Margin for Anheuser-Busch is calculated as follows, also see Table 39:

$$\text{Average Profit Margin} = \text{Average Net Income/Average Sales}$$

The Average Profit Margin for Anheuser-Busch is calculated as 7.72% (or 0.0772)

The Average Asset Turnover ratio is calculated as follows, also see Table 40:

$$\text{Average Asset Turnover ratio} = \text{Average Sales/Average Total Assets}$$

The Average Asset Turnover ratio for Anheuser-Busch is calculated as 1.16.

The Average Equity Multiplier is calculated as follows, also see Table 41:

$$\text{Average Equity Multiplier} = \text{Average Total Assets/Average Total Equity}$$

The average Total Average Equity Multiplier for Anheuser-Busch is calculated as 2.45.

We are now able to substitute our data into the equation to calculate Anheuser-Busch's sustainable growth rate:

$$S^* = 0.6781 * 0.0772 * 1.16 * 2.45$$

Sustainable growth rate for Anheuser-Busch is calculated as 14.88%.

(3) *Sales Regression*

The sales regression method used will regress the sales figures of Anheuser-Busch over the trailing 20-year period, Table 42:

The regression output of the sales regression is found in Table 43:

The sales growth rate as developed by the log regression model is the X variable, or 5.89%.

When we analyze the regression out put above, we can pick up on a few important aspects of the regression model. The $R^2 = 79.03\%$, which indicates a relatively strong "goodness of fit"; the independent variable explains 79.03% of the variability in the dependent variable.

We can also analyze the significance of both the intercept and the coefficient at a 95% confidence level, by noting the respective *t*-statistic for each. We see that the *t*-statistic for both the coefficient and the intercept are larger than the critical *t*-value (approximately 2 at a 5% level of significance), indicating they are both statistically different from zero.

We gain comfort with the statistical significance of the model as a whole (test that the coefficients are *simultaneously* different than zero at a 5% level of significance) by analyzing the F-statistic. The relatively large *F*-statistic indicates that the coefficients are simultaneously different from zero.

Using the boundaries established in the table, we are able to construct a prediction interval (upper and lower boundaries) for the estimated sales growth figure. With 95% confidence, the sales growth figure will range between:

4.39% and 7.39%

We estimate the prediction interval with the data provided in the regression table, under the heading Lower 95% and Upper 95%, respectively. To verify these figures, we consider the formula for the calculating a prediction interval:

$$\text{Prediction Interval} = \text{Coefficient} \pm (\text{Critical } t\text{-value})*(\text{Standard Error})$$

$$\text{Upper Boundary} = 0.0589 + (2.101)*(0.007156725) = 0.074 \text{ or } 7.4\%$$

$$\text{Lower Boundary} = 0.0589 - (2.101)*(0.007156725) = 0.0439 \text{ or } 4.39\%$$

Selection of the Growth Rate

Out of the three sales growth rates calculated above, we will select the growth rate obtained by using the Percentage Change Average method, of 7.26%. This is a relatively conservative growth rate, when compared to the sustainable growth rate of over 14%. The 7.26% also appears to be the most realistic. Over the past 20 years, this rate is the most representative of sales growth, and therefore will be used to forecast sales growth in the future.

Using the 7.26% sales growth rate, Table 44 illustrates the projected sales figures for Anheuser-Busch between fiscal years 2000 and 2010.

Now that the sales growth rate has been calculated, we are now able to enter the known data variables in the equation, see Table 45:

By using the data in Table 45, we are able to calculate the unknown variables in Table 45:

$$\begin{aligned} \text{Sales}_t &= \text{Sales}_{t-1} * (1 + \text{GCALS}_t) \\ &= 11{,}703.7 * (1.0726) \\ &= 12{,}553.38 \end{aligned} \tag{1}$$

$$\begin{aligned} \text{EBIT}_t &= \text{REBIT}_{t-1} * \text{Sales}_t \\ &= 0.1967 * 12{,}553.38 \\ &= 2{,}469.25 \end{aligned} \tag{2}$$

$$\begin{aligned} \text{CA}_t &= \text{RCA}_{t-1} * \text{Sales}_t \\ &= 0.1368 * 12{,}553.38 \\ &= 1{,}717.30 \end{aligned} \tag{3}$$

$$\begin{aligned} \text{FA}_t &= \text{RFA}_{t-1} * \text{Sales}_t \\ &= 0.6805 * 12{,}553.38 \\ &= 8{,}542.58 \end{aligned} \tag{4}$$

$$\begin{aligned} \text{A}_t &= \text{CA}_t + \text{FA}_t \\ &= 1{,}717.30 + 8{,}542.58 \\ &= 10{,}259.88 \end{aligned} \tag{5}$$

$$\begin{aligned} \text{CL}_t &= \text{RCL}_{t-1} * \text{Sales}_t \\ &= 0.1698 * 12{,}553.38 \\ &= 2{,}131.56 \end{aligned} \tag{6}$$

$$NF_t = (A_t - CL_t - PFDSK_t) - (L_{t-1} - LR_t) - S_{t-1} - R_{t-1} - b_t^*\{(1 - T_t) \times [EBIT_t - i_{t-1}(L_{t-1} - LR_t)] - PFDIV_t\}$$

$$= (10{,}259.88 - 2{,}131.56 - 0) - (4{,}880.60 - 553.70) - 716.1 - 9{,}006.20 - 0.6054^*\{(1 - 0.3524)^*(2{,}469.25 - 0.0631) ^*(4{,}880.60 - 553.70) - 0] - 0\}$$

$$= -6{,}781.92 \quad (7)$$

$$i_tL_t = i_0(L_0 - LR_t) + i_t^e{}^*NL_t$$

$$= 0.0631^*(4{,}880.60 - 553.70) + 0.0631^*NL_t$$

$$= 273.03 + 0.0631^*NL_t \quad (12)$$

$$NF_t + b_t(1 - T)[iNL_t + U_t^lNL_t] = NL_t + NS - 6{,}781.92 + 0.6054(1 - 0.3524) \times (0.0631NL_t + 0.0631NL_t)$$

$$= NL_t + NS - 6{,}781.92 + 0.0365NL$$

$$= NL + NS$$

(a) $NS_t + 0.9635NL = -6{,}781.92$ (8)

$$L_t = L_{t-1} - LR + NL$$

(b) $L_t = 4{,}880.60 - 553.70 + NL$

$L_t - NL = 4{,}326.90$ (9)

$$S_t = S_t - 1 + NS$$

(c) $-NS + S_t = 716.1$ (10)

$$R_t = R_{t-1} + b_t\{(1 - T_t)[EBIT - i_tL_t - U_t^lNL_t] - PFDIV\}$$

$$= 9{,}006.20 + 0.6054\{0.6476[2{,}469.25 - i_tL_t - 0.03NL]\} \quad (11)$$

Substitute (12) into (11) . . .

$$R_t = 9{,}006.20 + 0.654\{0.6476[2{,}469.25 - (273.027 + 0.0631NL) - 0.03NL]\}$$

$$= 9{,}006.20 + 861.04 - 0.0357NL$$

(d) $Rt = 9{,}867.24 - 0.0357NL$

$$L_t = (S_t - R_t)K_t$$

$$L_t = 1.2446S_t + 1.2446R_t \quad (13)$$

(e) $L_t - 1.2446S_t - 1.2446R_t = 0$

(b)–(e) = (f)

$= (L_t - NL_t - 4{,}326.90) - (L_t = 1.2446S_t + 1.2446R_t)$

$= 1.2446S_t + 1.2446R_t - NL - 4{,}326.90$

(f) − k(c) = (g)

$= (1.2446S_t - 1.2446R_t - NL_t = 4{,}326.90)$

$- 1.2446(-NS_t + S_t = 716.1)$

$= 1.2446NS_t - NL_t + 1.2446R_t = 3{,}435.64$

(g)–k(d) = (h)

$= (1.2446NS_t - NL_t + 1.2446R_t = 3{,}435.64)$

$- 1.2446(0.0494NL_t + R_t = 9{,}867.24)$

$= 1.2446NS_t - 1.06148NL_t = -8{,}845.13$

(h) − k(a) = (i)

$= (1.2446NS_t - 1.06148NL_t = -8{,}845.13)$

$- 1.2446(NS_t + 0.9505NL_t = -6{,}781.92)$

$= NL_t = 180.15$

Substitute NL_t in (a) . . .

$NS_t + 0.9635(180.149) = -6{,}781.92$

$NS_t = -6{,}955.49$

Substitute NL_t in (b) . . .

$L_t = 4{,}880.60 - 553.70 + 180.149$

$L_t = 4{,}507.05$

Substitute NS_t in (c) . . .

$6{,}955.49 + S_t = 716.1$

$S_t = -6{,}239.39$

Substitute NL in (d) . . .

$R_t = 9{,}867.24 - 0.0357(180.149)$

$R_t = 9{,}860.81$

Substitute NL_tL_t in (12) . . .

$$i_t(4{,}507.05) = 273.027 + 0.0631(180.149)$$

$$i_t = .0631$$

$$\begin{aligned} EAFCD &= (1 - T)(EBIT - i_L - U_t^l NL_t) \\ &= 0.64760(2{,}469.25 - (0.0631)(4{,}507.05) - 0.0631(180.149)) \\ &= 1{,}407.55 \end{aligned} \quad (14)$$

$$\begin{aligned} CMDIV &= (1 - b)EAFCD \\ &= 0.3946(1{,}407.55) \\ &= 555.42 \end{aligned} \quad (15)$$

$$NUMCS_t = X_1 = NUMCS_{t-1} + NEWCS$$

$$X_1 = 461.10 + NEWCS \quad (16)$$

$$NEWCS = X_2 = NS_t/(1 - U_t^s)P_t$$

$$X_2 = 10{,}158.55/(1 - 0.1016)P_t \quad (17)$$

$$P_t = X_3 = m_tEPS$$

$$X_3 = 23.70(EPS) \quad (18)$$

$$EPS_t = X_4 = EAFCD/NUMCS$$

$$X_4 = 1{,}407.55/NUMCS \quad (19)$$

$$DPS_t = X_5 = CMDIV/NUMCS$$

$$X_5 = 555.42/NUMCS \quad (20)$$

(A) = For (18) and (19) we obtain $X_3 = 23.70(1{,}407.55)/NUMCS$

Substitute (A) into Eq. (17) to calculate (B). . .

$(B) = -6{,}955.49/(0.8984)(23.70)(1{,}407.55)/X_1$

$(B) = 0.2321X_1$

Substitute (B) into Eq. (16) to calculate (C) . . .

$(C) = X_1 = 461.10 - 0.2321X_1$

$(C) = X_1 = 374.24$

Substitute (C) into (B) . . .

$(B) = 0.2321X_1$

$(B) = 86.86$

From Eqs (19) and (20) we obtain X_4, X_5 and X_3 . . .

$X_4 = 1{,}407.55/374.24 = 3.76$

$X_5 = 555.42/374.24 = 1.48$

$X_3 = 23.70(3.76) = 89.11$

The results of the above calculations allow us to forecast the following information regarding Anheuser-Busch in the 2000 fiscal year ($ in thousands, except for per share data):

- Sales = $12,553.38
- Current Assets = $1,717.30
- Fixed Assets = $8,542.58
- Total Assets = $10,259.88
- Current Payables = $2,131.56
- Needed Funds = ($6,781.92)
- Earnings Before Interest and Taxes = $2,469.25
- New Debt = $180.15
- New Stock = ($6,955.49)
- Total Debt = $4,507.05
- Common Stock = ($6,239.39)
- Retained Earnings $9,858.34
- Interest Rate on Debt = 6.31%
- Earnings Available for Common Dividends = $1,407.55
- Common Dividends = $555.42
- Number of Common Shares Outstanding = 374.24
- New Common Shares Issued = 86.86
- Price per Share = $89.11
- Earnings per Share = $3.76
- Dividends per Share = $1.48

One of the most interesting aspects of the results of the model is the negative value for funds needed. This indicates that Anheuser-Busch is retaining a larger than necessary amount of funds.

Anheuser-Busch should look to make better use of these funds, possibly by exploring one or more of the following:

- Increase dividends per share
- Stock buy back in the public market
- Retire a portion of its long-term debt
- Invest in new fixed assets
- Invest in other projects

By making better use of its internal funds, Anheuser-Busch could improve the performance of its company and/or increase its market value.

Another interesting result of the Warren and Shelton model is the projected price per share of $89.11. Due to a stock split that occurred in September of 2000, the non-split adjusted price per share as of December 15 was approximately $94 per share. The model correctly forecasted an increase in the stock price, varying by 5%.

The Warren and Shelton model was also calculated using the Financial Plan model obtained from Professor Lee's website at http://rbs.rutgers.edu/~lee. The result of the Financial Plan is detailed in Table 46:

The pro forma income statement results of the Financial Plan are outlined in Table 47:

The pro forma balance sheet results of the Financial Plan are outlined in Table 48:

Results from the Financial Plan are very consistent with those of the manual calculations, as shown in Table 49:

The accuracy of the model is further supported when comparing the estimated 2000 stock price of $89.11 per share to the actual stock price (pre-split) on December 29, 2000 of $91.00 per share. The forecasted P/E ratio for the Company was (89.11/4.09) 21.78x, and the actual P/E at year-end 2000 was approximately (91.00/3.50) 26x. Again, the forecasted values are relatively consistent with actuals.

8. CONCLUSION

The financial analyses contained within this paper allow an individual to better understand the financial structure of Anheuser-Busch. In the financial ratio analysis section, we analyzed and compared seven different ratios of Anheuser-Busch to those of the Alcoholic Beverage industry. We recall the following:

- *Current Ratio* – Anheuser-Busch consistently lagged the industry's current ratio average. This means that the firms in the industry, on average, had greater current assets than current liabilities on their respective balance sheets, in comparison to Anheuser-Busch. One cannot, however, simply assume that the company is in danger of bankruptcy. Rather, it is important to analyze these financial ratios in conjunction with others, as one can develop a greater and more accurate, understanding of the company.
- *Debt to Total Assets* – Although Anheuser-Busch lagged the industry in the early part of the 1990s, the industry average debt to total assets ratio fell below Anheuser-Busch. This indicates that Anheuser-Busch maintained a

greater dollar amount of debt relative to total assets, in comparison to other firms in the industry.

- *Asset Utilization* – The asset utilization ratio (indicating the productiveness of a firm's assets) for Anheuser Busch is significantly lower than the industry average. One explanation for this could be that Anheuser-Busch has a greater percentage of newly purchased equipment on its balance sheet compared to the industry. This would mean that Anheuser-Busch would have more expensive assets on its balance, decreasing the apparent productivity via asset utilization, when compared to firms with a lower asset base. This holds true when one considers the definition of the asset utilization ratio: sales/net assets. The lower the asset-value on a firm's balance sheet, the greater the asset utilization ratio. As such, if Anheuser-Busch has newly purchased equipment on its balance sheet (thus increasing the asset value), it would be difficult to match the asset utilization ratio of other firms.
- *Return on Total Assets* – Anheuser-Busch and the industry average were relatively consistent over the decade.
- *Payout Ratio* – Anheuser-Busch and the industry average were relatively consistent over the decade.
- *Price/Earnings Ratio* – Anheuser-Busch and the industry average were relatively consistent over the decade.
- *Market to Book Value* – Anheuser-Busch held a slightly higher market to book value than firms in the industry. This is an indication that the market is satisfied with the future prospects of the company, as demonstrated by its stock price trading at a premium to book, and greater than that of other companies in the industry.

Dynamic ratio analysis was performed on two of the above mentioned ratios: current ratio and price earnings ratio. Using dynamic forecasting, the current ratio for fiscal year 2000 was calculated to be 1.3404. The current ratio forecasted using the Warren and Shelton model, however, was only 0.81. By analyzing the data used for both computations, it appears the dynamic ratio analysis result of 1.3404 may be more accurate. The reason being, dynamic ratio analysis used 10-years worth of data in constructing its forecast, whereas the Warren and Shelton model made projections based on 1999 results.

Dynamic ratio analysis was also used to forecast the 2000 price earnings ratio. The price earnings ratio was calculated as 19.39. Under the Warren and Shelton model, the 2000 price earnings ratio was estimated at 23.70. As of December 15, 2000, the company was trading at a trailing price earnings ratio of approximately 26. While the historical data used in dynamic ratio analysis for the calculation of the current ratio was superior (in some respects) to the prior year data used by the Warren and Shelton model, the Warrant and Shelton model appears to have been more sensitive to changing economic conditions (regarding market place valuation), than the dynamic ratio analysis model.

An analysis of per share data was also performed on Anheuser-Busch. Upon review of the quarterly stock price, one notices an upward trend over the years. The trend-line for quarterly dividends is also moving upward, however, the slope is much more predictable (as the company has been increasing dividends every four quarters, consistently). The earnings per share chart is somewhat more interesting than the price per share and dividends per share. Upon closer analysis, the earnings per share line has both seasonal and trend components. Typically, the first three quarters of the Company's fiscal year are higher (and greater than the last) than the fourth quarter, which is consistently lower than the others. For the 10-year period analyzed, however, earnings per share is still trending upward (in that, as an example, the earnings per share in fiscal year 1998 were greater than that in 1992). One might draw the conclusion that in the summer months, more alcoholic beverages are consumed, in comparison to the winter months.

The cost of capital to Anheuser-Busch was also calculated. The capital asset pricing model was used to determine the firm's cost. The cost of capital equation takes into account the market risk premium, as well as the volatility of the firm's stock price. The cost of capital of Anheuser-Busch was calculated as 10.16%.

The sustainable growth rate is another important calculation. This equation allows investors to determine the rate at which a firm can sustain growth without necessitating new funds. The sustainable growth rate for Anheuser-Busch was calculated at 14.88%. This is consistent with our results generated from the Warren and Shelton model, indicating that the firm has considerable excess funds, lending itself to the belief that it could grow at a rate greater than it is currently experiencing.

Option pricing theory was used to calculate the call and put options for Anheuser-Busch. The variation between the computed results and the actual market premium was largely due to our calculation of the stock's variance. Whereas for this exercise we calculated variance (and standard deviation) based on the stock price return over the trailing 30-day period, the market (one may argue) was calculating variance over a longer period.

The dividend forecasting analysis allowed us forecast the next dividend payment of Anheuser-Busch. This was made possible by using a multiple regression analysis, in which current earnings per share figures were regressed against prior period dividend payments. The result was a dividend forecast of approximately \$0.28 a share, which appears reasonable in light of the most recent dividend payments.

In the financial planning and forecasting section, sales growth rate was forecasted using three separate models. The Percentage Change Average Method result was used for the Warren and Shelton 20-equation model, as opposed to the sustainable growth rate and regression output. The Percentage Change Average Method result was selected because it more closely reflected the Company's growth in sales over the trailing 10-year period.

The Warren and Shelton model, (explained in greater detail in Section 8) allows an individual to construct pro forma income statements and balance sheets. Based on upon the output solicited from this model, it appears that Anheuser-Busch has a tremendous amount of untapped financial resource. Should the company decide to decrease its funds reserve, it is quite possible the 20% sustainable growth rate would be realized, resulting in greater stock price appreciation.

REFERENCES

The following sources were used in the preparation of this case-study:

Anheuser-Busch Companies 1999 Annual Report.

Brealey, R. A., & Myers, S. C. (2000). *Principles of Corporate Finance* (6th ed., pp. 161–165). Burr Ridge, IL: McGraw-Hill.

COMPUSTAT (2000). Burr Ridge, IL: McGraw-Hill.

Frees, E. W. (1996). *Data Analysis Using Regression Models: The Business Perspective* (pp. 516–559). Upper Saddle River, NJ: Prentice Hall.

http://rd.yahoo.com/dir/?http://finance.yahoo.com/

http://rbs.rutgers.edu/ ~ lee

http://www.frbchi.org/securities/rates.html

Lee, C. F., Lee, J. C., & Lee, A. C. (2000). *Statistics for Business and Financial Economics* (2nd ed., pp. 290, 738–740, 813–814, 835–836). World Scientific Publishing, Singapore.

Lee, C. F. (1984). *Financial Analysis and Planning: Theory and Application* (pp. 167–176, 627–631). Reading, Mass.: Addison-Wesley Publishing Company.

TABLES

Table 1. Balance Sheet.

ANHEUSER-BUSCH COS INC
ANNUAL BALANCE SHEET

TICKER:	**BUD**	**($ MILLIONS)**
SIC:	**2082**	
GICS:	**30201010**	

	Dec-99	Dec-98	Dec-97	Dec-96	Dec-95	Dec-94	Dec-93	Dec-92	Dec-91	Dec-90	Dec-89
ASSETS											
Cash & Equivalents	152.1	224.8	147.3	93.6	93.6	156.4	127.4	215	97.3	95.3	36.4
Net Receivables	629	610.1	713.4	632.7	544.3	784.6	751.1	649.8	654.8	562.6	527.8
Inventories	623.8	623.4	550.2	531.1	582.7	624.8	626.7	660.7	635.6	567.2	531.7
Prepaid Expenses	0	0	0	0	0	0	0	0	0	0	0
Other Current Assets	195.7	182.1	173	208.4	290	295.8	290	290.3	240	201.2	181
Total Current Assets	1,600.60	1,640.40	1,583.90	1,465.80	1,510.60	1,861.60	1,795.20	1,815.80	1,627.70	1,426.30	1,276.9(
Gross Plant,Property & Equipment	14,379.60	13,837.70	13,227.60	12,214.70	11,319.70	12,224.10	11,727.10	11,385.10	10,589.60	10,016.70	9,187.9(
Accumulated Depreciation	6,415.00	5,988.70	5,477.00	5,006.50	4,556.70	4,676.40	4,230.00	3,861.40	3,393.10	2,952.90	2,516.6(
Net Plant,Property & Equipment	7,964.60	7,849.00	7,750.60	7,208.20	6,763.00	7,547.70	7,497.10	7,523.70	7,196.50	7,063.80	6,671.3(
Investments at Equity	2,012.50	1,880.60	1,296.80	741.2	178.2	177.5	136.1	171.6	116.9	100.8	87.4
Other Investments	119	116.4	128.1	129.3	618.6	634.9	645.3	164.8	159.9	151.4	141.1
Intangibles	425	442.2	451.9	435.8	443.8	483.4	495.9	505.7	519.9	533.6	536.8
Deferred Charges	518.7	555.7	515.8	483.3	312.7	340.3	310.7	@CF	@CF	@CF	@CF
Other Assets	0	0	0	0	764	0	0	356.3	365.6	358.4	312.2
TOTAL ASSETS	12,640.40	12,484.30	11,727.10	10,463.60	10,590.90	11,045.40	10,880.30	10,537.90	9,986.50	9,634.30	9,025.7(
LIABILITIES											
Long Term Debt Due In One Year	@NA	@CF	@CF	@CF	@CF	@CF	@CF	@CF	@CF	@CF	104
Notes Payable	242.3	0	0	0	0	0	0	0	0	0	0
Accounts Payable	932.6	905.7	791.8	726.8	682.8	850.9	812.5	737.4	709.8	711.2	608
Taxes Payable	164.2	193.6	183.9	233	0	0	91	38.8	45.2	79.2	40
Accrued Expenses	263	256.3	224.3	227.6	333.3	448.9	609.7	426.7	392.7	391.1	337.6
Other Current Liabilities	385.1	374.7	300.7	243.5	225.9	369.2	302.4	256.9	255.1	230.4	213
Total Current Liabilities	1,987.20	1,730.30	1,500.70	1,430.90	1,242.00	1,669.00	1,815.60	1,459.80	1,402.80	1,411.90	1,302.6(
Long Term Debt	4,880.60	4,718.60	4,365.60	3,270.90	3,270.10	3,078.40	3,031.70	2,642.50	2,644.90	3,147.10	3,307.3(
Deferred Taxes	1,344.70	1,303.60	1,293.60	1,208.10	1,132.80	1,258.20	1,170.40	1,276.90	1,500.70	1,396.20	1,315.9(
Investment Tax Credit	0	0	0	0	0	0	0	0	0	0	0
Minority Interest	@IF	@IF	@IF	0	0	0	0	0	0	0	0
Other Liabilities	506.4	515.8	525.4	524.6	512.1	624.3	607.1	538.3	0	0	0
TOTAL LIABILITIES	8,718.90	8,268.30	7,685.30	6,434.50	6,157.00	6,629.90	6,624.80	5,917.50	5,548.40	5,955.20	5,925.8(
	Dec-99	**Dec-98**	**Dec-97**	**Dec-96**	**Dec-95**	**Dec-94**	**Dec-93**	**Dec-92**	**Dec-91**	**Dec-90**	**Dec-89**
EQUITY											
Preferred Stock - Redeemable	0	0	0	0	0	0	0	0	0	0	0
Preferred Stock - Nonredeemable	0	0	0	0	0	0	0	0	0	0	0
Total Preferred Stock	0	0	0	0	0	0	0	0	0	0	0
Common Stock	716.1	712.7	709.3	705.8	347.3	343.8	342.5	341.3	338.5	335.7	333.9
Capital Surplus	1,030.50	870.3	734.9	613.8	665.1	479.4	402.2	328.5	193.3	73.9	7.2
Retained Earnings	9,006.20	8,115.10	7,390.90	6,915.70	6,857.50	6,634.90	5,990.40	5,793.50	5,230.50	4,592.60	3,995.6(
Less: Treasury Stock	6,831.30	5,482.10	4,793.30	4,206.20	3,436.00	3,042.60	2,479.60	1,842.90	1,324.20	1,323.10	1,236.8(
Common Equity	3,921.50	4,216.00	4,041.80	4,029.10	4,433.90	4,415.50	4,255.50	4,620.40	4,438.10	3,679.10	3,099.9(
TOTAL EQUITY	3,921.50	4,216.00	4,041.80	4,029.10	4,433.90	4,415.50	4,255.50	4,620.40	4,438.10	3,679.10	3,099.9(
TOTAL LIABILITIES & EQUITY	12,640.40	12,484.30	11,727.10	10,463.60	10,590.90	11,045.40	10,880.30	10,537.90	9,986.50	9,634.30	9,025.7(
COMMON SHARES OUTSTANDING	461.1	476.6	487.02	497.357	507.952	514.58	534.074	556.804	570.104	564.612	565.97‹

Table 2. Balance Sheet (continued).

ANHEUSER-BUSCH COS INC
ANNUAL BALANCE SHEET

TICKER: BUD
SIC: 2082
GICS: 30201010

($ MILLIONS)

	Dec-90	Dec-89	Dec-88	Dec-87	Dec-86	Dec-85	Dec-84	Dec-83	Dec-82	Dec-81	Dec-80
ASSETS											
Cash & Equivalents	95.3	36.4	63.9	111.3	69.4	169.6	78.6	218.4	21.5	93.6	14
Net Receivables	562.6	527.8	463.1	382.5	373	301.7	275.6	283.6	243.5	147.7	142.7
Inventories	567.2	531.7	512.2	451.9	427.8	337.7	315.9	298.8	307.8	228.4	233.5
Prepaid Expenses	0	0	0	0	0	0	0	0	0	0	0
Other Current Assets	201.2	181	155.1	179.6	150.4	156.5	106.2	96.8	119	69.6	49
Total Current Assets	1,426.30	1,276.90	1,194.30	1,125.30	1,020.60	965.5	776.3	897.6	691.8	539.3	439.2
Gross Plant,Property & Equipment	10,016.70	9,187.90	7,643.00	6,816.60	6,099.30	5,340.80	4,800.60	4,313.90	3,980.40	3,101.30	2,696.40
Accumulated Depreciation	2,952.90	2,516.60	2,175.30	1,902.50	1,671.70	1,454.90	1,285.60	1,109.70	991.5	843.7	749
Net Plant,Property & Equipment	7,063.80	6,671.30	5,467.70	4,914.10	4,427.60	3,885.90	3,515.00	3,204.20	2,988.90	2,257.60	1,947.40
Investments at Equity	100.8	87.4	82.3	146.6	99.7	56.7	42.9	57.7	58.9	46.8	35.4
Other Investments	151.4	141.1	34.9	13.9	16.5	16.5	18.1	9.1	9.1	9.1	9.1
Intangibles	533.6	536.8	104.9	120.4	137.8	99.3	85.3	87.9	77.4	0	0
Deferred Charges	@CF	@CF	@CF	@CF	@CF	@CF	@CF	@CF	@CF	@CF	@CF
Other Assets	358.4	312.2	225.7	171.3	131.6	97.5	87.1	73.7	76.7	22.4	18.7
TOTAL ASSETS	9,634.30	9,025.70	7,109.80	6,491.60	5,833.80	5,121.38	4,524.70	4,330.18	3,902.80	2,875.20	2,449.80
LIABILITIES											
Long Term Debt Due In One Year	@CF	104	29	23.8	23.1	24.5	15.9	14.9	4.9	49	34.9
Notes Payable	0	0	0.7	0.9	34.7	0	0	0	25	29.5	16.3
Accounts Payable	711.2	608	568.7	539.6	491.7	425.3	338.2	327.8	306.2	209.8	168
Taxes Payable	79.2	40	75.2	45.5	71.8	31.3	39	48.4	26.4	5.3	21.6
Accrued Expenses	391.1	337.6	339	295.5	274.7	264.1	220.7	236.7	223.6	168.8	128.2
Other Current Liabilities	230.4	213	166.5	137.1	119.6	92.6	82.2	94.7	59.9	31	31.3
Total Current Liabilities	1,411.90	1,302.60	1,179.10	1,042.40	1,015.60	837.8	696	722.5	646	493.4	400.3
Long Term Debt	3,147.10	3,307.30	1,615.30	1,396.50	1,126.80	861.3	835.8	961.4	969	817.3	743.8
Deferred Taxes	1,396.20	1,315.90	1,212.50	1,160.50	1,090.80	961.7	755	573.2	455.1	357.7	267.7
Investment Tax Credit	0	0	0	0	0	0	0	0	0	0	0
Minority Interest	0	0	0	0	@CF	@CF	0	20.6	21.1	0	0
Other Liabilities	0	0	0	0	0	0	0	0	0	0	0
TOTAL LIABILITIES	5,955.20	5,925.80	4,006.90	3,599.40	3,233.20	2,660.80	2,286.80	2,277.70	2,091.20	1,668.40	1,411.80

	Dec-90	Dec-89	Dec-88	Dec-87	Dec-86	Dec-85	Dec-84	Dec-83	Dec-82	Dec-81	Dec-80
EQUITY											
Preferred Stock - Redeemable	0	0	0	0	286.9	287.6	@NA	@NA	@NA	@NA	@NA
Preferred Stock - Nonredeemable	0	0	0	0	0	0	0	0	0	0	0
Total Preferred Stock	0	0	0	0	286.9	287.6	286.9	286	285	0	0
Common Stock	335.7	333.9	331	326.9	295.3	146.6	48.6	48.5	48.4	45.5	45.2
Capital Surplus	73.9	7.2	428.5	332.4	6.1	90.4	173.2	167.2	162.7	66.4	57.5
Retained Earnings	4,592.60	3,995.60	3,455.80	2,928.40	2,473.10	2,137.90	1,822.70	1,551.70	1,316.40	1,094.90	935.3
Less: Treasury Stock	1,323.10	1,236.80	1,112.40	695.5	460.8	201.9	93.5	0.9	0.9	@CF	@CF
Common Equity	3,679.10	3,099.90	3,102.90	2,892.20	2,313.70	2,173.00	1,951.00	1,766.50	1,526.60	1,206.80	1,038.00
TOTAL EQUITY	3,679.10	3,099.90	3,102.90	2,892.20	2,600.60	2,460.60	2,237.90	2,052.50	1,811.60	1,206.80	1,038.00
TOTAL LIABILITIES & EQUITY	9,634.30	9,025.70	7,109.80	6,491.60	5,833.80	5,121.38	4,524.70	4,330.18	3,902.80	2,875.20	2,449.80
COMMON SHARES OUTSTANDING	564.612	565.974	566.812	585.998	537.73	554.08	564.936	580.74	579.504	545.856	542.208

Table 3. Income Statement.

ANHEUSER-BUSCH COS INC
ANNUAL INCOME STATEMENT

TICKER:	BUD	**($ MILLIONS, EXCEPT PER SHARE)**
SIC:	2082	
GICS:	30201010	

	Dec-99	Dec-98	Dec-97	Dec-96	Dec-95	Dec-94	Dec-93	Dec-92	Dec-91	Dec-90	Dec-89
Sales	11,703.70	11,245.80	11,066.20	10,883.70	10,340.50	12,053.80	11,505.30	11,393.70	10,996.30	10,743.60	9,481.30
Cost of Goods Sold	6,477.40	6,424.10	6,413.20	6,370.70	6,225.40	7,156.90	6,825.60	6,756.30	6,628.80	6,612.00	5,869.40
Gross Profit	5,226.30	4,821.70	4,653.00	4,513.00	4,115.10	4,896.90	4,679.70	4,637.40	4,367.50	4,131.60	3,611.90
Selling, General, & Administrative Expense	2,147.00	1,958.00	1,916.30	1,890.00	1,756.60	2,370.30	2,308.70	2,308.90	2,126.10	2,051.10	1,876.80
Operating Income Before Deprec.	3,079.30	2,863.70	2,736.70	2,623.00	2,358.50	2,526.60	2,371.00	2,328.50	2,241.40	2,080.50	1,735.10
Depreciation, Depletion, & Amortization	777	738.4	683.7	593.9	565.6	627.5	594.1	552.8	519.9	481.5	406.4
Operating Profit	2,302.30	2,125.30	2,053.00	2,029.10	1,792.90	1,899.10	1,776.90	1,775.70	1,721.50	1,599.00	1,328.70
Interest Expense	307.8	291.5	261.2	232.8	225.9	221.4	207.8	199.6	238.5	283	177.9
Non-Operating Income/Expense	170.6	103.8	91	41.9	54.7	29.4	46.3	39.1	37.6	36.1	75.9
Special Items	0	@CF	0	54.7	-160	0	-565	0	0	0	0
Pretax Income	2,165.10	1,937.60	1,882.80	1,892.90	1,461.70	1,707.10	1,050.40	1,615.20	1,520.60	1,352.10	1,226.70
Total Income Taxes	762.9	704.3	703.6	736.8	575.1	675	455.9	621	580.8	509.7	459.5
Minority Interest	@IF	@IF	@IF	0	0	0	0	0	0	0	0
Income Before Extraordinary Items & Discontinued Operations	1,402.20	1,233.30	1,179.20	1,156.10	886.6	1,032.10	594.5	994.2	939.8	842.4	767.2
Preferred Dividends	0	0	0	0	0	0	0	0	0	0	0
Available for Common	1,402.20	1,233.30	1,179.20	1,156.10	886.6	1,032.10	594.5	994.2	939.8	842.4	767.2
Savings Due to Common Stock Equivalents	0	0	0	0	0	0	0	0	0	0	0
Adjusted Available for Common	1,402.20	1,233.30	1,179.20	1,156.10	886.6	1,032.10	594.5	994.2	939.8	842.4	767.2
Extraordinary Items	0	0	-10	0	0	0	0	-76.7	0	0	0
Discontinued Operations	0	0	0	33.8	-244.3	0	0	0	0	0	0
Adjusted Net Income	1,402.20	1,233.30	1,169.20	1,189.90	642.3	1,032.10	594.5	917.5	939.8	842.4	767.2

PER SHARE DATA	Dec-99	Dec-98	Dec-97	Dec-96	Dec-95	Dec-94	Dec-93	Dec-92	Dec-91	Dec-90	Dec-89
Earnings Per Share Basic - Excluding Extra Items & Disc Op	2.99	2.56	2.39	2.28	1.72	1.96	1.09	1.74	1.63	1.48	1.34
Earnings Per Share Basic - Including Extra Items & Disc Op	2.99	2.56	2.37	2.35	1.25	1.96	1.09	1.61	1.63	1.48	1.34
Earnings Per Share Diluted- Excluding Extra Items & Disc Op	2.94	2.53	2.36	2.27	1.71	1.94	1.09	1.73	1.63	1.48	1.34
Earning Per Share Diluted - Including Extra Items & Disc Op	2.94	2.53	2.34	2.34	1.25	1.94	1.09	1.6	1.63	1.48	1.34
EPS Basic from Operations	2.99	2.57	2.39	2.15	1.91	1.96	1.72	1.74	1.63	1.48	1.34
EPS Diluted from Ops	2.94	2.54	@NA	@NA	@NA	@NA	@NA	@NA	@NA	@NA	@NA
Dividends Per Share	1.16	1.08	1	0.92	0.84	0.76	0.68	0.6	0.53	0.47	0.4
Com Shares for Basic Eps	469.5	482.1	492.6	505.8	515.8	528.2	548.6	571.6	575.8	569.2	572.4
Com Shares for Diluted EPS	476.8	487.5	499.7	510.6	524.4	538	558.6	581.6	585.8	579.4	@NA

Table 4. Income Statement (continued).

ANHEUSER-BUSCH COS INC
ANNUAL INCOME STATEMENT

TICKER:	BUD	MILLIONS, EXCEPT PER SHARE)
SIC:	2082	
GICS:	30201010	

	Dec-89	Dec-88	Dec-87	Dec-86	Dec-85	Dec-84	Dec-83	Dec-82	Dec-81	Dec-80
Sales	9,481.30	8,924.10	8,258.40	7,677.20	7,000.30	6,501.20	6,034.20	4,576.60	3,847.20	3,295.40
Cost of Goods Sold	5,869.40	5,469.80	4,998.60	4,695.00	4,442.50	4,213.10	3,927.90	3,198.50	2,866.80	2,454.50
Gross Profit	3,611.90	3,454.30	3,259.80	2,982.20	2,557.80	2,288.10	2,106.30	1,378.10	980.4	840.901
Selling, General, & Administrative Expense	1,876.80	1,834.50	1,819.00	1,702.90	1,491.90	1,332.30	1,220.20	752	515	428.6
Operating Income Before Deprec.	1,735.10	1,619.80	1,440.80	1,279.30	1,065.90	955.802	886.1	626.099	465.4	412.301
Depreciation, Depletion, & Amortization	406.4	355.7	311.7	274.2	233.6	201.1	185.3	133.2	108.7	99.4
Operating Profit	1,328.70	1,264.10	1,129.10	1,005.10	832.301	754.701	700.8	492.899	356.7	312.901
Interest Expense	177.9	141.6	124.4	96.9	93.4	102.7	111.4	89.2	89.6	75.6
Non-Operating Income/Expense	75.9	37.6	51.4	33	41.6	37.8	26.6	50.1	58.1	34.2
Special Items	0	0	0	@CF	@CF	@CF	0	20.4	0	0
Pretax Income	1,226.70	1,160.10	1,056.10	941.2	780.5	689.8	616	474.2	325.2	271.5
Total Income Taxes	459.5	444.2	441.4	423.2	336.8	298.3	268	186.9	107.8	99.7
Minority Interest	0	0	@CF	@CF	@CF	@CF	@IF	@IF	0	0
Income Before Extraordinary Items & Discontinued Operations	767.2	715.9	614.7	518	443.7	391.5	348	287.3	217.4	171.8
Preferred Dividends	0	0	20.9	27.9	28	27.9	30.7	0	0	0
Available for Common	767.2	715.9	593.8	490.1	415.7	363.6	317.3	287.3	217.4	171.8
Savings Due to Common Stock Equivalents	0	0	20.9	27.9	28	27.9	30.7	0	0	0
Adjusted Available for Common	767.2	715.9	614.7	518	443.7	391.5	348	287.3	217.4	171.8
Extraordinary Items	0	0	0	0	0	0	0	0	0	0
Discontinued Operations	0	0	0	0	0	0	0	0	0	0
Adjusted Net Income	767.2	715.9	614.7	518	443.7	391.5	348	287.3	217.4	171.8

PER SHARE DATA	Dec-89	Dec-88	Dec-87	Dec-86	Dec-85	Dec-84	Dec-83	Dec-82	Dec-81	Dec-80
Earnings Per Share Basic - Excluding Extra Items & Disc Op	1.34	1.23	1.02	0.85	0.71	0.62	0.54	0.5	0.4	0.32
Earnings Per Share Basic - Including Extra Items & Disc Op	1.34	1.23	1.02	0.85	0.71	0.62	0.54	0.5	0.4	0.32
Earnings Per Share Diluted- Excluding Extra Items & Disc Op	1.34	1.23	1.02	0.85	0.71	0.62	0.54	0.49	0.38	0.32
Earning Per Share Diluted - Including Extra Items & Disc Op	1.34	1.23	1.02	0.85	0.71	0.62	0.54	0.49	0.38	0.32
EPS Basic from Operations	1.34	1.23	@NA	@NA	@NA	@NA	@NA	@NA	@NA	@NA
EPS Diluted from Ops	@NA	@NA	@NA	@NA	@NA	@NA	@NA	@NA	@NA	@NA
Dividends Per Share	0.4	0.33	0.27	0.22	0.18	0.16	0.14	0.11	0.09	0.08
Com Shares for Basic Eps	572.4	584.4	603	613.246	625.2	634.8	642	577.2	544.8	542.4
Com Shares for Diluted EPS	@NA	@NA	@NA	@NA	@NA	@NA	@NA	@NA	@NA	@NA

Table 5. Cash Flow.

ANHEUSER-BUSCH COS INC					
ANNUAL STATEMENT OF CASH FLOWS					
TICKER:	BUD		**($ MILLIONS)**		
SIC:	2082				
GICS:	30201010				
	Dec-99	**Dec-98**	**Dec-97**	**Dec-96**	**Dec-95**
INDIRECT OPERATING ACTIVITIES					
Income Before Extraordinary Items	1,402.20	1,233.30	1,179.20	1,156.10	886.6
Depreciation and Amortization	777	738.4	683.7	593.9	565.6
Extraordinary Items and Disc. Operations	0	0	0	52	-11
Deferred Taxes	40.3	34.5	91.4	93.8	51.3
Equity in Net Loss (Earnings)	-155.5	-53.7	-49.9	@CF	@CF
Sale of Property, Plant, and Equipment and Sale of Investments - Loss (Gain)	0	0	0	-33.4	0
Funds from Operations - Other	38.6	-27.1	-93.2	-75.2	184.4
Receivables - Decrease (Increase)	-18.9	103.3	-80.7	-88.4	54.2
Inventory - Decrease (Increase)	-0.4	-73.2	-19.1	51.6	-51.9
Accounts Payable and Accrued Liabs - Inc (Dec)	33.6	145.9	61.7	24.6	-126.2
Income Taxes - Accrued - Increase (Decrease)	-29.4	9.7	-49.1	146.7	@CF
Other Assets and Liabilities - Net Change	-3.2	64.9	92.6	99.2	-138.1
Operating Activities - Net Cash Flow	2,084.30	2,176.00	1,816.60	2,020.90	1,414.90
INVESTING ACTIVITIES					
Investments - Increase	0	0	0	0	0
Sale of Investments	0	0	0	0	0
Short-Term Investments - Change	0	0	0	0	0
Capital Expenditures	865.3	817.5	1,199.30	1,084.60	952.5
Sale of Property, Plant, and Equipment	@CF	0	0	@CF	0
Acquisitions	7	566.5	683.3	135.7	82.9
Investing Activities - Other	59.6	0	0	116.6	0
Investing Activities - Net Cash Flow	-812.7	-1,384.00	-1,882.60	-1,103.70	-1,035.40
FINANCING ACTIVITIES					
Sale of Common and Preferred Stock	129.9	107.4	95.1	113.4	159
Purchase of Common and Preferred Stock	1,349.20	688.8	587.1	770.2	393.4
Cash Dividends	544.7	521	492.6	458.9	429.5
Long-Term Debt - Issuance	973.4	451.5	1,245.90	773.6	597.6
Long-Term Debt - Reduction	553.7	63.6	141.6	575.1	363.6
Current Debt - Changes	@CF	@CF	@CF	@CF	@CF
Financing Activities - Other	0	0	0	0	0
Financing Activities - Net Cash Flow	-1,344.30	-714.5	119.7	-917.2	-429.9
Exchange Rate Effect	0	0	0	0	0
Cash and Equivalents - Change	-72.7	77.5	53.7	0	-50.4
DIRECT OPERATING ACTIVITIES					
Interest Paid - Net	286.9	263.3	205.1	208	198
Income Taxes Paid	706.2	644.3	609.5	533.6	546.6
SUPPLEMENTAL STATEMENT OF FINANCIAL POSITION					
Total Funds from Operations	@NA	@NA	@NA	@NA	@NA
Other Sources of Funds	@NA	@NA	@NA	@NA	@NA
Total Sources of Funds	@NA	@NA	@NA	@NA	@NA
Total Working Capital Change	@NA	@NA	@NA	@NA	@NA
Other Uses of Funds	@NA	@NA	@NA	@NA	@NA
Total Uses of Funds	@NA	@NA	@NA	@NA	@NA
Working Capital Changes - Other - Inc (Dec)	@NA	@NA	@NA	@NA	@NA
Format Code	7	7	7	7	7
ANNUAL STATEMENT OF CASH FLOWS FOOTNOTE DESCRIPTIONS					
Capital	Dec-99				
Expend	Dec-98				
Note	Dec-97				
Dec-96					

Table 6. Retained Earnings Statement.

CONSOLIDATED STATEMENT OF CHANGES IN SHAREHOLDERS EQUITY
Anheuser-Busch Companies and Subsidiaries

YEAR ENDED DECEMBER 31 (in millions, except per share)

	1999	1998	1997
COMMON STOCK			
Balance, beginning of period	$712.7	$709.3	$705.8
Shares issued under stock plans	3.4	3.4	3.5
Balance, end of period	$716.1	$712.7	$709.3
CAPITAL IN EXCESS OF PAR VALUE			
Balance, beginning of period	$1,117.5	$1,017.0	$929.2
Shares issued under stock plans	123.5	100.5	87.8
Balance, end of period	$1,241.0	$1,117.5	$1,017.0
RETAINED EARNINGS			
Balance, beginning of period	$8,320.7	$7,604.9	$6,924.5
Net income	1,402.2	1,233.3	1,169.2
Common dividend paid (per share: 1999 - $1.16; 1998 - $1.08; 1997 - $1.00)	(544.7)	(521.0)	(492.6)
Shares issued under stock plans	3.0	3.5	3.8
Balance, end of period	$9,181.2	$8,320.7	$7,604.9
TREASURY STOCK			
Balance, beginning of period	($5,482.1)	($4,793.3)	($4,206.2)
Treasuru stock acquired	1,349.2	688.8	587.1
Balance, end of period	($6,831.3)	($5,482.1)	($4,793.3)
ESOP DEBT GUARANTEE			
Balance, beginning of period	($247.2)	($282.1)	($315.4)
Annual debt service	36.7	34.9	33.3
Balance, end of period	($210.5)	($247.2)	($282.1)
ACCUMULATED OTHER COMPREHENSIVE INCOME			
Balance, beginning of period	($205.6)	($214.0)	($8.8)
Foreign currency translation adjustment	30.6	8.4	(205.2)
Balance, end of period	($175.0)	($205.6)	($214.0)
TOTAL SHAREHOLDERS EQUITY	$3,921.5	$4,216.0	$4,041.8
COMPREHENSIVE INCOME			
Net income	$1,402.2	$1,233.3	$1,169.2
Foreign currency translation adjustment	30.6	8.4	(205.2)
TOTAL COMPREHENSIVE INCOME	$1,432.8	$1,241.7	$964.0

Table 7. Current Ratio Results – Mean Calculation.

Current Ratio Results - Mean Calculation

Year	Anheuser-Busch
1990	1.01
1991	1.16
1992	1.24
1993	0.99
1994	1.12
1995	1.22
1996	1.02
1997	1.06
1998	0.95
1999	0.81
Total	10.58
Number of Years	10
Mean	**1.058**

Table 8. Price/Earnings Ratio Results – Mean Calculation..

Price/Earnings Ratio Results - Mean Calculation

Year	Anheuser-Busch
1990	11.36
1991	15.07
1992	14.83
1993	18.90
1994	11.21
1995	26.75
1996	17.02
1997	18.57
1998	25.63
1999	23.70
Total	183.04
Number of Years	10
Mean	**18.304**

Table 9. Current Ratio Results – Median Calculation.

Current Ratio Results - Median Calculation	
Year	**Anheuser-Busch**
1990	1.01
1991	1.16
1992	1.24
1993	0.99
1994	1.12
1995	1.22
1996	1.02
1997	1.06
1998	0.95
1999	0.81
Midpoint Avgs	1.17
Median	**1.17**

Table 10. Price/Earnings Ratio Results – Median Calculation.

Price/Earnings Ratio Results - Median Calculation	
Year	**Anheuser-Busch**
1990	11.36
1991	15.07
1992	14.83
1993	18.90
1994	11.21
1995	26.75
1996	17.02
1997	18.57
1998	25.63
1999	23.70
Midpoint Avgs	18.98
Median	**18.98**

Table 11. Current Ratio Results – Variance Calculation.

Current Ratio Results - Variance Calculation

Anheuser-Busch

Year	Results (X_i)	Mean (X_{bar})	$(X_i - X_{bar})^2$
1990	1.01	1.058	0.0023
1991	1.16	1.058	0.0104
1992	1.24	1.058	0.0331
1993	0.99	1.058	0.0046
1994	1.12	1.058	0.0038
1995	1.22	1.058	0.0262
1996	1.02	1.058	0.0014
1997	1.06	1.058	0.0000
1998	0.95	1.058	0.0117
1999	0.81	1.058	0.0615
			0.1552
		Divide by n-1 observations	9
		Variance	0.01724

Table 12. Price/Earnings Results – Variance Calculation.

Price/Earnings Results - Variance Calculation

Anheuser-Busch

Year	Results (X_i)	Mean (X_{bar})	$(X_i - X_{bar})^2$
1990	11.36	18.30	48.2191
1991	15.07	18.30	10.4588
1992	14.83	18.30	12.0687
1993	18.90	18.30	0.3552
1994	11.21	18.30	50.3248
1995	26.75	18.30	71.3349
1996	17.02	18.30	1.6487
1997	18.57	18.30	0.0708
1998	25.63	18.30	53.6703
1999	23.70	18.30	29.1168
			277.2680
	Divide by n-1 observations		9
		Variance	30.8076

Table 13. Current Ratio – Standard Deviation.

Current Ratio - Standard Deviation

	Anheuser-Busch
Variance	0.01724
Std Dev.	**0.1313**

Table 14. Price/Earnings Ratio – Standard Deviation.

Price/Earnings Ratio - Standard Deviation

	Anheuser-Busch
Variance	30.8076
Std Dev.	**5.5505**

Table 15. Current Ratio – Coefficient of Variation Calculation.

Current Ratio - Coefficient of Variation Calculation

	Anheuser-Busch
Standard Deviation	0.1313
Mean	1.058
Coefficient of Variation (CV)	**0.1241**

Table 16. Price/Earnings Ratio – Coefficient of Variation Calculation.

Price/Earnings Ratio - Coefficient of Variation Calculation

	Anheuser-Busch
Standard Deviation	5.5505
Mean	18.3
Coefficient of Variation (CV)	**0.3033**

Table 17. Current Ratio Results – Skewness Calculation.

Current Ratio Results - Skewness Calculation

Anheuser-Busch

Year	Results (X_i)	Mean (X_{bar})	$(X_i - X_{bar})^3$
1990	1.01	1.058	-0.0001
1991	1.16	1.058	0.0011
1992	1.24	1.058	0.0060
1993	0.99	1.058	-0.0003
1994	1.12	1.058	0.0002
1995	1.22	1.058	0.0043
1996	1.02	1.058	-0.0001
1997	1.06	1.058	0.0000
1998	0.95	1.058	-0.0013
1999	0.81	1.058	-0.0153
			-0.0054
		Divide by n observations	10
		Skewness	-0.0005413

Table 18. Price/Earnings Results – Skewness Calculation.

Price/Earnings Results - Skewness Calculation

Anheuser-Busch

Year	Results (X_i)	Mean (X_{bar})	$(X_i - X_{bar})^3$
1990	11.36	18.3	-334.2554
1991	15.07	18.3	-33.6983
1992	14.83	18.3	-41.7819
1993	18.9	18.3	0.2160
1994	11.21	18.3	-356.4008
1995	26.75	18.3	603.3511
1996	17.02	18.3	-2.0972
1997	18.57	18.3	0.0197
1998	25.63	18.3	393.8328
1999	23.7	18.3	157.4640
			386.6501
		Divide by n observations	10
		Skewness	38.665009

Table 19. Current Ratio – Coefficient of Skewness Calculation.

Current Ratio - Coefficient of Skewness Calculation

	Anheuser-Busch
Skewness	-0.000541
Standard Deviation	0.1313
Coefficient of Skewness (CS)	**-0.004123**

Table 20. Price/Earnings Ratio – Coefficient of Skewness Calculation.

Price/Earnings Ratio - Coefficient of Skewness Calculation

	Anheuser-Busch
Skewness	38.665009
Standard Deviation	5.5505
Coefficient of Skewness (CS)	**6.966041**

Table 21. Current Ratio Results – Kurtosis Calculation.

Current Ratio Results - Kurtosis Calculation

Anheuser-Busch

Year	Results (X_i)	Mean (X_{bar})	$(X_i - X_{bar})^4$
1990	1.01	1.058	0.0000
1991	1.16	1.058	0.0001
1992	1.24	1.058	0.0011
1993	0.99	1.058	0.0000
1994	1.12	1.058	0.0000
1995	1.22	1.058	0.0007
1996	1.02	1.058	0.0000
1997	1.06	1.058	0.0000
1998	0.95	1.058	0.0001
1999	0.81	1.058	0.0038
			0.0059
		Divide by n observations	10
		Kurtosis	0.00058565

Table 22. Price/Earnings Ratio Results – Kurtosis Calculation.

Price/Earnings Ratio Results - Kurtosis Calculation

		Anheuser-Busch	
Year	**Results (X_i)**	**Mean (X_{bar})**	**$(X_i - X_{bar})^4$**
1990	11.36	18.30	2,319.73
1991	15.07	18.30	108.85
1992	14.83	18.30	144.98
1993	18.90	18.30	0.13
1994	11.21	18.30	2,526.88
1995	26.75	18.30	5,098.32
1996	17.02	18.30	2.68
1997	18.57	18.30	0.01
1998	25.63	18.30	2,886.79
1999	23.70	18.30	850.31
			13,938.6795
		Divide by n observations	10
		Kurtosis	1,393.87

Table 23. Industry Results – Current Ratio & Price/Earnings Ratio.

Industry Results - Current Ratio & Price/Earnings Ratio

Year	Current Ratio	Price/Earnings Ratio
1990	1.11	10.41
1991	1.30	13.82
1992	1.39	14.91
1993	1.19	16.42
1994	1.29	9.81
1995	1.41	17.58
1996	1.26	18.88
1997	1.32	18.85
1998	1.21	25.49
1999	1.11	22.87
Total	12.59	169.04
Number of Years	10	10
Mean	**1.259**	**16.904**

Table 24. Current Ratio Results – Regression Calculation.

Current Ratio Results - Regression Calculation

Y_t	X_{t-1}	Y_{t-1}
1.24	1.11	1.16
0.99	1.30	1.24
1.12	1.39	0.99
1.22	1.19	1.12
1.02	1.29	1.22
1.06	1.41	1.02
0.95	1.26	1.06
0.81	1.32	0.95

Variable Definitions

Y_t - current ratio for Anheuser-Bush in period t

X_{t-1} - industry average for current ratio in period t-1

Y_{t-1} - current ratio for Anheuser-Busch in period t-1

Table 25. Summary Output.

SUMMARY OUTPUT

Regression Statistics	
Multiple R	0.4948
R Square	0.2449
Adjusted R	-0.0572
Standard Er	0.1465
Observation	8

ANOVA

	df	*SS*	*MS*	*F*	*Significance F*
Regression	2	0.0348	0.0174	0.8106	0.4955
Residual	5	0.1073	0.0215		
Total	7	0.1421			

	Coefficients	*Standard Error*	*t Stat*	*P-value*	*Lower 95%*	*Upper 95%*	*Lower 95.0%*	*Upper 95.0%*
Intercept	1.6760	1.2634	1.3266	0.2420	-1.5717	4.9237	-1.5717	4.9237
Xt-1	-0.6180	0.6383	-0.9682	0.3774	-2.2588	1.0228	-2.2588	1.0228
Yt-1	0.1540	0.5887	0.2616	0.8041	-1.3593	1.6673	-1.3593	1.6673

Table 26. Price/Earnings Results – Regression Calculation.

Price/Earnings Results - Regression Calculation

Y_t	X_{t-1}	Y_{t-1}
15.07	10.41	11.36
14.83	13.82	15.07
18.90	14.91	14.83
11.21	16.42	18.90
26.75	9.81	11.21
17.02	17.58	26.75
18.57	18.88	17.02
25.63	18.85	18.57

Variable Definitions

Y_t - price/earnings ratio for Anheuser-Bush in period t

X_{t-1} - industry average for price/earnings ratio in period t-1

Y_{t-1} - price/earnings ratio for Anheuser-Busch in period t-1

Table 27. Summary Output.

SUMMARY OUTPUT

Regression Statistics	
Multiple R	0.2489
R Square	0.0620
Adjusted R	-0.3132
Standard Er	6.1198
Observation	8

ANOVA

	df	*SS*	*MS*	*F*	*Significance F*
Regression	2	12.3716	6.1858	0.1652	0.8522
Residual	5	187.2609	37.4522		
Total	7	199.6326			

	Coefficients	*Standard Error*	*t Stat*	*P-value*	*Lower 95%*	*Upper 95%*	*Lower 95.0%*	*Upper 95.0%*
Intercept	20.3988	10.0982	2.0200	0.0994	-5.5595	46.3571	-5.5595	46.3571
Xt-1	0.3011	0.9836	0.3061	0.7719	-2.2275	2.8296	-2.2275	2.8296
Yt-1	-0.3855	0.6986	-0.5518	0.6048	-2.1813	1.4104	-2.1813	1.4104

Table 28. Current Ratio – Dynamic Analysis Comparison.

	Current Ratio - Dynamic Analysis Comparison	
	Anheuser-Busch	**PSE&G**
Mean	1.058	0.683
Median	1.17	0.673
Variance	0.01724	0.009
Standard Deviation	0.1313	0.095
Coefficient of Variation	0.1241	1.4
Skewness	-0.0005413	-0.551
Coefficient of Skewness	-0.004123	635.188
Kurtosis	0.00058565	0.308
2000 Forecast	**1.3464**	**0.6054**

Table 29. Price/Earnings Ratio – Dynamic Analysis Comparison.

	Price/Earnings Ratio - Dynamic Analysis Comparison	
	Anheuser-Busch	**PSE&G**
Mean	18.304	8.495
Median	18.98	8.211
Variance	30.8076	5.48
Standard Deviation	5.5505	2.341
Coefficient of Variation	0.3033	0.276
Skewness	38.665009	0.574
Coefficient of Skewness	6.966041	0.045
Kurtosis	1393.87	0.015
2000 Forecast	**19.39**	**11.93**

Table 30. Calculation of Average Monthly Return.

Calculation of Average Monthly Return

	Anheuser-Busch			S&P 500		
Date	Open	Close	Return	Open	Close	Return
Oct-00	42.13	45.75	0.0861	1,436.52	1,429.40	-0.0050
Sep-00	39.38	42.31	0.0746	1,517.68	1,436.51	-0.0535
Aug-00	40.28	39.41	-0.0214	1,430.83	1,517.68	0.0607
Jul-00	37.20	40.09	0.0778	1,454.60	1,430.83	-0.0163
Jun-00	38.47	37.20	-0.0332	1,420.60	1,454.60	0.0239
May-00	34.88	38.60	0.1067	1,452.43	1,420.60	-0.0219
Apr-00	31.00	35.00	0.1290	1,498.58	1,452.43	-0.0308
Mar-00	31.81	30.88	-0.0292	1,366.42	1,498.58	0.0967
Feb-00	33.45	31.74	-0.0511	1,394.46	1,366.42	-0.0201
Jan-00	34.75	33.33	-0.0409	1,469.25	1,394.46	-0.0509
Dec-99	37.03	35.00	-0.0550	1,388.91	1,469.25	0.0578
Nov-99	35.34	36.94	0.0452	1,362.93	1,389.07	0.0192
Oct-99	34.67	35.37	0.0204	1,282.71	1,362.93	0.0625
Sep-99	37.86	34.45	-0.0901	1,320.41	1,282.71	-0.0286
Aug-99	38.63	37.86	-0.0198	1,328.72	1,320.41	-0.0063
Jul-99	34.99	38.66	0.1050	1,372.71	1,328.72	-0.0320
Jun-99	35.88	34.74	-0.0316	1,301.84	1,372.71	0.0544
May-99	35.67	35.78	0.0032	1,335.18	1,301.84	-0.0250
Apr-99	37.13	35.67	-0.0394	1,286.37	1,335.18	0.0379
Mar-99	37.41	37.13	-0.0073	1,238.33	1,286.37	0.0388
Feb-99	34.07	37.41	0.0981	1,279.64	1,238.33	-0.0323
Jan-99	31.91	34.34	0.0761	1,229.23	1,279.64	0.0410
Dec-98	29.60	31.88	0.0769	1,163.63	1,229.23	0.0564
Nov-98	28.64	29.45	0.0283	1,098.67	1,163.63	0.0591
Oct-98	25.74	28.76	0.1174	1,017.01	1,098.67	0.0803
Sep-98	22.30	26.10	0.1707	957.28	1,017.01	0.0624
Aug-98	24.82	22.60	-0.0894	1,120.67	957.28	-0.1458
Jul-98	22.75	24.91	0.0951	1,133.84	1,120.67	-0.0116
Jun-98	22.14	22.69	0.0244	1,090.82	1,133.84	0.0394
May-98	21.99	22.08	0.0043	1,111.75	1,090.82	-0.0188
Apr-98	22.26	21.90	-0.0161	1,101.75	1,111.75	0.0091
Mar-98	22.35	22.11	-0.0107	1,049.34	1,101.75	0.0499
Feb-98	21.39	22.41	0.0477	980.28	1,049.34	0.0704
Jan-98	20.62	21.36	0.0360	970.43	980.28	0.0102
Dec-97	20.53	20.91	0.0188	955.40	970.43	0.0157
Nov-97	18.92	20.53	0.0848	914.62	955.40	0.0446
Oct-97	21.08	18.86	-0.1050	947.28	914.62	-0.0345
Sep-97	20.22	21.31	0.0540	899.47	947.28	0.0532
Aug-97	20.01	20.13	0.0059	954.29	899.47	-0.0574
Jul-97	19.75	20.16	0.0208	885.14	954.31	0.0781
Jun-97	20.13	19.69	-0.0219	848.28	885.14	0.0435
May-97	19.90	20.13	0.0116	801.34	848.28	0.0586
Apr-97	19.49	20.02	0.0269	757.12	801.34	0.0584
Mar-97	20.48	19.26	-0.0598	790.82	757.12	-0.0426
Feb-97	19.61	20.78	0.0591	786.16	790.82	0.0059
Jan-97	18.69	19.73	0.0559	740.74	786.16	0.0613
Dec-96	19.50	18.57	-0.0476	757.02	740.74	-0.0215
Nov-96	17.82	19.67	0.1038	705.27	757.02	0.0734
Oct-96	17.42	17.77	0.0199	687.31	705.27	0.0261
Sep-96	17.39	17.42	0.0017	651.99	687.33	0.0542
Aug-96	17.13	17.48	0.0200	639.95	651.99	0.0188
Jul-96	17.19	17.13	-0.0033	670.63	639.95	-0.0457
Jun-96	16.50	17.19	0.0417	669.12	670.63	0.0023
May-96	15.29	16.33	0.0685	654.17	669.12	0.0229
Apr-96	15.40	15.29	-0.0074	645.50	654.17	0.0134
Mar-96	15.27	15.34	0.0051	640.43	645.50	0.0079
Feb-96	15.23	15.07	-0.0103	636.02	640.43	0.0069
Jan-96	14.78	15.45	0.0451	615.93	636.02	0.0326
		Total	1.2759		Total	0.9075
	Number of Observations		58	Number of Observations		58
	Average Monthly Return		0.0220	Average Monthly Return		0.0156

Table 31. Calculation of Variance.

Calculation of Variance

	Anheuser-Busch			S&P 500		
Date	Return (X_i)	Mean (X_{bar})	$(X_i - X_{bar})^2$	Return (X_i)	Mean (X_{bar})	$(X_i - X_{bar})^2$
Oct-00	0.0861	0.0220	0.0041	-0.0050	0.0156	0.0004
Sep-00	0.0746	0.0220	0.0028	-0.0535	0.0156	0.0048
Aug-00	-0.0214	0.0220	0.0019	0.0607	0.0156	0.0020
Jul-00	0.0778	0.0220	0.0031	-0.0163	0.0156	0.0010
Jun-00	-0.0332	0.0220	0.0030	0.0239	0.0156	0.0001
May-00	0.1067	0.0220	0.0072	-0.0219	0.0156	0.0014
Apr-00	0.1290	0.0220	0.0114	-0.0308	0.0156	0.0022
Mar-00	-0.0292	0.0220	0.0026	0.0967	0.0156	0.0066
Feb-00	-0.0511	0.0220	0.0053	-0.0201	0.0156	0.0013
Jan-00	-0.0409	0.0220	0.0040	-0.0509	0.0156	0.0044
Dec-99	-0.0550	0.0220	0.0059	0.0578	0.0156	0.0018
Nov-99	0.0452	0.0220	0.0005	0.0192	0.0156	0.0000
Oct-99	0.0204	0.0220	0.0000	0.0625	0.0156	0.0022
Sep-99	-0.0901	0.0220	0.0126	-0.0286	0.0156	0.0019
Aug-99	-0.0198	0.0220	0.0018	-0.0063	0.0156	0.0005
Jul-99	0.1050	0.0220	0.0069	-0.0320	0.0156	0.0023
Jun-99	-0.0316	0.0220	0.0029	0.0544	0.0156	0.0015
May-99	0.0032	0.0220	0.0004	-0.0250	0.0156	0.0016
Apr-99	-0.0394	0.0220	0.0038	0.0379	0.0156	0.0005
Mar-99	-0.0073	0.0220	0.0009	0.0388	0.0156	0.0005
Feb-99	0.0981	0.0220	0.0058	-0.0323	0.0156	0.0023
Jan-99	0.0761	0.0220	0.0029	0.0410	0.0156	0.0006
Dec-98	0.0769	0.0220	0.0030	0.0564	0.0156	0.0017
Nov-98	0.0283	0.0220	0.0000	0.0591	0.0156	0.0019
Oct-98	0.1174	0.0220	0.0091	0.0803	0.0156	0.0042
Sep-98	0.1707	0.0220	0.0221	0.0624	0.0156	0.0022
Aug-98	-0.0894	0.0220	0.0124	-0.1458	0.0156	0.0260
Jul-98	0.0951	0.0220	0.0053	-0.0116	0.0156	0.0007
Jun-98	0.0244	0.0220	0.0000	0.0394	0.0156	0.0006
May-98	0.0043	0.0220	0.0003	-0.0188	0.0156	0.0012
Apr-98	-0.0161	0.0220	0.0015	0.0091	0.0156	0.0000
Mar-98	-0.0107	0.0220	0.0011	0.0499	0.0156	0.0012
Feb-98	0.0477	0.0220	0.0007	0.0704	0.0156	0.0030
Jan-98	0.0360	0.0220	0.0002	0.0102	0.0156	0.0000
Dec-97	0.0188	0.0220	0.0000	0.0157	0.0156	0.0000
Nov-97	0.0848	0.0220	0.0039	0.0446	0.0156	0.0008
Oct-97	-0.1050	0.0220	0.0161	-0.0345	0.0156	0.0025
Sep-97	0.0540	0.0220	0.0010	0.0532	0.0156	0.0014
Aug-97	0.0059	0.0220	0.0003	-0.0574	0.0156	0.0053
Jul-97	0.0208	0.0220	0.0000	0.0781	0.0156	0.0039
Jun-97	-0.0219	0.0220	0.0019	0.0435	0.0156	0.0008
May-97	0.0116	0.0220	0.0001	0.0586	0.0156	0.0018
Apr-97	0.0269	0.0220	0.0000	0.0584	0.0156	0.0018
Mar-97	-0.0598	0.0220	0.0067	-0.0426	0.0156	0.0034
Feb-97	0.0591	0.0220	0.0014	0.0059	0.0156	0.0001
Jan-97	0.0559	0.0220	0.0011	0.0613	0.0156	0.0021
Dec-96	-0.0476	0.0220	0.0048	-0.0215	0.0156	0.0014
Nov-96	0.1038	0.0220	0.0067	0.0734	0.0156	0.0033
Oct-96	0.0199	0.0220	0.0000	0.0261	0.0156	0.0001
Sep-96	0.0017	0.0220	0.0004	0.0542	0.0156	0.0015
Aug-96	0.0200	0.0220	0.0000	0.0188	0.0156	0.0000
Jul-96	-0.0033	0.0220	0.0006	-0.0457	0.0156	0.0038
Jun-96	0.0417	0.0220	0.0004	0.0023	0.0156	0.0002
May-96	0.0685	0.0220	0.0022	0.0229	0.0156	0.0001
Apr-96	-0.0074	0.0220	0.0009	0.0134	0.0156	0.0000
Mar-96	0.0051	0.0220	0.0003	0.0079	0.0156	0.0001
Feb-96	-0.0103	0.0220	0.0010	0.0069	0.0156	0.0001
Jan-96	0.0451	0.0220	0.0005	0.0326	0.0156	0.0003
		Total	0.1960		Total	0.1175
	Number of Observations - 1		57	Number of Observations - 1		57
	Average Monthly Return		0.0034	Average Monthly Return		0.0021

Table 32.

Calculation of Covariance

Date	(A) Anheuser-Busch Monthly Return	(B) S&P 500 Monthly Return	(A) * (B)
Oct-00	0.0861	-0.0050	-0.0004
Sep-00	0.0746	-0.0535	-0.0040
Aug-00	-0.0214	0.0607	-0.0013
Jul-00	0.0778	-0.0163	-0.0013
Jun-00	-0.0332	0.0239	-0.0008
May-00	0.1067	-0.0219	-0.0023
Apr-00	0.1290	-0.0308	-0.0040
Mar-00	-0.0292	0.0967	-0.0028
Feb-00	-0.0511	-0.0201	0.0010
Jan-00	-0.0409	-0.0509	0.0021
Dec-99	-0.0550	0.0578	-0.0032
Nov-99	0.0452	0.0192	0.0009
Oct-99	0.0204	0.0625	0.0013
Sep-99	-0.0901	-0.0286	0.0026
Aug-99	-0.0198	-0.0063	0.0001
Jul-99	0.1050	-0.0320	-0.0034
Jun-99	-0.0316	0.0544	-0.0017
May-99	0.0032	-0.0250	-0.0001
Apr-99	-0.0394	0.0379	-0.0015
Mar-99	-0.0073	0.0388	-0.0003
Feb-99	0.0981	-0.0323	-0.0032
Jan-99	0.0761	0.0410	0.0031
Dec-98	0.0769	0.0564	0.0043
Nov-98	0.0283	0.0591	0.0017
Oct-98	0.1174	0.0803	0.0094
Sep-98	0.1707	0.0624	0.0107
Aug-98	-0.0894	-0.1458	0.0130
Jul-98	0.0951	-0.0116	-0.0011
Jun-98	0.0244	0.0394	0.0010
May-98	0.0043	-0.0188	-0.0001
Apr-98	-0.0161	0.0091	-0.0001
Mar-98	-0.0107	0.0499	-0.0005
Feb-98	0.0477	0.0704	0.0034
Jan-98	0.0360	0.0102	0.0004
Dec-97	0.0188	0.0157	0.0003
Nov-97	0.0848	0.0446	0.0038
Oct-97	-0.1050	-0.0345	0.0036
Sep-97	0.0540	0.0532	0.0029
Aug-97	0.0059	-0.0574	-0.0003
Jul-97	0.0208	0.0781	0.0016
Jun-97	-0.0219	0.0435	-0.0010
May-97	0.0116	0.0586	0.0007
Apr-97	0.0269	0.0584	0.0016
Mar-97	-0.0598	-0.0426	0.0025
Feb-97	0.0591	0.0059	0.0004
Jan-97	0.0559	0.0613	0.0034
Dec-96	-0.0476	-0.0215	0.0010
Nov-96	0.1038	0.0734	0.0076
Oct-96	0.0199	0.0261	0.0005
Sep-96	0.0017	0.0542	0.0001
Aug-96	0.0200	0.0188	0.0004
Jul-96	-0.0033	-0.0457	0.0002
Jun-96	0.0417	0.0023	0.0001
May-96	0.0685	0.0229	0.0016
Apr-96	-0.0074	0.0134	-0.0001
Mar-96	0.0051	0.0079	0.0000
Feb-96	-0.0103	0.0069	-0.0001
Jan-96	0.0451	0.0326	0.0015
		Total	0.0551
		Number of Observations - 1	57
		Covariance	0.0010

Table 33. Option Prices Table.

Options: Dec-00 | **Jan-01** | Mar-01 | Jun-01 | Jan-02 | Jan-03

Calls							Strike Price	Puts						
Symbol	Last Trade	Chg	Bid	Ask	Vol	Open Int		Symbol	Last Trade	Chg	Bid	Ask	Vol	Open Int
BUDAD.X	**28 1/8**	0	26 7/8	27 3/8	0	82	20	BUDMD.X	**0**	0	0	8-Jan	0	442
BUDAE.X	**23 1/8**	0	22	22 1/2	0	406	25	BUDME.X	**8-Jan**	0	0	8-Jan	0	1,958
BUDAF.X	**18 5/8**	0	17	17 3/8	0	241	30	BUDMF.X	**16-Mar**	0	16-Jan	16-Mar	0	1,128
BUDAZ.X	**15 3/4**	0	14 5/8	15	0	290	32.5	BUDMZ.X	**16-Mar**	0	8-Jan	4-Jan	0	521
BUDAG.X	**13 1/4**	0	12 1/8	12 1/2	0	1,712	35	BUDMG.X	**16-May**	0	16-Mar	16-May	0	2,255
BUDAU.X	**10 3/4**	0	9 5/8	10	0	972	37.5	BUDMU.X	**4-Jan**	0	4-Jan	8-Mar	0	681
BUDAH.X	**8 3/8**	0	7 1/4	7 5/8	0	4,075	40	BUDMH.X	**16-Jul**	0	16-Jul	16-Sep	0	2,545
BUDAV.X	**6 1/8**	0	5 1/8	5 1/2	0	1,303	42.5	BUDMV.X	**4-Mar**	0.0625	8-May	13/16	300	575
BUDAI.X	**4 1/2**	0	3 1/2	3 3/4	0	1,127	45	BUDMI.X	**1**	0	1 1/4	1 7/16	0	616
BUDAW.X	**2 9/16**	0	1 15/16	2 1/8	0	520	47.5	BUDMW.X	**2 1/16**	0	2 3/8	2 5/8	0	111
BUDAJ.X	**1 3/8**	0	15/16	1 1/8	0	1,560	50	BUDMJ.X	**3 3/8**	0	3 7/8	4 1/8	0	116
BUDAX.X	**8-May**	0	8-Mar	2-Jan	0	276	52.5	BUDMX.X	**5 1/4**	0	5 3/4	6 1/8	0	0
BUDAK.X	**8-Mar**	0	16-Mar	16-May	0	12	55	BUDMK.X	**7 3/8**	0	8	8 3/8	0	0

Table 34. Variance Calculation.

Day Count	Date	Stock Price Open	Stock Price Close	(a) Daily Rate of Return	(b) Mean Daily Rate of Return	[(a) - (b)]^2
1	12/14/00	$47.50	$47.44	-0.001316	0.004897	0.000039
2	12/13/00	46.13	47.50	0.029810	0.004897	0.000621
3	12/12/00	46.00	46.25	0.005435	0.004897	0.000000
4	12/11/00	46.25	45.94	-0.006757	0.004897	0.000136
5	12/8/00	48.00	46.19	-0.037760	0.004897	0.001820
6	12/7/00	45.81	48.06	0.049113	0.004897	0.001955
7	12/6/00	46.94	45.81	-0.023968	0.004897	0.000833
8	12/5/00	46.88	46.88	0.000000	0.004897	0.000024
9	12/4/00	47.13	46.63	-0.010610	0.004897	0.000240
10	12/1/00	47.38	47.13	-0.005277	0.004897	0.000104
11	11/30/00	47.00	47.44	0.009309	0.004897	0.000019
12	11/29/00	48.00	47.38	-0.013021	0.004897	0.000321
13	11/28/00	47.63	48.00	0.007874	0.004897	0.000009
14	11/27/00	48.38	48.06	-0.006460	0.004897	0.000129
15	11/24/00	48.88	48.94	0.001279	0.004897	0.000013
16	11/22/00	49.25	48.88	-0.007614	0.004897	0.000157
17	11/21/00	47.75	49.81	0.043194	0.004897	0.001467
18	11/20/00	48.00	48.06	0.001302	0.004897	0.000013
19	11/17/00	48.06	47.63	-0.009103	0.004897	0.000196
20	11/16/00	46.44	47.56	0.024226	0.004897	0.000374
21	11/15/00	45.75	46.44	0.015027	0.004897	0.000103
22	11/14/00	46.88	47.44	0.012000	0.004897	0.000050
23	11/13/00	47.13	46.56	-0.011936	0.004897	0.000283
24	11/10/00	46.00	46.88	0.019022	0.004897	0.000200
25	11/9/00	45.31	46.25	0.020690	0.004897	0.000249
26	11/8/00	44.19	45.06	0.019802	0.004897	0.000222
27	11/7/00	44.50	44.31	-0.004213	0.004897	0.000083
28	11/6/00	44.09	45.09	0.022600	0.004897	0.000313
29	11/3/00	43.90	44.15	0.005674	0.004897	0.000001
30	11/2/00	43.84	43.78	-0.001421	0.004897	0.000040
			Sum Total	0.146899		0.0100
			n =	30	n-1 =	29
			Mean Stock Price	0.004897	**Variance**	**0.000345**

Table 35. Data Set.

Data Set

t	DPS_t	EPS_t	DPS_{t-1}
1	0.11	0.22	0.11
2	0.11	0.32	0.11
3	0.13	0.45	0.11
4	0.13	0.46	0.13
5	0.13	0.25	0.13
6	0.13	0.35	0.13
7	0.14	0.50	0.13
8	0.14	0.50	0.14
9	0.14	0.28	0.14
10	0.14	0.24	0.14
11	0.16	0.53	0.14
12	0.16	0.54	0.16
13	0.16	0.29	0.16
14	0.16	0.34	0.16
15	0.18	0.55	0.16
16	0.18	-0.14	0.18
17	0.18	0.31	0.18
18	0.18	0.38	0.18
19	0.2	0.60	0.18
20	0.2	0.62	0.2
21	0.2	0.34	0.2
22	0.2	0.41	0.2
23	0.22	0.63	0.2
24	0.22	0.33	0.22
25	0.22	-0.47	0.22
26	0.22	0.53	0.22
27	0.24	0.76	0.22
28	0.24	0.74	0.24
29	0.24	0.30	0.24
30	0.24	0.51	0.24
31	0.26	0.76	0.24
32	0.26	0.79	0.26
33	0.26	0.28	0.26
34	0.26	0.54	0.26
35	0.28	0.80	0.26
36	0.28	0.84	0.28
37	0.28	0.35	0.28
38	0.28	0.66	0.28
39	0.3	0.90	0.28

Table 36. Summary Output.

SUMMARY OUTPUT

Regression Statistics	
Multiple R	0.990885003
R Square	0.981853089
Adjusted R Square	0.980844927
Standard Error	0.007652027
Observations	39

ANOVA

	df	*SS*	*MS*	*F*	*Significance F*
Regression	2	0.114051048	0.057025524	973.9043612	4.55458E-32
Residual	36	0.002107927	5.85535E-05		
Total	38	0.116158974			

	Coefficients	*Standard Error*	*t Stat*	*P-value*	*Lower 95%*	*Upper 95%*	*Lower 95.0%*	*Upper 95.0%*
Intercept	0.002656047	0.004618475	0.575091705	0.568806433	-0.006710642	0.012022736	-0.006710642	0.012022736
EPSt	0.01729273	0.00512746	3.372572113	0.001792278	0.006893772	0.027691688	0.006893772	0.027691688
DPSt-1	0.971233165	0.024523402	39.60434092	2.77173E-31	0.921497467	1.020968864	0.921497467	1.020968864

Table 36. Continued.

RESIDUAL OUTPUT

Observation	*Predicted DPSt*	*Residuals*	*Standard Residuals*
1	0.113296095	-0.003296095	-0.442551517
2	0.115025368	-0.005025368	-0.674733023
3	0.117273423	0.012726577	1.708738718
4	0.136871014	-0.006871014	-0.922539328
5	0.133239541	-0.003239541	-0.434958166
6	0.134968814	-0.004968814	-0.667139672
7	0.137562723	0.002437277	0.327241919
8	0.147275055	-0.007275055	-0.976788029
9	0.143470654	-0.003470654	-0.465988716
10	0.142778945	-0.002778945	-0.373116114
11	0.147793837	0.012206163	1.638865218
12	0.167391427	-0.007391427	-0.992412828
13	0.163068245	-0.003068245	-0.411959064
14	0.163932881	-0.003932881	-0.528049816
15	0.167564355	0.012435645	1.66967672
16	0.175057034	0.004942966	0.663669214
17	0.182838763	-0.002838763	-0.381147562
18	0.184049254	-0.004049254	-0.543674616
19	0.187853654	0.012146346	1.63083377
20	0.207624172	-0.007624172	-1.023662426
21	0.202782208	-0.002782208	-0.37355421
22	0.203992699	-0.003992699	-0.536081264
23	0.2077971	0.0122029	1.638427122
24	0.222033944	-0.002033944	-0.273088257
25	0.20819976	0.01180024	1.58436379
26	0.22549249	-0.00549249	-0.737451268
27	0.229469818	0.010530182	1.413838967
28	0.248548626	-0.008548626	-1.147784627
29	0.240939825	-0.000939825	-0.126186002
30	0.244571299	-0.004571299	-0.613767164
31	0.248894481	0.011105519	1.49108677
32	0.268837926	-0.008837926	-1.186627577
33	0.260018634	-1.8634E-05	-0.002501898
34	0.264514744	-0.004514744	-0.606173813
35	0.269010854	0.010989146	1.475461971
36	0.289127226	-0.009127226	-1.225470527
37	0.280653788	-0.000653788	-0.087781148
38	0.286014535	-0.006014535	-0.807543816
39	0.29016479	0.00983521	1.320528268

Table 37. Sales Growth Rate Calculation.

SALES GROWTH RATE CALCULATION

	Date	Sales	Annual Growth From Prior Year
1	Dec-80	3,295.40	n/a
2	Dec-81	3,847.20	16.74%
3	Dec-82	4,576.60	18.96%
4	Dec-83	6,034.20	31.85%
5	Dec-84	6,501.20	7.74%
6	Dec-85	7,000.30	7.68%
7	Dec-86	7,677.20	9.67%
8	Dec-87	8,258.40	7.57%
9	Dec-88	8,924.10	8.06%
10	Dec-89	9,481.30	6.24%
11	Dec-90	10,743.60	13.31%
12	Dec-91	10,996.30	2.35%
13	Dec-92	11,393.70	3.61%
14	Dec-93	11,505.30	0.98%
15	Dec-94	12,053.80	4.77%
16	Dec-95	10,340.50	-14.21%
17	Dec-96	10,883.70	5.25%
18	Dec-97	11,066.20	1.68%
19	Dec-98	11,245.80	1.62%
20	Dec-99	11,703.70	4.07%
	Average Growth Rate		7.26%

Table 38. Average Dividend Payout Ratio Calculation.

Average Dividend Payout Ratio Calculation				
	Date	Dividends per Share	Earnings per Share	Avg Dividend Payout Ratio
1	Dec-80	0.08	0.32	25.00%
2	Dec-81	0.09	0.38	23.68%
3	Dec-82	0.11	0.49	22.45%
4	Dec-83	0.14	0.54	25.93%
5	Dec-84	0.16	0.62	25.81%
6	Dec-85	0.18	0.71	25.35%
7	Dec-86	0.22	0.85	25.88%
8	Dec-87	0.27	1.02	26.47%
9	Dec-88	0.33	1.23	26.83%
10	Dec-89	0.40	1.34	29.85%
11	Dec-90	0.47	1.48	31.76%
12	Dec-91	0.53	1.63	32.52%
13	Dec-92	0.60	1.74	34.48%
14	Dec-93	0.68	1.72	39.53%
15	Dec-94	0.76	1.96	38.78%
16	Dec-95	0.84	1.91	43.98%
17	Dec-96	0.92	2.15	42.79%
18	Dec-97	1.00	2.39	41.84%
19	Dec-98	1.08	2.57	42.02%
20	Dec-99	1.16	2.99	38.80%
		Average Dividend Payout Ratio		32.19%

Table 39. Average Profit Margin Calculation.

Average Profit Margin Calculation

	Date	Net Income	Sales	Average Profit Margin
1	Dec-80	171.80	3,295.40	5.21%
2	Dec-81	217.40	3,847.20	5.65%
3	Dec-82	287.30	4,576.60	6.28%
4	Dec-83	348.00	6,034.20	5.77%
5	Dec-84	391.50	6,501.20	6.02%
6	Dec-85	443.70	7,000.30	6.34%
7	Dec-86	518.00	7,677.20	6.75%
8	Dec-87	614.70	8,258.40	7.44%
9	Dec-88	715.90	8,924.10	8.02%
10	Dec-89	767.20	9,481.30	8.09%
11	Dec-90	842.40	10,743.60	7.84%
12	Dec-91	939.80	10,996.30	8.55%
13	Dec-92	917.50	11,393.70	8.05%
14	Dec-93	594.50	11,505.30	5.17%
15	Dec-94	1,032.10	12,053.80	8.56%
16	Dec-95	642.30	10,340.50	6.21%
17	Dec-96	1,189.90	10,883.70	10.93%
18	Dec-97	1,169.90	11,066.20	10.57%
19	Dec-98	1,233.30	11,245.80	10.97%
20	Dec-99	1,402.20	11,703.70	11.98%
		Average Profit Margin		7.72%

Table 40. Average Asset Turnover Calculation.

Average Asset Turnover Calculation

	Date	Sales	Total Assets	Avg Asset Turnover
1	Dec-80	3,295.40	2,449.80	1.35
2	Dec-81	3,847.20	2,875.20	1.34
3	Dec-82	4,576.60	3,902.80	1.17
4	Dec-83	6,034.20	4,330.18	1.39
5	Dec-84	6,501.20	4,524.70	1.44
6	Dec-85	7,000.30	5,121.38	1.37
7	Dec-86	7,677.20	5,833.80	1.32
8	Dec-87	8,258.40	6,491.60	1.27
9	Dec-88	8,924.10	7,109.80	1.26
10	Dec-89	9,481.30	9,025.70	1.05
11	Dec-90	10,743.60	9,634.30	1.12
12	Dec-91	10,996.30	9,986.50	1.10
13	Dec-92	11,393.70	10,537.90	1.08
14	Dec-93	11,505.30	10,880.30	1.06
15	Dec-94	12,053.80	11,045.40	1.09
16	Dec-95	10,340.50	10,590.90	0.98
17	Dec-96	10,883.70	10,463.60	1.04
18	Dec-97	11,066.20	11,727.10	0.94
19	Dec-98	11,245.80	12,484.30	0.90
20	Dec-99	11,703.70	12,640.40	0.93
		Average Asset Turnover Ratio		1.16

Table 41. Average Equity Multiplier Calculation.

Average Equity Multiplier Calculation

	Date	Total Assets	Total Equity	Avg Equity Multiplier
1	Dec-80	2,449.80	1,038.00	2.36
2	Dec-81	2,875.20	1,206.80	2.38
3	Dec-82	3,902.80	1,811.60	2.15
4	Dec-83	4,330.18	2,052.50	2.11
5	Dec-84	4,524.70	2,237.90	2.02
6	Dec-85	5,121.38	2,460.60	2.08
7	Dec-86	5,833.80	2,600.60	2.24
8	Dec-87	6,491.60	2,892.20	2.24
9	Dec-88	7,109.80	3,102.90	2.29
10	Dec-89	9,025.70	3,099.90	2.91
11	Dec-90	9,634.30	3,679.10	2.62
12	Dec-91	9,986.50	4,438.10	2.25
13	Dec-92	10,537.90	4,620.40	2.28
14	Dec-93	10,880.30	4,255.50	2.56
15	Dec-94	11,045.40	4,415.50	2.50
16	Dec-95	10,590.90	4,433.90	2.39
17	Dec-96	10,463.60	4,029.10	2.60
18	Dec-97	11,727.10	4,041.80	2.90
19	Dec-98	12,484.30	4,216.00	2.96
20	Dec-99	12,640.40	3,921.50	3.22
		Average Equity Multiplier		2.45

Table 42. Sales Data.

Sales Data

t	Year	Sales	ln
	Dec-80	3,295.40	8.10
1	Dec-81	3,847.20	8.26
2	Dec-82	4,576.60	8.43
3	Dec-83	6,034.20	8.71
4	Dec-84	6,501.20	8.78
5	Dec-85	7,000.30	8.85
6	Dec-86	7,677.20	8.95
7	Dec-87	8,258.40	9.02
8	Dec-88	8,924.10	9.10
9	Dec-89	9,481.30	9.16
10	Dec-90	10,743.60	9.28
11	Dec-91	10,996.30	9.31
12	Dec-92	11,393.70	9.34
13	Dec-93	11,505.30	9.35
14	Dec-94	12,053.80	9.40
15	Dec-95	10,340.50	9.24
16	Dec-96	10,883.70	9.30
17	Dec-97	11,066.20	9.31
18	Dec-98	11,245.80	9.33
19	Dec-99	11,703.70	9.37

Table 43. Summary Output.

SUMMARY OUTPUT

Regression Statistics	
Multiple R	0.889031524
R Square	0.79037705
Adjusted R Square	0.778731331
Standard Error	0.184554716
Observations	20

ANOVA

	df	*SS*	*MS*	*F*	*Significance F*
Regression	1	2.311629845	2.311629845	67.86846048	1.60957E-07
Residual	18	0.613087978	0.034060443		
Total	19	2.924717823			

	Coefficients	*Standard Error*	*t Stat*	*P-value*	*Lower 95%*	*Upper 95%*	*Lower 95.0%*	*Upper 95.0%*
Intercept	8.409089441	0.085731471	98.08637767	5.12661E-26	8.228974165	8.589204717	8.228974165	8.589204717
X Variable 1	0.058958758	0.007156725	8.238231635	1.60957E-07	0.043923025	0.07399449	0.043923025	0.07399449

Table 44. Sales Forecast.

	Actual	Forecast @ 7.26%										
	1999	2000	2001	2002	2003	2004	2005	2006	2007	2008	2009	2010
Sales	$11,704	$12,553	$13,465	$14,442	$15,491	$16,615	$17,822	$19,116	$20,503	$21,992	$23,589	$25,301

Table 45. Input Data.

INPUT DATA

Variable Number	Data*	Variable	Description
21	11,703.7	EBITt-1	Sales in 1999
22	0.0726	GCALSt	Growth in Sales
23	0.1368	RCAt-1	Current Assets as a Percent of Sales
24	0.6805	RFAt-1	Fixed Assets as a Percent of Sales
25	0.1698	RCLt-1	Current Payables as a Percent of Sales
26	0.0	PFDSKt-1	Preferred Stock
27	0.0	PFDIVt-1	Preferred Dividends
28	4,880.6	Lt-1	Debt in Previous Period
29	553.7	LRt-1	Debt Repayment
30	716.1	St-1	Common Stock in Previous Period
31	9,006.2	Rt-1	Retained Earnings in Previous Period
32	0.6054	bt-1	Retention Rate
33	0.3524	Tt-1	Average Tax Rate
34	0.0631	it-1	Average Interest Rate in Previous Period
35	0.0631	iet-1	Expected Interest Rate on New Debt
36	0.1967	REBITt-1	Operating Income as a Percentage of Sales
37	0.0631	UD	Underwriting Cost of Debt
38	0.1016	UE	Underwriting Cost of Equity
39	1.2446	Kt	Ratio of Debt to Equity
40	461.1	NUMCSt-1	Number of Common Shares Outstanding in Previous Period
41	23.7	mt-1	Price-Earnings Ratio

***Data obtained from Anheuser-Busch Balance Sheets and Income Statements**

Table 46. FINPLAN Input

FINPLAN input
1999

Value of Data	**Variable Number**	**Beginning Period**	**Last Period**
11703.7	2	0	0
716.1	15	0	0
9006.2	17	0	0
0.0631	10	0	0
461.1	16	0	0
4	1	0	0
4880.6	9	0	0
0.0726	3	1	4
0.1368	6	1	4
0.6805	7	1	4
0.1698	8	1	4
0.1967	4	1	4
553.7	12	1	4
0.6054	18	1	4
1.2446	19	1	4
23.7	20	1	4
0.3524	5	1	4
0.0631	11	1	4
0.0631	21	1	4
0.0726	22	1	4

Table 47. Pro Forma Income Statement

Pro Forma Income Statement

	1999	2000	2001	2002	2003
Sales	$11,703.70	12,553.39	13,464.76	14,442.31	15,490.82
Operating income	0	2,469.25	2,648.52	2,840.80	3,047.04
Interest expense	0	284.39	305.04	327.19	350.94
Underwriting commission -- debt	0	11.37	55.59	57.08	58.69
Income before taxes	0	2,173.49	2,287.89	2,456.53	2,637.41
Taxes	0	765.94	806.25	865.68	929.42
Net income	0	1,407.55	1,481.64	1,590.85	1,707.99
Preferred dividends	0	0.00	0.00	0.00	0.00
Available for common dividends	0	1,407.55	1,481.64	1,590.85	1,707.99
Common dividends	0	555.42	584.65	627.75	673.97
Debt repayments	0	553.70	553.70	553.70	553.70
Actl funds needed for investment	0	(6,773.01)	246.83	223.56	198.60

Table 48. Pro Forma Balance Sheet

Pro Forma Balance Sheet

	1999	**2000**	**2001**	**2002**	**2003**
Assets					
Current assets	$0.00	1,717.30	1,841.98	1,975.71	2,119.14
Fixed assets	0.00	8,542.58	9,162.77	9,827.99	10,541.50
Total assets	0.00	10,259.88	11,004.75	11,803.70	12,660.65
Liabilities and net worth					
Current liabilities	0.00	2,131.57	2,286.32	2,452.30	2,630.34
Long term debt	4,880.60	4,507.04	4,834.25	5,185.22	5,561.67
Preferred stock	0.00	0.00	0.00	0.00	0.00
Common stock	716.10	(6,237.05)	(6,871.13)	(7,552.24)	(8,283.79)
Retained earnings	9,006.20	9,858.33	10,755.32	11,718.42	12,752.43
Total liabilities and net worth	0.00	10,259.88	11,004.75	11,803.70	12,660.65
Computed DBT/EQ	0.00	1.24	1.24	1.24	1.24
Int. rate on total debt	0.06	0.06	0.06	0.06	0.06
Per share data					
Earnings	0.00	3.74	0.01	4.39	4.81
Dividends	0.00	1.48	1.58	1.73	1.90
Price	0.00	88.61	95.09	104.08	113.93

Table 49. Manual Calculation vs. Financial Plan Model

Category	Manual Calculation	Financial Plan Model	Variance
INCOME STATEMENT			
Sales	12,553.38	12,553.39	0.0%
Operating Income	2,469.25	2,469.25	0.0%
Interest Expense	284.39	284.39	0.0%
Income before taxes	2,173.49	2,173.49	0.0%
Taxes	765.94	765.94	0.0%
Net Income	1,407.55	1,407.55	0.0%
Common Dividends	555.42	555.42	0.0%
Debt Repayments	553.70	553.70	0.0%
BALANCE SHEET			
Assets			
Current Assets	1,717.30	1,717.30	0.0%
Fixed Assets	8,542.58	8,542.58	0.0%
Total Assets	10,259.88	10,259.88	0.0%
LIABILITIES AND NET WORTH			
Current Payables	2,131.56	2,131.57	0.0%
Total Debt	4,507.05	4,507.04	0.0%
Common Stock	(6,237.07)	(6,237.06)	0.0%
Retained Earnings	9,858.34	9,858.33	0.0%
Total Liabilities and Net Worth	10,259.88	10,259.88	0.0%
PER SHARE DATA			
Price per Share	89.11	88.61	0.6%
Earnings per Share (EPS)	3.76	3.74	0.6%
Dividends per Share (DPS)	1.48	1.48	0.3%

FIGURES

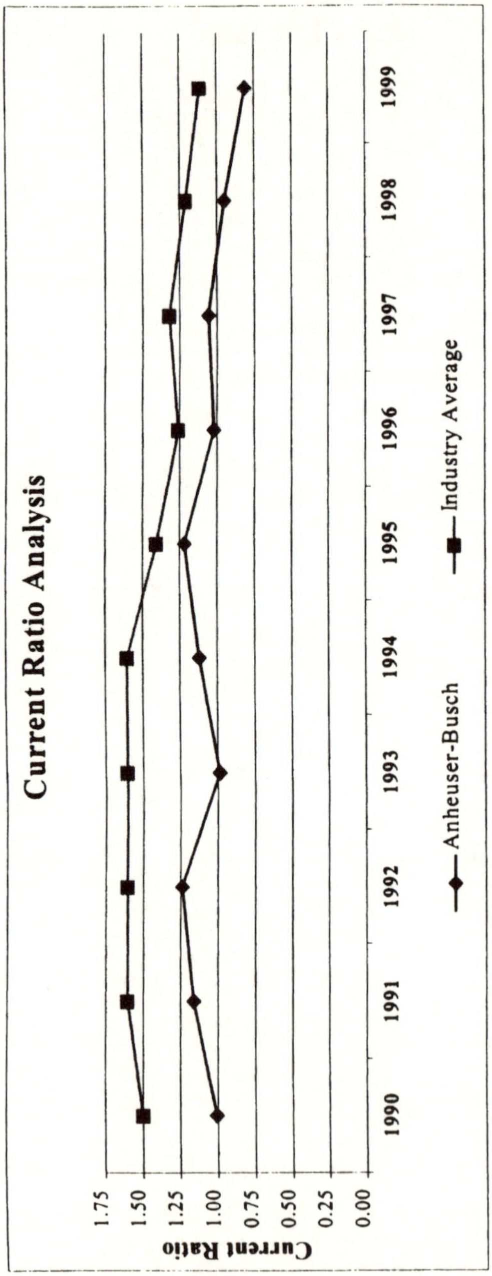

Fig. 1. Current Ratio Analysis.

Anheuser-Busch Cos., Inc.

	1990	1991	1992	1993	1994	1995	1996	1997	1998	1999
Current Assets	1,426.3	1,627.7	1,815.8	1,795.2	1,861.6	1,510.6	1,465.8	1,583.9	1,640.4	1,600.6
Current Liabilities	1,411.9	1,402.8	1,459.8	1,815.6	1,669.0	1,242.0	1,430.9	1,500.7	1,730.3	1,987.2
Current Ratio	1.01	1.16	1.24	0.99	1.12	1.22	1.02	1.06	0.95	0.81

Alcoholic-Beverage Indusrty Data

	1990	1991	1992	1993	1994	1995	1996	1997	1998	1999
Current Ratio	1.5	1.60	1.6	1.6	1.6	1.41	1.26	1.32	1.21	1.11

Note: Anheuser-Busch data obtained from Balance Sheet. Alcoholic-Beverage Industry Data obtained from Ratio Analysis

Fig. 2. Current Ratio Analysis Data.

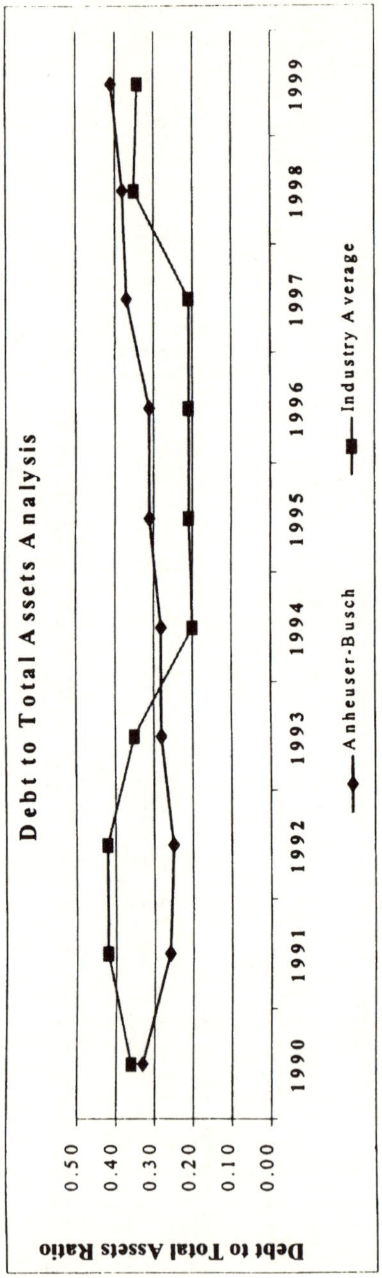

Fig. 3. Debt to Total Asset Analysis.

Anheuser-Busch Cos., Inc.

	1990	1991	1992	1993	1994	1995	1996	1997	1998	1999
Total Debt*	3,147.1	2,644.9	2,642.5	3,031.7	3,078.4	3,270.1	3,270.9	4,365.6	4,718.6	5,122.9
Total Assets	9,634.3	9,986.5 #	10,537.9	10,880.3	11,045.4 #	10,590.9	10,463.6	11,727.1	12,484.3	12,640.4
Debt to Total Assets	0.33	0.26	0.25	0.28	0.28	0.31	0.31	0.37	0.38	0.41

Alcoholic-Beverage Indusrty Data

	1990	1991	1992	1993	1994	1995	1996	1997	1998	1999
Debt to Total Assets	0.36	0.42	0.42	0.35	0.20	0.21	0.21	0.21	0.35	0.34

Note: Anheuser-Busch data obtained from Balance Sheet. Alcoholic-Beverage Industry Data obtained from Ratio Analysis

*Total debt consists of long-term debt and notes payable.

Fig. 4. Debt to Total Assets Data.

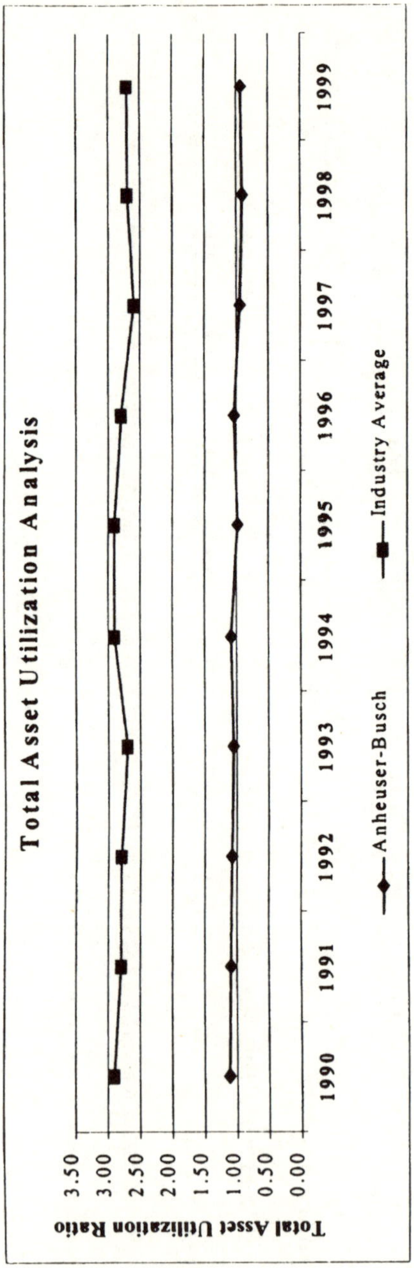

Fig. 5. Total Asset Utilization Analysis.

Anheuser-Busch Cos., Inc.

	1990	1991	1992	1993	1994	1995	1996	1997	1998	1999
Net Sales	10,743.6	10,996.3	11,393.7	11,505.3	12,053.8	10,340.5	10,883.7	11,066.2	11,245.8	11,703.7
Total Assets	9,634.3	9,986.5 #	10,537.9	10,880.3	11,045.4 #	10,590.9	10,463.6	11,727.1	12,484.3	12,640.4
Total Asset Utilization Ratio	1.12	1.10	1.08	1.06	1.09	0.98	1.04	0.94	0.90	0.93

Alcoholic-Beverage Indusrty Data

	1990	1991	1992	1993	1994	1995	1996	1997	1998	1999
Total Asset Utilization Ratio	2.9	2.8	2.8	2.7	2.9	2.9	2.8	2.6	2.7	2.7

Note: Anheuser-Busch data obtained from Balance Sheet and Income Statement. Alcoholic-Beverage Industry Data obtained from Ratio Analysis.

Fig. 6. Total Asset Utilization Data.

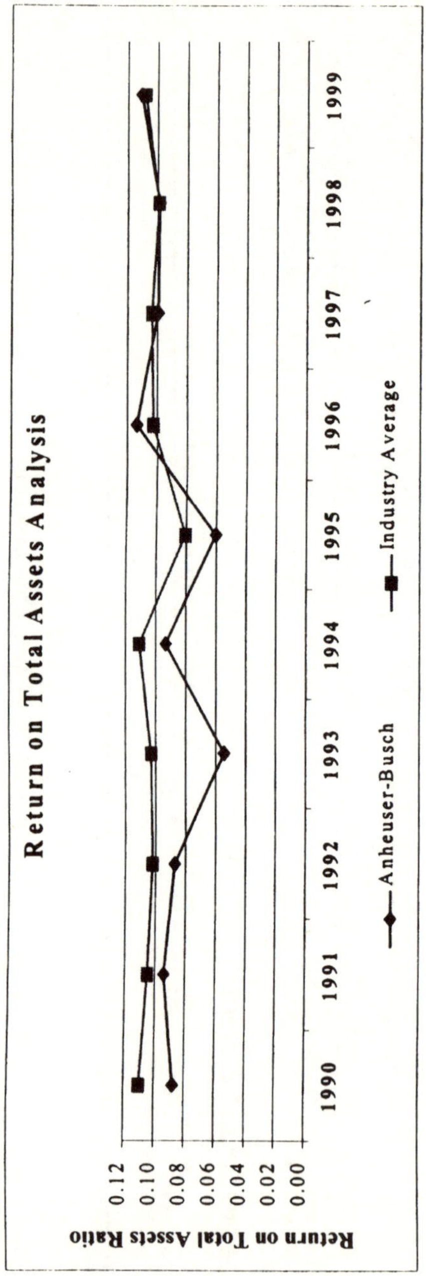

Fig. 7. Return on Total Assets Analysis.

Anheuser-Busch Cos., Inc.

	1990	1991	1992	1993	1994	1995	1996	1997	1998	1999
Net Income	842.4	939.8	917.5	594.5	1,032.1	642.3	1,189.9	1,169.2	1,233.3	1,402.2
Total Assets	9,634.3	9,986.5 #	10,537.9	10,880.3	11,045.4 #	10,590.9	10,463.6	11,727.1	12,484.3	12,640.4
Return on Total Assets	0.0874	0.0941	0.0871	0.0546	0.0934	0.0606	0.1137	0.0997	0.0988	0.1109

Alcoholic-Beverage Indusrty Data

	1990	1991	1992	1993	1994	1995	1996	1997	1998	1999
Return on Total Assets	0.11	0.105	0.102	0.103	0.111	0.0805	0.1028	0.1037	0.0992	0.1082

Note: Anheuser-Busch data obtained from Balance Sheet anc Income Statement. Alcoholic-Beverage Industry Data obtained from Ratio Analysis.

Fig. 8. Return on Total Assets Data.

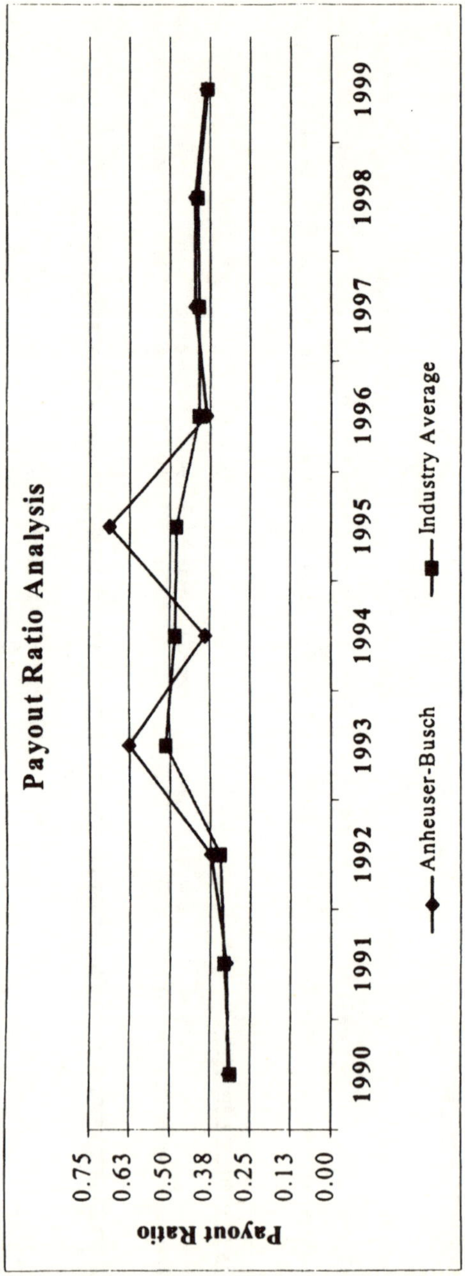

Fig. 9. Payout Ratio Analysis.

Anheuser-Busch Cos., Inc.

	1990	1991	1992	1993	1994	1995	1996	1997	1998	1999
Dividends	267.5	305.2	343.0	373.0	401.4	429.5	458.9	492.6	521.0	544.7
Net Income	842.4	939.8	917.5	594.5	1,032.1	642.3	1,189.9	1,169.2	1,233.3	1,402.2
Payout Ratio	0.3176	0.3247	0.3738	0.6275	0.3889	0.6687	0.3857	0.4213	0.4224	0.3885

Alcoholic-Beverage Indusrty Data

	1990	1991	1992	1993	1994	1995	1996	1997	1998	1999
Payout Ratio	0.3122	0.3310	0.3452	0.5120	0.4812	0.4802	0.4097	0.4091	0.4125	0.3826

Note: Anheuser-Busch data obtained from Income Statement. Alcoholic-Beverage Industry Data obtained from Ratio Analysis

Fig. 10. Payout Ratio Data.

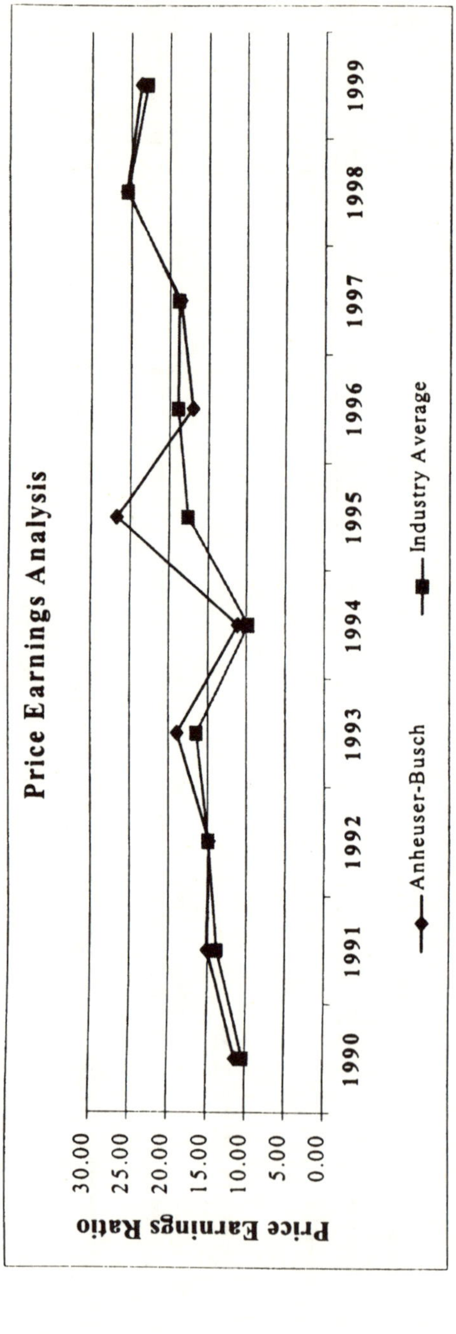

Fig. 11. Price Earnings Analysis.

Anheuser-Busch Cos., Inc.

	1990	1991	1992	1993	1994	1995	1996	1997	1998	1999
Market Price per Share	16.81	24.56	23.87	20.60	21.97	33.44	40.00	44.00	65.62	70.87
Earnings Per Share*	1.48	1.63	1.61	1.09	1.96	1.25	2.35	2.37	2.56	2.99
Price/Earnings Ratio	11.36	15.07	14.83	18.90	11.21	26.75	17.02	18.57	25.63	23.70

Alcoholic-Beverage Indusrty Data

	1990	1991	1992	1993	1994	1995	1996	1997	1998	1999
Price/Earnings Ratio	10.41	13.82	14.91	16.42	9.81	17.58	18.88	18.85	25.49	22.87

Note: P/E Ratio calculated based on Stock Price prior to split adjustment. Anheuser-Busch data obtained from Income Statement and Industry Data . Alcoholic-Beverage Industry data obtained from Ratio Analysis.

*Represents diluted EPS

Fig. 12. Price Earnings Data.

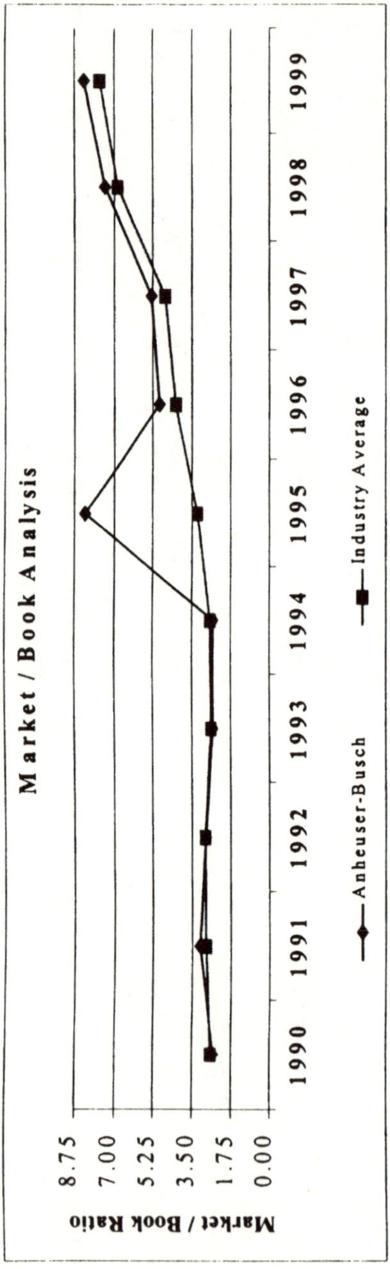

Fig. 13. Market/Book Analysis.

Anheuser-Busch Cos., Inc.

	1990	1991	1992	1993	1994	1995	1996	1997	1998	1999
Total Equity	3,679.1	4,438.1	4,620.4	4,255.5	4,415.5	4,433.9	4,029.1	4,041.8	4,216.0	3,921.5
Shares Outstanding	564.6	570.1	556.8	534.1	514.6	508.0	497.4	487.0	476.6	461.1
Book Value per Share	6.52	7.78	8.30	7.97	8.58	8.73	8.10	8.30	8.85	8.50
Market Price per Share	16.81	24.56	23.87	20.60	21.97	33.44	40.00	44.00	65.62	70.87
Book Value per Share	6.52	7.78	8.30	7.97	8.58	8.73	8.10	8.30	8.85	8.50
Market / Book Value	2.58	3.15	2.88	2.59	2.56	3.83	4.94	5.30	7.42	8.33

Alcoholic-Beverage Indusrty Data

	1990	1991	1992	1993	1994	1995	1996	1997	1998	1999
Market / Book Value	2.68	2.89	2.90	2.65	2.68	3.25	4.23	4.68	6.84	7.63

Note: Anheuser-Busch data obtained from Balance Sheet and Industry Data. Alcoholic-Beverage Industry data obtained from Ratio Analysis

Fig. 14. Market/Book Data.

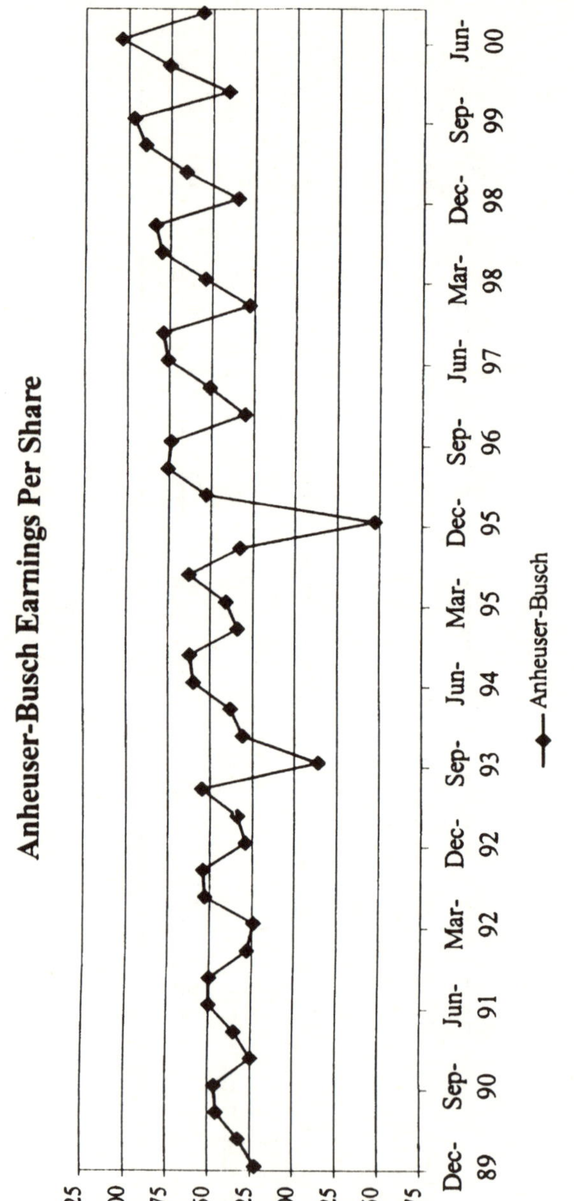

Fig. 15. Earnings Per Share.

Anheuser-Busch Earnings Per Share: 1989 - 2000

Date	Diluted Earnings per Share	Date	Diluted Earnings per Share	Date	Diluted Earnings per Share
Dec-89	0.22	Sep-93	-0.14	Jun-97	0.76
Mar-90	0.32	Dec-93	0.31	Sep-97	0.79
Jun-90	0.45	Mar-94	0.38	Dec-97	0.28
Sep-90	0.46	Jun-94	0.60	Mar-98	0.54
Dec-90	0.25	Sep-94	0.62	Jun-98	0.80
Mar-91	0.35	Dec-94	0.34	Sep-98	0.84
Jun-91	0.50	Mar-95	0.41	Dec-98	0.35
Sep-91	0.50	Jun-95	0.63	Mar-99	0.66
Dec-91	0.28	Sep-95	0.33	Jun-99	0.90
Mar-92	0.24	Dec-95	-0.47	Sep-99	0.97
Jun-92	0.53	Mar-96	0.53	Dec-99	0.41
Sep-92	0.54	Jun-96	0.76	Mar-00	0.76
Dec-92	0.29	Sep-96	0.74	Jun-00	1.04
Mar-93	0.34	Dec-96	0.30	Sep-00	0.56
Jun-93	0.55	Mar-97	0.51		

Fig. 16. Earnings Per Share.

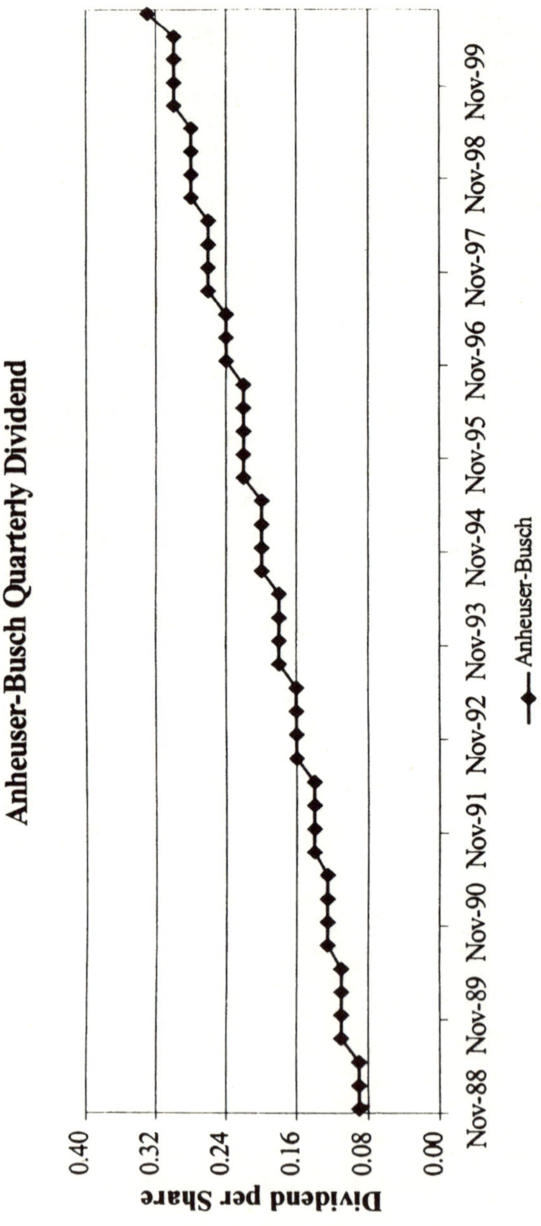

Fig. 17. Quarterly Dividend.

Anheuser-Busch Dividend Per Share: 1989 - 2000

Date	Dividend per Share	Date	Dividend per Share	Date	Dividend per Share
Aug-00	0.33	Nov-96	0.24	May-93	0.16
May-00	0.30	Aug-96	0.24	Feb-93	0.16
Feb-00	0.30	May-96	0.22	Nov-92	0.16
Nov-99	0.30	Mar-96	0.61	Aug-92	0.16
Aug-99	0.30	Feb-96	0.22	May-92	0.14
May-99	0.28	Nov-95	0.22	Feb-92	0.14
Feb-99	0.28	Aug-95	0.22	Nov-91	0.14
Nov-98	0.28	May-95	0.20	Aug-91	0.14
Aug-98	0.28	Feb-95	0.20	May-91	0.13
May-98	0.26	Nov-94	0.20	Feb-91	0.13
Feb-98	0.26	Aug-94	0.20	Nov-90	0.13
Nov-97	0.26	May-94	0.18	Aug-90	0.13
Aug-97	0.26	Feb-94	0.18	May-90	0.11
May-97	0.24	Nov-93	0.18	Feb-90	0.11
Feb-97	0.24	Aug-93	0.18	Nov-89	0.11

Fig. 18. Dividend Per Share.

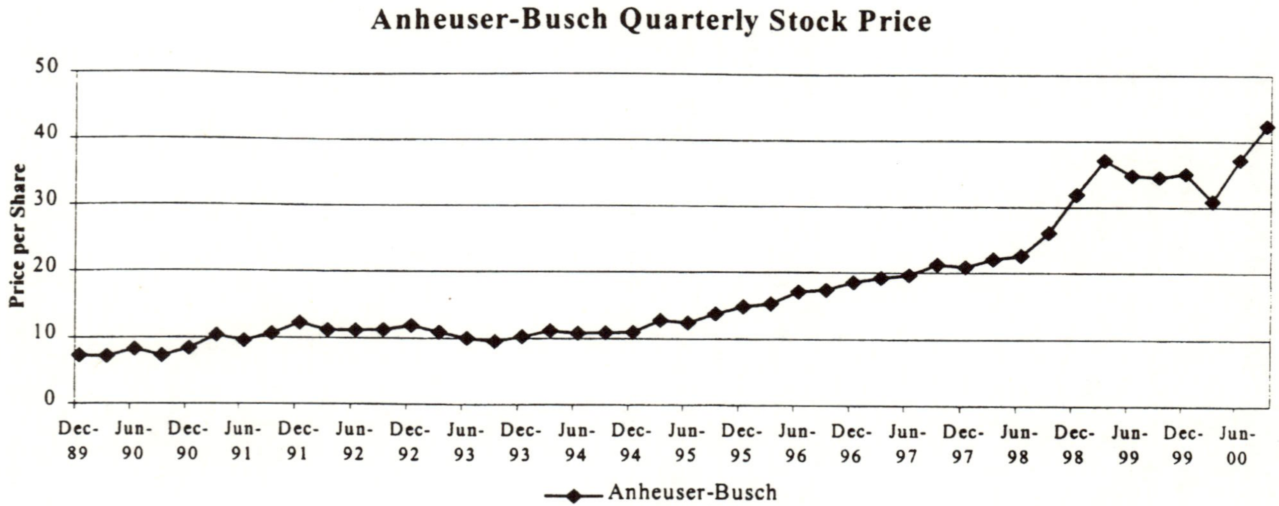

Fig. 19. Quarterly Stock Price.

Anheuser-Busch Price Per Share: 1989 - 2000

Date	Price per Share	Date	Price per Share	Date	Price per Share	Date	Price per Share	Date	Price per Share	Date	Price per Share
Sep-00	42.31	Oct-98	28.76	Nov-96	19.67	Dec-94	10.99	Jan-93	11.99	Feb-91	9.27
Aug-00	39.41	Sep-98	26.10	Oct-96	17.77	Nov-94	10.61	Dec-92	11.93	Jan-91	8.65
Jul-00	40.09	Aug-98	22.60	Sep-96	17.42	Oct-94	10.87	Nov-92	12.21	Dec-90	8.41
Jun-00	37.20	Jul-98	24.91	Aug-96	17.48	Sep-94	10.90	Oct-92	11.51	Nov-90	7.82
May-00	38.60	Jun-98	22.69	Jul-96	17.13	Aug-94	11.68	Sep-92	11.26	Oct-90	7.16
Apr-00	35.00	May-98	22.08	Jun-96	17.19	Jul-94	11.11	Aug-92	10.93	Sep-90	7.28
Mar-00	30.88	Apr-98	21.90	May-96	16.33	Jun-94	10.79	Jul-92	11.14	Aug-90	7.72
Feb-00	31.74	Mar-98	22.11	Apr-96	15.29	May-94	11.56	Jun-92	11.19	Jul-90	8.06
Jan-00	33.33	Feb-98	22.41	Mar-96	15.34	Apr-94	11.43	May-92	10.84	Jun-90	8.32
Dec-99	35.00	Jan-98	21.36	Feb-96	15.07	Mar-94	11.19	Apr-92	10.61	May-90	8.30
Nov-99	36.94	Dec-97	20.91	Jan-96	15.45	Feb-94	10.51	Mar-92	11.19	Apr-90	7.10
Oct-99	35.37	Nov-97	20.53	Dec-95	14.87	Jan-94	10.27	Feb-92	11.41	Mar-90	7.24
Sep-99	34.45	Oct-97	18.86	Nov-95	14.73	Dec-93	10.30	Jan-92	11.38	Feb-90	6.74
Aug-99	37.86	Sep-97	21.31	Oct-95	14.57	Nov-93	10.32	Dec-91	12.28	Jan-90	7.20
Jul-99	38.66	Aug-97	20.13	Sep-95	13.77	Oct-93	9.91	Nov-91	10.53	Dec-89	7.34
Jun-99	34.74	Jul-97	20.16	Aug-95	12.61	Sep-93	9.55	Oct-91	10.78		
May-99	35.78	Jun-97	19.69	Jul-95	12.18	Aug-93	9.94	Sep-91	10.63		
Apr-99	35.67	May-97	20.13	Jun-95	12.46	Jul-93	9.70	Aug-91	10.80		
Mar-99	37.13	Apr-97	20.02	May-95	12.95	Jun-93	10.01	Jul-91	10.12		
Feb-99	37.41	Mar-97	19.26	Apr-95	12.65	May-93	10.76	Jun-91	9.53		
Jan-99	34.34	Feb-97	20.78	Mar-95	12.78	Apr-93	9.82	May-91	10.25		
Dec-98	31.88	Jan-97	19.73	Feb-95	12.26	Mar-93	10.90	Apr-91	10.10		
Nov-98	29.45	Dec-96	18.57	Jan-95	11.82	Feb-93	11.31	Mar-91	10.40		

Fig. 20. Price Per Share.

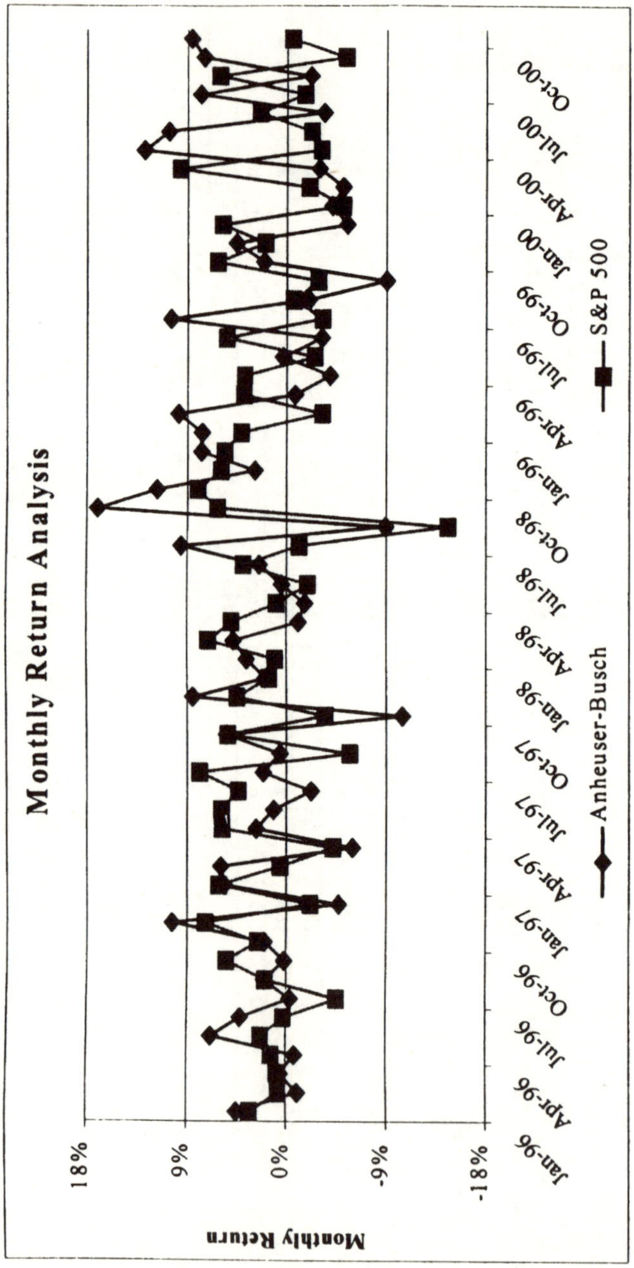

Fig. 21. Monthly Return Analysis.

Valuation of Stock Option

S (current stock price)=	48.875
X (exercise price)=	47.5
r (risk-free interest rate)=	0.0604
σ(volatility of stock)=	0.0186
T (time to expiration)=	0.0959
d_1=	5.9627
d_2=	5.9570
C (the European call option price)=	**1.65**
P (the European put option price)=	**1.40**

Fig. 22. Valuation of Stock Option.

10. WHAT CAUSES MEMORY IN MULTI-PERIOD CONTRACTS?

Bin Srinidhi and Kaustav Sen

ABSTRACT

This paper uses a stylized two period principal-agent model to examine the circumstances under which the second period compensation depends on the output of the first period (defined as memory). We show that if the agent exhibits a temporally split utility function, the outputs are not correlated, the first period action does not affect the second period output and there is no consumption smoothing, then the memory effect is not manifested. In all other cases, the optimal compensation contract exhibits memory effect. We also examine the influence of output correlation and utility trade off on the memory effect. This analysis provides the benchmark for delineating the effect of multi-period phenomena such as renegotiation relevant in understanding accounting and finance research issues from the mechanical effects of the model like consumption smoothing and utility trade-offs on compensation contracts.

1. INTRODUCTION

Research questions in finance and accounting often require the analysis of managerial compensation contracts in a multi-period setting. In accounting, researchers typically address multi-period issues such as earnings management, participative budgeting and auditor low-balling.[1] Finance researchers are also concerned with multi-period equilibrium processes in credit markets.[2] In all

Advances in Quantitative Analysis of Finance and Accounting, Volume 10, pages 255–269.

ISBN: 0-7623-0969-5

these cases, the analysis requires assumptions on inter-period utility trade-offs of contracting parties, correlation between outputs of consecutive periods and the contracting parties' ability to commit or not to commit to renegotiation of contracts. These assumptions play a very important role in determining their conclusion. In this paper, we examine how the assumptions of utility trade-off and association between outputs of consecutive periods influence the role of historical performance in determining current compensation. The inclusion of historical performance as a determiner of current compensation in multi-period contracts has been referred to as memory in the contract.

The causes of memory in multi-period contracts are important in order to understand the results of the model. By far, most of the executive compensation literature on delayed compensation deals with the case in which action in one period has an effect on the output in a future period. In such a case, the future compensation must depend on the past outputs that are noisy signals of past efforts. While it is true that the future effects of actions result in the compensation contracts that depend on past outputs, the question addressed in this paper is the converse one. If we observe a (presumably optimal) contract in which the compensation is dependent on past outputs, can we attribute this solely to actions that have long-term effects? We show that even in a setting in which the current action has no effect on future output, it is possible to have an optimal contract with memory. To what other effects is memory attributable? Could it be that even if the actions do not directly affect future outputs, the outputs themselves are correlated? This would cause memory in compensation contracts. We go one step further. Let us assume that there is no long-term effect of action and the outputs are not correlated either. Even in such a case, we show that memory can exist. We show that memory can exist because of the way utility is often modeled. A single attribute utility function defined over more than one period assumes that there is a consistent way in which utility can be traded off between different periods. We show that this assumption is enough to result in memory in the compensation contract. Banker, Datar and Maindiratta (1987) show that it is not generally true that such utility trade-offs can be assumed.

The importance of our results is that when a paper models a multi-period setting and attributes the optimality of a contract with memory to either the deferred effect of past actions or to correlations between outputs, they might be missing out on the effect of utility trade-offs. Many papers model multi-period contracts that might involve possibly unintended memory effects. For example, in Lambert (1980), the advantages of a long-term contract could be partially due to the mechanical improvement caused by unintended memory effect. However, in some other papers like Indjejikan and Nanda (1999), the intended specific memory effect might be affected by the mechanical memory effect that may not be explicitly modeled.

There are several papers where it is important either to eliminate any extraneous cause of memory or introduce memory explicitly to prove a point. Demski and Frimor (1999) show that there is no value to communication at the end of the first period if there is an option to renegotiate the contract. In order to prove their result, they had to ensure that there was no other source of memory. Antle and Fellingham (1990) explore inefficiencies (organizational slack) in an investment (resource rationing) context. If the owner commits to a multi-period contact, the slack is reduced. However, for this to be true, the multi-period contract needs to have memory. Rey and Salanie (1996) show that under asymmetric information, a limited commitment two period contract (short-term) is more efficient than a spot contract. Long-term efficiency is achieved by a set of short-term contracts than a set of spot contracts due to two reasons – smoothing in the symmetric setting and ratchet effects (information rents) in the asymmetric setting. Implicit in the short-term contract is the notion of memory, since all future rents are incorporated in the contract.

In this paper, our objective is to "peel off" the different effects that might result in memory in compensation contracts and finally arrive at a setting when the optimal compensation in any one period depends solely on the output of that period. This will serve as a benchmark to assess whether a model has a mechanical source of memory not caused by other model considerations. It will be an important assessment tool to evaluate the results and conclusions of analyzing any multi-period model.

Consumption smoothing by the agent has been advocated as another reason for memory in compensation contracts. In the situation where the agent could not borrow and lend freely or where the cost of borrowing is greater for the agent than the principal, compensation contracts with memory can effectively exploit this friction. Lambert (1980) shows that even in the absence of consumption smoothing, memory exists in moral hazard settings. In his model, the principal can diversify the risk from agent's actions by using multiple period compensations based on the output and effectively reduce the total risk premium paid the agent. This is possible because the agent can trade off his utility in one period with his utility in other periods. Rogerson (1985) uses the same idea of utility trade-off in a two period model and shows that the optimal compensation function equates the expected reciprocals of the marginal utilities in the first and the second periods. This is different from the pure consumption-smoothing model in which the expected marginal utilities of the two periods are equated. Christensen and Frimor (1997) identify the main factors contributing to memory as insufficient period-by-period punishment possibilities, inter-temporal correlation and consumption smoothing over time. Focusing on the last factor, they expand on Rogerson's (1985) result that memory does not arise solely from the desire to smooth consumption but rather as a cost minimizing allocation of consumption.

In this paper, we suppress consumption smoothing and examine sufficient conditions to efficiently implement a two-period compensation contract without memory. Though Fellingham, Newman and Suh (1985) identify sufficient conditions for optimal memory-less two period contracts, their conditions are restrictive, requiring either risk neutrality or CARA utility functions in addition to additive or multiplicative separability.

In contrast, we find sufficient conditions under more general utility functions for the agent that gives a memory-less contract. The conditions are:

(a) the agent cannot trade off his utilities in the two periods; and
(b) there is no inter-temporal correlation between the outputs.

Condition (a) is satisfied if the agent has a multi-attribute utility function with the utilities in the two periods being the two attributes. We describe such a utility function as a "temporally split" utility function. Banker, Data and Maindiratta (1988) analyze a setting that considers multi-attribute utility preferences.[3] They convincingly argue that for any individual (in their case, principal), a single attribute utility function is representative if and only if any certain stream of cash flows in future (vectors) can be converted to a current period monetary equivalent r(s). This is valid if the individual's borrowing and lending rates are independent of the levels of cash flow. These assumptions are not always fulfilled.[4] This provides the basis for the split utility function.

It is important to note that we do not claim that agents in the real world typically exhibit temporally split utility function. However, our exposition on the temporally split utility function is important when analyzing memory in long-term contracts. Researchers should be very cautious in interpreting the reason for the superiority of long-term contracts when a common (as opposed to the split) utility function is assumed. Long-term contracts become superior "mechanically" because the agents do not exhibit split utility functions.[5]

We first examine the case where the agent exhibits a temporally split utility function and the outputs are inter-temporally uncorrelated. We show that this case does not exhibit memory. Next we examine the case where the agent still exhibits temporally split utility function but the outputs are inter-temporally correlated. In this case, we show that memory plays a role. The third case we examine has inter-temporally uncorrelated outputs but the agent has a single attribute utility function that spans both the periods. Again, we show that memory plays a role. The last combination is the case where the agent displays a single attribute utility function and there is an inter-temporal correlation between outputs. Though we do not explicitly examine this setting, it is clear from the analysis and earlier literature (such as Lambert, 1980) that memory plays an important role in compensation contracts.

In the second section, we develop the models for all three cases and derive the results. In the third section, we provide a discussion and conclusions from the results.

2. MODEL DEVELOPMENT

Consider a two-period agency contract where the output at the end of each period is stochastically determined by the agent's action choices. Let the output x_t at time t be determined by action a_t where $t \in \{1, 2\}$, i.e. the action in the first period does not affect output in the second period. Denote the agent's reservation utility in time t by $\bar{u}_t$. Let the agent's utility in time t be $u(s_t, a_t) = u(s_t) - v(a_t)$ where s_t is the compensation for time t. In general, we allow s_2 to be a function of both x_1 and x_2. Furthermore, $u'(s_t) > 0$, $u''(s_t)$ and a_t is the action such that $v'(a_t) > 0$, $v''(a_t) > 0$. Let the conditional outcome density function be denoted by $f(x_1 | a_1)$ for the first period. The conditional outcome density function for the second period is denoted by $g(x_2 | a_2)$ if the outcomes in the two periods are assumed to be inter-temporally uncorrelated and by $g(x_2 | a_2, x_1)$ if they are inter-temporally correlated.

Case 1: No inter-temporal correlation of outputs and the agent displays a temporally split utility function.

Because the agent displays a temporally split utility function, he does not trade off his utilities between the two periods. Both the individual rationality constraints and the incentive constraints have to be individually satisfied for the two periods.

The formulation is given by:

Program P1:

$$\text{Min} \int s_1 f(x_1 | a_1)\, dx_1 + \int s_2 f(x_2 | a_2) g(x_2 | a_2)\, dx_1\, dx_2$$

Subject to

$$\int u(s_1)f(x_1 \mid a_1)\,dx_1 - v(a_1) \geq \bar{u}_1 \qquad (IR_1)$$

$$\int u(s_2)f(x_1 \mid a_1)g(x_2 \mid a_2)\,dx_1\,dx_2 - v(a_2) \geq \bar{u}_2 \qquad (IR_2)$$

$$\int u(s_1)f_{a1}(x_1 \mid a_1)\,dx_1 - v'(a_1) = 0 \qquad (IC_1)$$

$$\int u(s_2)f_{a_1}(x_1 \mid a_1)g(x_2 \mid a_2)\,dx_1\,dx_2 = 0 \qquad (IC_{2a})$$

$$\int u(s_2)f(x_1 \mid a_1)g_{a_2}(x_2 \mid a_2)\,dx_1\,dx_2 - v'(a_2) = 0 \qquad (IC_{2b})$$

In the above formulation, f_{a1} and g_{a2} denote the first derivatives of functions f and g with respect to a_1 and a_2 respectively. There are two reservation wage constraints, IR_1 for period 1 and IR_2 for period 2. Also there are three incentive constraints, IC_1 to induce a_1 in period 1, IC_{2a} to ensure that a_1 is incentive compatible for period 2 and IC_{2b} to induce a_2 in period 2. The separation of the reservation utility constraints for the two periods is the direct consequence of the temporally split utility function. Note that the distribution of the second period output is conditioned only on a_2 because by construction, the first period effort does not affect the second period output. Moreover, there is no association between the first period output and the second period output. This is captured in the second period output distribution function g that is conditioned only on a_2 and not on x_1.

Let $s_1^*(x_1)$, $s_2^*(x_1, x_2)$, a_1^*, a_2^* be the optional solution to the problem. Now consider $s_1^{**}(x_2)$ such that $s_2^{**}(x_2) = u^{-1}[\int u[s_2^*(x_1, x_2)]f(x_1 \mid a_1^*)\,dx_1]$. Consider the solution set $s_1^*(x_1)$, $s_2^{**}(x_2)$, a_1^* and a_2^*. Note that the transformation of the second period compensation retains the *same* expected utilities in the two periods. In other words, for any given action, the expected utilities that the agent receives from the new compensation function are the same as the ones that he would have received under the earlier compensation function. Therefore, these compensation changes do not result in any change in the actions a_1^* and a_2^*. This solution set clearly satisfies IR_1 and IC_1.

IR_2 is satisfied because

$$\int u(s_2^{**})f(x_1 | a_1)g(x_2 | a_2)\, dx_1\, dx_2 = \int\left[\int u(s_2^{**})f(x_1 | a_1)\, dx_1\right]g(x_2 | a_2)\, dx_2$$

$$= \int\left[\int u(s_2^{*})f(x_1 | a_1^{*})\, dx_1\right]g(x_2 | a_2^{*})\, dx_2 \geq \bar{u}_2.$$

IC_{2a} is easily satisfied because

$$\int u(s_2^{**})f_a(x_1 | a_1)g(x_2 | a_2)\, dx_1\, dx_2 = \int\left[\int f_a(x_1 | a_1)\, dx_1\right]u_2(s_2^{**})g(x_2 | a_2)\, dx_2 = 0$$

Note that the term in [ ] can be simplified as

$$\frac{\partial}{\partial a_1}\int f(x_1 | a_1)\, dx_1 = \frac{\partial}{\partial a_1}(1) = 0,$$

implying that this constraint is satisfied for any value of f_{a1}.

IC_{2b} is satisfied because

$$\int u(s_2^{**})f(x_1 | a_1)g_{a_2}(x_2 | a_2)\, dx_1\, dx_2 = \int\left[\int u(s_2^{**})f(x_1 | a_1)\, dx_1\right]g_{a_2}(x_2 | a_2)\, dx_2$$

$$= \int\left[\int u(s_2^{*})f(x_1 | a_1)\, dx_1\right]g_{a_2}(x_2 | a_2)\, dx_2$$

$$= v'(a_2)$$

Therefore the second solution set is feasible. Now, we will compare the objective function in the two cases. Define

$$Es_2^{*} = \int s_2^{*}f(x_1 | a_1)g(x_2 | a_2)\, dx_1\, dx_2$$

and

$$Es_2^{**} = \int s_2^{**}f(x_1 | a_1)g(x_2 | a_2)\, dx_1\, dx_2 = \int s_2^{**}g(x_2 | a_2)\, dx_2$$

Because of the optimality of s_2^*, $Es_2^* \leq Es_2^{**}$. From the definition of $u(s_2^{**})$, we have

$$\int u(s_2^*)f(x_1 | a_1)\, dx_1 = u(s_2^{**}).$$

By Jensen's inequality, we know that

$$\int u(s_2^*)f(x_1 | a_1)\, dx_1 < u\left[\int s_2^* f(x_1 | a_1)\, dx_1\right].$$

Therefore, because

$$u'(.) > 0,\ s_2^{**} < \int s_2^* f(x_1 | a_{1\_}\, dx_1.$$

$$Es_2^{**} = \int s_2^{**} g(x_2 | a_2)\, dx_2 < \int s_2^* f(x_1 | a_1) g(x_2 | a_2)\, dx_1\, dx_2 = Es_2^*$$

i.e. $Es_2^{**} < Es_2^*$.

Therefore s_2^* could not have been optimal. In other words, the optimal s_2^* is a function of x_2 only. Thus we note that the optimal compensation contract does not exhibit memory.

Proposition 1: The optimal solution to a multi-period agency contract does not exhibit memory when there is no inter-temporal correlation of outputs and the agent displays a temporally split utility function.

Case 2: Inter-temporal correlation of outputs and the agent displays temporally split utility function.

The formulation is given by:

Program P2:

$$\text{Min} \int s_1 f(x_1 | a_1)\, dx_1 + \int s_2 f(x_1 | a_1) g(x_2 | a_2, x_1)\, dx_1\, dx_2$$

subject to

$$\int u(s_1)f(x_1 | a_1)\, dx_1 - v(a_1) \geq \bar{u}_1 \qquad (IR_1)$$

$$\int u(s_2)f(x_1 | a_1)g(x_2 | a_2, x_1)\, dx_1\, dx_2 - v(a_2) \geq \bar{u}_2 \qquad (IR_2)$$

$$\int u(s_1)f_{a_1}(x_1 | a_1)dx_1 - v'(a_1) = 0 \qquad (IC_1)$$

$$\int u(s_2)f_{a_2}(x_1 | a_1)g(x_2 | a_2, x_1)\, dx_1\, dx_2 = 0 \qquad (IC_{2a})$$

$$\int u(s_2)f(x_1 | a_1)g_{a_2}(x_2 | a_2, x_1)\, dx_1\, dx_2 - v'(a_2) = 0 \qquad (IC_{2b})$$

Optimizing w.r.t. s_1

$$f(x_1 | a_1) - \lambda_1 u'(s_1)f(x_1 | a_1) - \mu_1 u'(s_1)f_{a_1}(x_1 | a_1) = 0$$

$$\Rightarrow \frac{1}{u'(s_1)} = \lambda_1 + \mu_1 \frac{f_{a_1}(x_1 | a_1)}{f(x_1 | a_1)} \qquad (1)$$

Optimizing w.r.t. s_2

$$f(x_1 | a_1)g(x_2 | a_2, x_1) - \lambda_2 u'(s_2)f(x_1 | a_1)g(x_2 | a_2, x_1) - \mu_{1a} u'(s_2)f_{a_1}(x_1 | a_1)g(x_2 | a_2, x_1)$$
$$- \mu_{2b} u'(s_2)f(x_1 | a_1)g_{a_{21}}(x_2 | a_2, x_1) = 0$$

$$\Rightarrow \frac{1}{u'(s_2)} = \lambda_2 + \mu_{2a} \frac{f_{a_1}(x_1 | a_1)}{f(x_1 | a_1)} - \mu_{2b} \frac{g_{a_1}(x_2 | a_2, x_1)}{g(x_2 | a_2, x_1)} \qquad (2)$$

Suppose s_2 is a function of only x_2. Then, IC_{2a} can be written as follows:

$$\int f_{a1}(x_1 | a_1)\, dx_1 \int u(s_2)g(x_2 | a_2)\, dx_2 = 0.$$

The first part of the above constraint is the derivative of 1 and therefore identically equal to zero. Therefore, this constraint is inactive (non-binding at all points of all variables). Therefore, $\mu_{2a} = 0$.[6] From the above equation, the term multiplying μ_{2b} is 0 because g is not a function of a_1. Then s_2 = constant and

$$IC_{2b} = u(s_2) \int f(x_1 | a_1) g_{a_2}(x_2 | a_2)\, dx_1\, dx_2 - v'(a_2) \neq 0.$$

The incentive constraint IC_{2b} will be violated. By contradiction, we have proved that s_2 is a function of x_1.

Proposition 2: The optimal solution to a multi-period agency contract exhibits memory when there is inter-temporal correlation of outputs and the agent displays a temporally split utility function.

Case 3: No inter-temporal correlation of outputs and the agent displays a common utility function over the two periods.

Let the discount rates for the principal and the agent be α and β respectively. The formulation is given by

Program 3:

$$\text{Min} \int s_1 f(x_1 | a_1)\, dx_1 + \alpha \int s_2 f(x_1 | a_1) g(x_2 | a_2)\, dx_1\, dx_2$$

Subject to

$$\int u(s_1) f(x_1 | a_1)\, dx_1 + \beta \int u(s_2) f(x_1 | a_1) g(x_2 | a_2)\, dx_1\, dx_2 - v(a_1) - \beta v(a_2) \geq \bar{u} \qquad \text{(IR)}$$

and

$$a_1, a_2 \in \text{Argmax}_{a_1, a_2} \int u(s_1) f(x_1 | a_1)\, dx_1 + \beta \int u(s_2) f(x_1 | a_1) g(x_2 | a_2)\, dx_1\, dx_2 - v(a_1) - \beta v(a_2) \qquad \text{(IC)}$$

Let the solution be a_1^*, a_2^*, $s_1{}^*(x_1)$ and $s_2^*(x_1, x_2)$.

The first order condition for the argmax constraint gives

$$\int u(s_1) f_{a_1}(x_1 | a_1^*)\, dx_1 + \beta \int u(s_2) f_{a_1}(x_1 | a_1^*) g(x_2 | a_2^*)\, dx_1\, dx_2 = v'(a_1^*) \qquad (IC_1)$$

and

$$\beta \int u(s_2)f(x_1 | a_1^*)g_{a_2}(x_2 | a_2^*)\, dx_1\, dx_2 = v'(a_2^*) \qquad (IC_2)$$

Let $s_1(x_1)$ and $s_2(x_1, x_2)$ be any feasible compensation function set which will induce a_1^*, a_2^*. Now, if we reduce s_1 by an amount k_1 such that $u(s_1 - k_1, a_1^*) = u(s_1, a_1^*) - u_k$ and increase s_2 by an amount k_2 such that

$$u(s_2 + k_2, a_2^*) = u(s_2, a_2^*) + \frac{u_k}{\beta}$$

i.e.

$$u(s_1, a_1^*) + \beta u(s_2, a_2^*) = u(s_1^*, a_1^*) + \beta u(s_2^*, a_2^*) = v(x_1, x_2)$$

The induced action set (a_1^*, a_2^*) does not change because the agent gets the same total utility. We can now solve a simpler problem in which the principal chooses among all sets of compensation contracts that induce (a_1^*, a_2^*).

Program 4:

$$\text{Min} \int s_1(x_1)f(x_1 | a_1^*)\, dx_1 + \alpha \int s_2(x_1, x_2)f(x_1 | a_1^*)g(x_2 | a_2^*)\, dx_1\, dx_2$$

Subject to

$$u(s_1(x_1) + \beta u(s_2(x_2)) = v(x_1, x_2) \forall (x_1, x_2)$$

$$L = \int s_1(x_1)f(x_1 | a_1^*)\, dx_1 + \alpha \int s_2(x_1, x_2)f(x_1 | a_1^*)g(x_2 | a_2^*)\, dx_1\, dx_2$$

$$+ \int \lambda(x_1, x_2)\{u(s_1(x_1)) + \beta(u(s_2(x_1, x_2)) - v(x_1, x_2)\}\, dx_2\, dx_2$$

From this, we get

$$f(x_1 | a_1^*) + u'(s_1) \int \lambda(x_1, x_2)\, dx_2 = 0 \,\forall\, x_1 \qquad (3)$$

$$\alpha g(x_2 | a_2^*)f(x_1 | a_1^*) + \beta\lambda(x_1, x_2)u'(s_2) = 0 \,\forall x_1, x_2 \qquad (4)$$

Substituting for $\lambda(x_1, x_2)$ from Eqs (4) in (3), we get

$$\frac{1}{u'(s_1(x_1))} = \frac{\alpha}{\beta} \int \frac{g(x_2 | a_2^*)}{u'(s_2(x_1, x_2))}\, dx_2 \,\forall\, x_1 \qquad (5)$$

If $s_2 = s_2(x_2)$, the RHS of the above expression is not a function of x_1. This leads to $s_1(x_1) = s_1 =$ constant for all x_1. If s_1 is a constant, the LHS of the IC_1 reduces to zero and cannot equal $v'(a_1^*)$ which by assumption is positive. Therefore s_2 is a function of both x_1 and x_2.

> *Proposition 3:* The optimal solution to a multi-period agency contract exhibits memory even when there is no inter-temporal correlation of outputs if the agent does not display a temporally split utility function.

3. DISCUSSION

3.1. Sensitivity of Memory in Compensation to the Correlation Between the Outputs

For the purpose of this discussion, consider case 2 with temporally split utility function and correlated outputs. In particular, let the utilities in each period be exponential and the outputs mean shifting bivariate normal as described below.

$$u(s) = -e^{-\varphi s},\ f(x_1 | a_1) = N(a_1, \sigma^2) \text{ and } g(x_2 | x_1, a_2) = N(\gamma x_1 + a_2, \sigma^2).$$

Note that the correlation coefficient ρ between x_1 and x_2 is given by

$$\rho = \frac{\gamma}{\sqrt{1+\gamma^2}}$$

From (2), after substitution, we get

$$\frac{1}{\varphi} e^{\varphi s_2} = k_1 + \frac{\mu_{2a} - \gamma\mu_{2b}}{\sigma^2} x_1 + \frac{\mu_{2b}}{\sigma^2} x_2$$

where

$$k_1 = \lambda_2 - \frac{\mu_{2a} a_1 + \mu_{2b} a_2}{\sigma^2}.$$

Furthermore, from proposition 1, when $\gamma = 0$, s_2 is a function of only x_2 and so, $\mu_{2a} = 0$. Therefore,

$$\frac{1}{\varphi} e^{\varphi s_2} = k_1 - \frac{\gamma\mu_{2b}}{\sigma^2} x_1 + \frac{\mu_{2b}}{\sigma^2} x_2 = k_1 + \frac{\mu_{2b}}{\sigma^2}(x_2 - \gamma x_1) \tag{6}$$

where

$$k_1 = \lambda_2 - \frac{\mu_{2b} a_2}{\sigma^2}.$$

Differentiating Eq. (6) with respect to x_1 and γ, we get

$$e^{\varphi s_2}\frac{\partial s_2}{\partial x_1} = -\frac{\gamma\mu_{2b}}{\sigma^2},\ e^{\varphi s_2}\frac{\partial s_2}{\partial \gamma} = -\frac{\mu_{2b}}{\sigma^2}x_1 \tag{7}$$

and

$$\varphi\left[k_1 - \frac{\gamma\mu_{2b}}{\sigma^2}x_1 + \frac{\mu_{2b}}{\sigma^2}x_2\right]\frac{\partial^2 s_2}{\partial x_1 \partial \gamma} = -\frac{\mu_{2b}}{\sigma^2}\left[1 - \varphi x_1 \frac{\partial s_2}{\partial x_1}\right] \tag{8}$$

From Eqs (6) to (8), given that μ_{2b} is positive, for a high correlation (i.e. large γ) s_2 will be a decreasing function of x_1 for a given x_2. It is also seen to be a decreasing function of γ for any $x_1 > 0$. In fact, $(x_2 - \gamma x_1)$ has an expected value of a_2. It is intuitive to make s_2 a function of this variable. Higher the value of ρ, greater is the independence of s_2 on x_1.

3.2. Memory Effect When the Agent has a One-dimensional Utility Function but the Outputs Are Not Correlated (Case 3)

Using exponential utility function and mean-shifting independent normal distributions of outputs in the two periods, it is easy to show that the discount rates α and β do not affect the slope of the resulting linear compensation contract. Using the same notation as in 3.1,

$$e^{\varphi s_2} = \varphi\tau\left[\left\{\lambda - \frac{\mu_{a_1}a_1 + \mu_{a_2}a_2}{\sigma^2}\right\} + \frac{\mu_{a_1}}{\sigma^2}x_1 + \frac{\mu_{a_2}}{\sigma^2}x_2\right]$$

where λ, μ_{a_1} and μ_{a_2} are the Lagrange multipliers of the constraints in Program P3 and $\tau = \beta/\alpha$, the ratio of the two discount rates. It is seen that

$$\frac{\partial s_2}{\partial x_1} = \tau\, e^{-\varphi s_2}\frac{\mu_{a_1}}{\sigma^2}$$

which is invariant with τ. From proposition 4, it is clear that $\mu_{a_1} > 0$. Therefore, we have

$$\frac{\partial s_2}{\partial x_1} > 0.$$

The slope of the compensation function is an increasing function of the precision of the outputs x_1 and x_2.

3.3. Memory Effect When Utilities Are Combined and the Outputs Are Correlated

The previous literature, as well as our analysis, shows that memory has a significant effect on the compensation in this case.

As before, using negative exponential utility functions and normal distributions for the outputs, we have a compensation function with the following structure:

$$e^{\varphi s_2} = \varphi\tau\left[k_1 = \frac{\mu_{a_1} - \gamma\mu_{a_2}}{\sigma^2}x_1 + \frac{\mu_{a_2}}{\sigma^2}x_2\right].$$

As in case 3, the memory effect, i.e. the variation of s_2 with x_1, is not affected by the discount rates α and β. As in case 2, for a high γ, s_2 is a decreasing function of x_1 given x_2 and decreases in γ for any $x_1 > 0$.

4. CONCLUSIONS

This paper investigates memory in multi-period agency contracts. We show that the sufficient conditions for lack of memory in optimal multi-period compensation contracts are (a) the agent is not able to trade-off utility over periods, i.e. he should display a temporally split utility function and (b) there is no correlation between the outputs of the periods. We showed that even in the absence of explicit trade off of utilities as in the case of consumption smoothing, violation of either of these conditions could result in memory being part of the optimal contract. Furthermore, when the agent displays split utility function, we showed how the memory effect is influenced by correlation between the outputs.

This paper is neutral on whether agents typically exhibit split utility functions. The purpose of this paper is to provide a benchmark case when the effects of multi-period phenomena such as learning and renegotiation on optimal compensation contracts are examined. The effect in the case of split utility function and no direct inter-temporal correlation between outputs is "pure" in the sense that memory in the contract is not caused by other factors. Such an analysis is essential for complementing our understanding of memory in multi-period contracts.

NOTES

1. Representative examples are Arya, Glover and Sunder (1998), Sivaramakrishnan (1994) and Antle and Nalebuff (1991) respectively.

2. See Chinporri, Macho, Rey and Salanie (1994).

3. They consider a situation where the contract uses two signals, one on the agent's unobserved action and the second on the unobserved outcome. They show that if the principal is intertemporally risk-neutral, only the first signal is useful and if not, then both signals are valuable.

4. In reality, low cash flows will result in a higher default risk assessment and therefore higher borrowing rates whereas high cash flows will result in lower borrowing rates. These rates are not even estimable currently. Similarly, low cash flows lead to low lending rates and higher cash flows lead to higher lending rates. Therefore, different cash flow streams get converted differently to current monetary equivalents. In other words, the same cash flow stream can be converted to different monetary equivalents.

5. Our objective is to identify a general set of sufficient conditions to ensure a memory-less contract in any setting. Demski and Frimor (1999) have controlled for all sources of interdependencies in a two period model. Since their model setting demonstrates that the interim report is not truthful, use of a split function is redundant.

6. Alternately, because this constraint is inactive, this can be removed from the program without affecting the solution. Equation (2) can now be re-written without the :$_{2a}$ term. The reasoning given in the text follows.

REFERENCES

Antle, R., & Fellingham, J. (1990). Resource Rationing and Organizational Slack in a Two-Period. *Journal of Accounting Research, 28* (Spring), 1–24.

Antle, A., & Nalebuff, B. (1991). Conservatism and Auditor-Client Negotiations. *Journal of Accounting Research*, (Supplement), 31–54.

Arya, A., Glover, J., & Sunder, S. (1998). Earnings Management and the Revelation Principle. *Review of Accounting Studies, 3*(1/2), 7–34.

Banker, R., Datar, S., & Maindiratta, A. (1988). Unobservable outcomes and multiattribute preferences in the evaluation of managerial performance. *Contemporary Accounting Research, 5*(1), 96–124.

Chinporri, P., Macho, I., Rey, P., & Salanie, B. (1994). Repeated Moral Hazard: The Tole of Memory, Commitment and the Access to Credit Markets. *European Economic Review, 38*(8), 1527–1553.

Christensen, P. O., & Frimor, H. (1997). Memory and Consumption Smoothing in Multi-period Agencies. Working Paper. Department of Management, Odenese University 5/1997 (pp. 1–29).

Demski, J., & Frimor, H. (1999). Performance measure garbling under renegotiation in multi-period agencies. *Journal of Accounting Research, 37*, 187–214.

Fellingham, J., Newman, P., & Suh, Y. S. (1985). Contracts without Memory in Multiperiod Agency Models. *Journal of Economic Theory, 37*, 340–355.

Lambert, R. (1983). Long term contracts and moral hazard. *Bell Journal of Economics, 14*, 441–452.

Rey, P., & Salanie, B. (1996). On the value of commitment with asymmetric information. *Econometrica, 64*(6), 1395–1414.

Rogerson, W. (1985). Repeated moral hazard. *Econometrica, 53*, 69–76.

Sivaramakrishnan, K. (1994). Information Asymmetry, Participation, and Long-term Contracts. *Management Science, 40*, 1228–1244.